ETHNOLOGICAL

AND

CULTURAL STUDIES

OF THE

Sex Life in England

Facsimile of the title-page to the catalogue of PISANUS FRAXI's *Million Dollar Library* of Erotic Classics, which that great collector and bibliographer courteously placed at the disposal of DR. IWAN BLOCH in the preparation of this work.

Ethnological *and* Cultural Studies

of the

Sex Life in England

As Revealed in Its

Erotic and Obscene
Literature and Art

Dr. IWAN BLOCH
Author of
120 DAYS OF SODOM
STRANGE SEXUAL PRACTISES
SEX LIFE OF OUR TIME
etc.

The Roman rants of heroes, gods and love,
The Briton purely paints the Art of Love.
—WM. KING

Translated and Edited by
RICHARD DENISTON

Fredonia Books
Amsterdam, The Netherlands

Ethnological and Cultural Studies of the Sex Life in
England as Revealed in Its Erotic and Obscene
Literature and Art

by
Dr. Iwan Bloch

ISBN: 1-58963-724-0

Reprinted from the 1934 edition

Fredonia Books
Amsterdam, the Netherlands
http://www.fredoniabooks.com

A Few of the Mass of Editorial Reviews
Enthusiastically Acclaiming the
Foreign Editions of this

PIONEER MASTERPIECE

From Leading Authorities in England,
France, Germany

❦

DR. A. EULENBURG, Professor of Medical History and Advisory Councillor to the Bureau of Public Welfare, Berlin, in the featured editorial of the *Deutsch-Medizin. Wochenschrift*:

We always look forward with keen anticipation to any new work by that indefatigable master of research, Dr. Iwan Bloch, for we are assured of his ever new and startling revelations of the cultural and ethnological significances of the sex life of a people or an epoch. But in this latest triumph of sexual ethnology Dr. Bloch has surpassed his previous valuable contributions to medical and legal pathology. As the author himself states, Sex Life in England will undoubtedly have a "four-fold appeal" to cultured circles of society. We would, however, here like to call attention to these sections of Dr. Bloch's treatise which are especially interesting to the medical profession. Dr. Bloch is perfectly justified in taking the standpoint that the vices and virtues of a people are best to be seen in their literary productions. He presents vividly and informatively those specific English—that is, Anglo-Saxon—sex practices that can be found in no other erotic literature in such detail and complexity. This is especially true of flagellation and defloration, which are veritable sex manias in England and as such are referred to time and time again in erotic and pornographic works.

Many important side-lights thus illuminate the etiology and nosology of sex perversions and perversities . . . No less fascinating are the chapters on the erotic art of the English in which we see graphically, and thus more clearly, portrayed all the erotic relations of a country that is notorious for its grossness and coarseness of expression . . . We can safely recommend this latest study by Dr. Bloch to our colleagues with the assurance that they will find it highly interesting as well as informative.

Dr. J. Pagel, Professor of Pathology, in the *Deutschen Aerztezeitung*:

Dr. Bloch gained a well-deserved continental reputation with his "epoch-making double-masterpiece," the 120 **Days of Sodom.** His latest work on the sex life in England is certain to spread his literary fame to all quarters of the civilized world. Dr. Bloch has utilized an ingenious method in alloying the most famous English eroticists and pornographists to present their own analyses of the sex life of the English people. This makes fascinating reading and Dr. Bloch has cleverly connected the absorbing chapters of his work with descriptive excurses that present an authoritative and well-rounded out panorama of the erotic nature of the English race . . .

8

DAVISON OTWAY, the noted critic, in the *Book-lovers' Quarterly*:

> We can explain our native authors' shameful neglect of so important a field of human relations only by frankly confessing that England has no scientist who can compare with the rank, stature and courage of Dr. Iwan Bloch. Some consolation may, however, be found in the unstinting assistance and collaboration by Sir H. Spencer Ashbee (Pisanus Fraxi) in the production of this monumental work on the "Sex Life in England". It is only too rarely that our collectors have come to the aid of literary and medical research and we cannot applaud too highly the generous action of Sir Ashbee in placing his magnificent library of erotica and pornography at the disposal of Dr. Bloch. (Bibliophiles will recall that Sir Ashbee's private library was recently evaluated at about £200,000.

> It is astounding to note how thoroughly and intimately Dr. Bloch is acquainted with the entire field of English literature. We might even say that this German savant has perfectly completed the lacunae in the classic work of the French critic Taine on English Life and Literature! Higher praise it is not in our power to bestow . . .

DR. ROHLEDER in the *Breslauer Morgenzeitung*:

> Dr. Bloch has irrevocably taken first place among the historians of human culture by the publication of his monumental study of the sexual life of the English people. The reasons for his indisputable superiority over other professional students of the sexual relations of mankind are not far to seek. As in his former work, the **120 Days of Sodom**, we immediately recognize the

9

intense serious nature of his undertaking that
brooks no obstacles, the fundamental moral motivation of his work, the critical clarity of his
analyses and descriptions, his objectivity in dis-
cussing the most pornographic books and authors, and the wealth of amazing material placed
before us. No reader—and the author is not
interested in piquanteries for the man-about-
town, but in authoritative research for cultured
students—can escape the conclusion that the intelligent public has before it for the first time a
solid and honorable work on the true conditions
of English morality, as it was and now is . . .

MAURICE SHIPLEY in the *Philobiblon*:

Dr. Bloch is certain to receive the enthusiastic
plaudits of scientists and collectors everywhere
for his monumental work on so important yet so
neglected a field as the sexual manners and
morals of the English people . . . An immediate
translation of this epochal German work is sorely
needed. Yet we regret to state that such an imposing contribution to the cultural achievements
of a nation is not likely to see publication in its
native land. For Dr. Bloch's "Das Geschlechst-
leben in England" (Sex Life in England Illustrated) demands: firstly, a publisher with courage who will not stint in issuing an unbowdler-
ized private edition; secondly, an editor and
translater who will faithfully render and complete Dr. Bloch's magnum opus; and lastly—
most important of all—an intelligent cultured
public who will understand and correctly evalu-
ate the decisive importance of such studies in
the making of modern civilized society. It seems
far more probable that the United States of
America by first issuing translations into English

will be privileged to reap the intellectual fruits of Dr. Bloch's magnificent researches into the entire field of sexual anthropology and ethnology. England is still tied to Victoria's stays while The States are more apt to recognize and acclaim the humanizing forces of the pioneer geniuses of mankind.

Dr. Ludwig Skerzy in the *Ungarische medizin. Presse*:

"The great and interesting History of Medicine would have had a huge void without the works of Dr. Iwan Bloch. This gifted scholar manifests an incomparable comprehension of the very interesting problems of the sex life and sex literature of the various ages and peoples and has an extraordinary ability to unearth difficult and invaluable data from which he creates works that are without question altogether singular and stand entirely alone in literature. The majority of these works are well known in medical circles, and his forelying masterpiece for that reason would be noteworthy in a high degree . . .

The *Zeitschrift fuer Buecherfreunde*:

. . . To Dr. Bloch it has, naturally, supreme worth from the standpoint of Psychopathia Sexualis, but it is besides a literary treasure of no small interest to Bibliophiles . . . The eminently cultural significance of his work is inestimable . . .

J. Grand-Carteret, in *La Parisienne*:

Dr. Bloch, who is a savant, demonstrates conclusively in his profound dissertations that if the sexual urge is the cause of many crimes and misdemeanors, it is also the inspiration of deeds of grandeur and it is intimately related to the sublime conceptions of art and poetry.

Explanatory Foreword

By Dr. Iwan Bloch

*on the ethnological and cultural significance of studies and
analyses of the foremost erotic and obscene classics as a
vital element in the examination of the national
characteristics of a race.*

THE FOUR-FOLD VALUE
AND APPEAL OF SUCH A WORK:

"To the psychologist and psychoanalyst; to the literary
critic, historian, philologist and bibliographer; to the fields
of medical science, pathology, law and medical jurisprudence; and to the entire world of art which has been for so
long bereft of many of the greatest erotic classics of
English art and genius."

Foreword

IF it seems strange that a foreigner should undertake a work of this national character, we need but reply with the Frenchman Taine's apologia for writing his classic "History of English Literature": "Possibly it would be better to leave my task to those who are natives of England; they are apt to say that they know our subject better because they are of his family. True, but in living with a person one is not apt to be keenly aware of his peculiarities. On the contrary, a stranger has one advantage— custom does not blunt his perceptions; he is immediately struck by the principal characteristics, and treats the subject with reference to them."

We were the more convinced of the necessity of our investigation into the nature and art of the sex life in England, as revealed in its erotic literature and art, since there has been *no work in any language* that discusses even in some slight measure this most important element of a national character. This deliberate neglect of so essential a part of the social relations of mankind is motivated by specific English characteristics, pride, prudery and hypocrisy, each of which is augmented in the ethos of England to such a degree that it may be called a mania.

Every country distinguishes itself from all others by a national character, "both mental and moral, which manifests itself at the beginning, and develops from epoch to epoch, preserving the same fundamental qualities from its origin to its decline". No country can long secrete itself from the eyes of its neighbours since "each of its literary productions is a picture in which we contemplate the nation itself. And this picture is more precious than a physical portrait, for it is a moral one. The poem of Beowulf and the 'Canterbury Tales', the dramatic works of the Renaissance and the Reformation, the various lines in prose and verse of authors who have followed each other, from Shakespeare and Bacon down to Tennyson, Dickens and Carlyle, place before us all the literary forms and poetical images, all the variations of thought, sentiment and expression, in which the soul of the English nation has found delight."

We are therefore completely justified in presenting an exposition of the sex life in England as portrayed in its literary productions in the field of eroticism. It is only in such works that there are clearly revealed the sexual relations of a people, their conception of a normal sex life, as well as their perversities and abnormalities. We can trace through these media the rise, growth, decline and resurrection of the "divine spark in man" through the course of the centuries, revealing to the discerning reader a direct parallel between the advance of civilization and the increasing freedom of the sex life.

Another important element that has nullified any previous attempt to render a faithful account of the sex life in England is the excessive rarity of the requisite works, the prohibitive cost of their acquisition, the inability of students and investigators to consult them at the national libraries, and the enormous expenditure of money, time and patience necessary to collect the famous English erotic classics. This last factor, in itself, would have made it impossible for any one person to set about such a pioneering task, and we would have considered such a work as hopeless had we not been granted the special privilege of consulting the astounding collection of erotica and pornography by that foremost erotic bibliographer of all time, Pisanus Fraxi, of London. In the course of his lifetime, and by the expenditure of £100,000, Fraxi had assembled a complete collection of all famous and important works that dealt in any way with the sex life in England. His gracious aid and generosity have immeasurably eased our labor. Fraxi's library was undoubtedly the most complete collection of English erotica the world has ever known. Although the books cost him "only" £100,000, his judgment and taste were so excellent that at his death his library was appraised at £210,000, over a million dollars!

But the greatest drawback to serious research in the field of eroticism in England is caused by the typically British distrust of the motives of students and collectors alike. With the appearance of the genuine erotic literature in England at the beginning of the eighteenth century, there was naturally a concomitant growth in the collection and sale of such work. This grew to such proportions that as early as 1814 James Caulfield, in his "Chalcographimania", bitterly decried the common practice of the foremost men in England who spend their patrimony in collecting erotic literature:

> *Nor pass we by that shameful band,*
> *Dispensing with a lib'ral hand,*
> *Large sums, indecent books to buy,*
> *And prints disgusting to the eye:*
> *Witness from Duke of first degree,*
> *E'en to old sporting Colonel T——:*
> *In fine, full many none suspect,*
> *On themes like these alone reflect,*
> *Disgracing thus the manly name,*
> *And blazon'd sons of guilt and shame.*

Caulfield however errs in ascribing indecent motives to the "erotobibliomaniacs" (a charming neologism coined by Octave Uzanne in his amusing "Caprices d'un Bibliophile" and which designates those booklovers who especially cultivate the field of erotic and pornographic literature). Such criticism pertains rather to that part of the public which is devoid of all literary or bibliophilic interest, and which therefore concerns itself only with the "pure sex" in this field. It is for such smuthounds that there are daily fabricated worthless pamphlets, brochures and cheap reprints which may cause great harm if they fall into the hands of the immature youth. And this is more than a minor tragedy. For the youth must perforce find his information in such gutter-works, since sane and reasonable explanations of the divine nature of the sex act are forbidden by the canting censors, who are on a par with the smuthounds in seeking only the "dirty parts", the more to inflame their own vile minds.

But we are here concerned with rare and expensive works in private editions which are placed beyond the reach of any possible injury to children. As for those adults who profess to be shocked and disgusted at the mere mention of such "filthy trash" we can express but sympathy and commiseration for the unclean state of their own imaginations. Even the most potent poisons are not discarded because of their possible misuse, but are guarded and distinguished for their salutary potentialities. Given the safeguards of costliness and privacy, there is no reason why the foremost classics in erotic literature should be forbidden to those who are in a position to appreciate and make use of them.

For it is not merely the rarity of the erotica in their original editions, nor the sumptuousness of their reprints and translations, that makes them desirable in the eyes of book-collectors (although there are indeed a good number of bibliophilists who collect such works for these reasons). It is far more the undeniably high literary, cultural and historical significance of the worthy works of this nature which portray the sexual relations and all the other relations of mankind from the standpoint of the sex life. No

other branch of literature performs this valuable
function of revealing the "vita sexualis" with
such truth and intimacy. Erotic works thus form
one of the most significant sources for the knowledge of a cultural epoch or an historical period.
We need but remind the student that Aretino's
"Ragionamenti", Restif de la Bretonne's innumerable obscene novels and the Marquis de Sade's
astounding work, the "120 Days of Sodom",
were true products of their period, born in a state
of revolutionary frenzy and affording the reader
a most comprehensive view of the sexual and social life of the time.

Most important of all, however, is the funda-
mentally important psychological and psycho-
analytical role played by erotica and pornography: firstly, in the numerous faithful descriptions of the sexual development of individuals
(as in Bretonne's autobiographical novels and in
Frank Harris' masterful three-volume "My Life
and Loves"), which have proven so valuable to
modern psychology; secondly, in the representation of the *normal* sex life, for, contrary to general uninformed opinion, the erotica of any country are mainly concerned with the normal sexual
practices of the natives, and it is usually in foreign
translations that strange perversions are encountered; thirdly, in the necessary use of erotica by
the literary critic, historian, philologist, bibli-
ographers and many, many other serious students
in their research work, which is often left in an
incomplete and fragmentary state because of
their inability to procure important classics which
are considered harmful to children and infantile
adults — and are hence forbidden to mature.

cultured adults, even when motivated by the most laudatory of scholarly projects; lastly, and perhaps most important of all, in the extraordinary value of erotica and pornography to medical science, pathology, lay and medical jurisprudence. The clearest light on the origination and development of all the pathological manifestations of a country is to be found in such works. Many physicians and jurists have learned far more about the treatment, possible cure, and the best "punishments" for sexual perversions from these "harmful" works than from regular textbooks with their scant mention or hasty dismissal of this fundamental problem in modern life. In England it was the erotic and pornographic work that brought home to the lawmakers the knowledge of the vast spread of flagellation throughout the land; in pensions, schools, boarding houses, in the army, etc. And yet lawmakers, jurists, counsellors, plus all the self-appointed specialists in the morals of other people, seek to ban their best weapons of defence. There are many more arguments on the decided value of erotica but we believe we have sufficiently indicated the importance of this subject and must rest the question at this point.

The many concepts and adjectives pertaining to the field of erotica have caused extreme confusion in both academic and legal circles. In its essence, eroticism is a subjective concept and hence depends upon the individual for a definite significance. "To the pure all things are pure" may be converted to "anything may be obscene to anyone". Such astounding nonsensicalities cannot be duplicated in any other field of human

research, for it is only the study of the sexual relations of mankind which has been forbidden
until modern times—and even now classic works
and scientific studies are disapproved of and
bowdlerized by many political jurists who have
the effrontery to suppress the most valuable in-
vestigations of the divinest principles of the
Creator.

The universal "erotic literature"—it is found
in every country and in every age, a fact which
alone sufficiently indicates its indispensability —
covers the entire field of the sexual relations of
mankind: it may be scientific in nature, as in sexology, anthropology, ethnology, etc., or literary
("real"), as in classic works, novels and belles
lettres which concern themselves with the representation of sexual sensations and situations. This
inclusive concept of erotic literature may be
further subdivided into the following classes:

Piquant literature. Piquant signifies piercing,
sharp, biting: it need not have an outspoken
erotic character. A striking fusion of situations
which evokes a sarcastic or ironical smile from
the reader is called piquant. But in general we
consider "piquant literature" to be the representation of erotic scenes, wittily treated and covered by a transparent veil.

Gallant literature. We speak of gallant adventures, gallant diseases, gallant dress and gallant conduct. In general we understand by "gallantry" the exercise of the art of love and seduction, the "savoir vivre" of the French, the "decorum" of the Romans.

Frivolous literature. Frivolity is the conscious
ridicule of the emotions and ideals of other per-

sons, a blasphemy or travesty of pure sensations in a boorish, coarse way or by forthright absurdities. In both cases it is the intention of the scoffer to wound the feelings of another and to incite his own laughter with mephistophelian sneers.

Obscene and Pornographic literature. It is only in recent times that an important and essential differentiation has been made between "obscenity" and "pornography". This distinction is vitally necessary to the advance of civilized society. Lawmakers and jurists, who are always behind literary geniuses in recognizing the potentialities of human progress, are just beginning to distinguish between the cultured and the vulgar use of "obscene" words.* The use of obscenity does not in itself, make a work obscene. We might just as well say that the use of cocaine and other drugs in medicine makes the afflicted patient a dope-fiend, the physician a criminal! The purpose and motive of the author and reader, physician and patient, are the essential elements. Literary methods, scenes and characters may demand the use of common argot for the full realization of the plot and motivation. It is only when an author uses "obscene" words for the purpose of perverse sexual excitation that a work can properly be called pornographic. This word itself (porne = prostitute, graphein = to write) characterizes its province as the deliberate de-

---

* "Ulysses" is now permissible in the United States of America as a modern classic, and the day is not far off when "Lady Chatterley's Lover" and "My Life and Loves" will be recognized as highly important and valuable contributions to the salvation of society.

scription of adventures that are closely connected
with the profession of prostitutes. Pornography
is erotic literature in its narrowest sense and is
rightfully condemned by society for its pernicious influence in arousing perverse lusts and desires in both young and old. We hold no brief
for such wretched trash and have avoided any
reference to this class of literature, except when
a few of these works are historically important
to students, and we have then given only the essential bibliographical details.

But such dregs from diseased minds are no excuse for impotent reformers and meddling mor-
alists deliberately to soil with their impure hands
the masterworks of the ancients and moderns as
if these ignorant pigmies know better than the
intellectual giants of the foremost races and eras
of society what is good or bad for mankind! A
book may be written in conscious opposition to
the "prevailing morals" and may nevertheless
afford us a more perfect explanation of the phys-
iological sex life, thus pointing a new path to a
more ideal state of sex relations than our present
system with all its attendant woes and abuses.
The arousing of sexual excitation by literature
may often be of the greatest aid to frigid or indifferent wives and husbands. In all cases the use
of such works is beneficial to the reader in that
it allows an outlet for his sexual emotions. This
is technically known to psychologists and physicians as katharsis, a principle which dates back
to Aristotle's discovery that the incestuous Athe-
nian tragedies rid the ancient Greeks of their
perverse desires and Oedipus complexes. It is
only when the reverse is true and the work at-

tempts to *arouse perverse desires,* not to relieve
them by sublimity of language, style, motive,
etc., that we can rightfully call the book pornographic, or, in the ambiguous legal sense, "obscene".

Thus the use of the word obscene in this present work should not be confused with the common and uncritical meaning. We are fully aware
that there may be border-line cases in which it
will be difficult to decide, but we believe that
the above distinctions represent a considerable
advance in clearing up the ambiguities and sub-
jectiveness of the various classes of erotic literature. As our lawmakers and jurists increasingly
turn to scientific studies, so will many of the
works discussed in this volume be removed from
the inferno of "forbidden books and pictures"
and restored to their rightful place in society.

The above clarification of the field of eroticism is also important to us in a personal sense.
For over thirty years we have studied sexology
in practically all its branches and have watched
its birth as a rickety hybrid and its growth to its
present status as a full-fledged science. We have
written over twenty-five books ranging from scientific monographs on the treatment and preven-
tion of syphilis to literary encyclopedias on the
sex life of modern times. But with none of these
works have we personally been so pleased as with
the present volume. We feel certain that the "Sex
Life in England Illustrated" (as revealed in its
erotic and obscene literature and art) will have
a four-fold value and appeal: to the psychologist and psychoanalyst; to the literary critic,
historian, philologist and bibliographer; to the

fields of medical science, pathology, law and medical jurisprudence; and to the entire world of art which has been for so long bereft of many of the greatest erotic classics of English art and genius. We take great pride in being the first student to explore the unpath'd waters of English eroticism, for we have personally experienced all the difficulties of scientists and collectors the world over in obtaining and describing these rare and valuable works. We can say with Fraxi: "To extract from them their pith and marrow, and to put the same in a useful, convenient, and readable form, so as to be a lasting and trustworthy record, is a noble and elevating pursuit, which requires tact, delicacy, discrimination, perspicuity, not to mention patience and untiring assiduity."

We hope in all humility that our "Sex Life in England" will remove the shackles of prudery from English scholars, turn their attention to this important and yet so neglected field of human erotics, and bring forth extended research in their own native country, just as our "120 Days of Sodom" opened the myopic eyes of French savants to an epoch-making genius of their own native land.

Dr. Iwan Bloch,
Professor of Genito-Urinary Diseases,
University of Berlin.
Author of "120 Days of Sodom",
"Strange Sexual Practises",
"Anthropologia Sexualis",
"Origin of Syphilis",
etc.. etc.. etc.

Contents

BOOK ONE

ETHNOLOGICAL *and* CULTURAL STUDIES
of the SEX LIFE IN ENGLAND
as revealed
in its EROTIC *and* OBSCENE LITERATURE

27

29

BOOK TWO
ETHNOLOGICAL and CULTURAL STUDIES
of the SEX LIFE IN ENGLAND
as revealed
in its EROTIC and OBSCENE ART

34

Book One

ETHNOLOGICAL

AND

CULTURAL STUDIES

OF THE

Sex Life in England

AS REVEALED IN ITS

Erotic and Obscene Literature

1.

General Character
of English Erotica and
Pornography

THE true character of a country is most clearly revealed in its literary productions. Modern psychology has satisfactorily explained the decisive role in literature in the interpretation of a national characteristic or a definite cultural period. Yet how much more strikingly does the erotic and pornographic output of a country indicate the temper of the people, its hidden foibles and idiosyncracies, its fads and perversions, its secret longings, practices and indiscretions.

"Of all the emotions treated of in literature," says George Brandes, "the erotic emotion is that which receives most attention, and as a rule makes most impression on the reader. Knowledge of the manner in which it is apprehended and represented is an important factor in any real understanding of the spirit of an age. In the age's conception of the passion of eroticism we have, as it were, a gauge by which we can measure with extreme accuracy the force, the nature, the temperament of its whole emotional life."

This universal agreement on the significance of eroticism in the prose and poetry of a people may best be tested for correctness of judgment by an examination of the crassest and grossest expression of eroticism as it is revealed in the so-called "obscene" literature, in the narrower sense. And, in fact, the character of the English people is mirrored very clearly and distinctly in their erotic literature. Those extreme developments of the English national character, brutality, grossness, eccentricity, stolid pride, are the elements which attract our immediate attention in a far greater degree than in the ordinary works of belles lettres and poesy which, in turn, expose the entire solidity, profundity, sentimentality, hypochondria and affected prudery of the inner mind of the English nation.

Boileau's famous statement: "Les Anglais dans les mots bravent l'honnêteté," therefore holds unrestrictedly only in the field of erotic and obscene literature. The foremost and profoundest scholar of English erotic literature, Pisanus Fraxi, has the following to say on this point: "English erotic stories are sorry products from the literary standpoint which alone can pardon them in the eyes of an educated person. It seems in fact that the English language is not adapted to the description of erotic scenes and that a delicate treatment of such subjects is impossible for us. That refined and sensitive sensuality which Eugène Sue, himself a great hero of debauchery, called the 'religion of the senses, not vulgar sensuality, illiterate, unintelligent, but that exquisite sensuality which is emotional and Attic in spirit,' is rarely, if ever, to be found among us. On the contrary our writers in this field have sought to extend themselves with the physical description of love, and that with the coarsest words and the most brutal and grossest expressions, so that their stories are more apt to repulse than to attract and can be qualified only with our highly expressive word 'bawdy'."

Fraxi further states that this repulsive character of English erotica is mostly due to the fact that in France, Italy and even Germany the most imposing writers and thinkers have not disdained entering the field of genuine eroticism; in England only the "veriest grubbians", mostly persons without any pretensions to literary or artistic talents, have placed their pens in the service of Venus and Priapus. The "greatest name of which England can boast" is John Cleland, the author of "Fanny Hill, or the Memoirs of a Woman of Pleasure", and he is but a star of minor magnitude compared to the shining lights of French pornography in his own time.

Matters became even worse as the influence of foreign, especially that of French, literature made itself felt in the course of the nineteenth century. The English eroticists and pornographists bodily took over all the perversities and perversions of the French but without their "raffinement" in form and expression. And so the more modern English eroticism represents a weird mixture of

commonest coarseness and grossest monstrous-
ness. "When we," says Fraxi, "compare such tales
as the 'Memoirs of a Woman of Pleasure' and
the 'Memoirs of a Coxcomb' with the 'Romance
of Lust', the 'Experimental Lecture' or the 'Lascivious Gems' then we note that in the first named
works the characters, scenes and incidents are
natural, the words and expressions not overly
vulgar. Cleland's characters, Fanny Hill, the
fop, the pimpesses and rakes whom she encounters, are all described from nature and do only
what they ordinarily would have done in the
natural circumstances in which they were placed,
whereas the persons of the last named works are
impossible products of a diseased phantasy whose
actions are improbable or impossible."

2.

Rich Erotic Vocabulary of the English

NOTHER clue to the ethos of a people is the nature and extent of the erotic vocabulary at its command. Although England cannot hope to equal France in the variety and delicate nuances of obscene argot, nevertheless there is quite an extensive erotic vocabulary in English literature, comparable in number to that of the French, and far superior to that of the German.

There have been a number of dictionaries published in England which contained erotic expressions. John Bee has collected a number of such words in his "Sportsman's Slang" (1825). But the classic work on the subject is the famous lexicon by Captain Grose, "A Classical Dictionary of the Vulgar Tongue". The first edition of this work appeared in 1785 and there have been many additions made to it, notably by Pierce Egan and Eric Partridge in recent times.

The erotic expressions in Grose's work were collected and published under the title "An Erotic English Dictionary" in the second volume of "Kryptadia". Since the last-named work is of great rarity, and since the words and expressions are of extreme importance to linguists, historians, critics and students of English literature (much of the best prose work of the eighteenth and nineteenth centuries cannot be understood without a knowledge of the meaning of such recondite terms) we reproduce at this point the "erotic dictionary" with the exception of a few words still current which might prove offensive to the reader:

Abbess, or **Lady Abbess**: Procuress or manageress of a bordel.
Academy, or **Pushing School**: Bordel.
Ankle: A pregnant girl is said to have "sprained her ankle".
Armour, to fight in: To use a condom.
Aunt: Procuress.

Backgammon player: Pederast.
Usher, or **gentleman of the back-door**: Pederast.
To Bagpipe: To irrumate.
Basketmaking: Copulation (cf. the German "Korbmachen").
Bawbles: Testicles.
Beard-splitter: Rake.
Beast with two backs: Man and woman in act of copulation.
Blower: Whore.
Bobtail: Whore, Eunuch.
Brim: Prostitute.
Brother Starling: One who sleeps with the same woman.
Brush, to have a, with a woman: Copulation.
Buck-fitch: A lecherous old man.

Buggery: Pederasty.
Bumbo: Negro word for vulva.
Buttered Bun: A man who directly follows another man in copulation with a girl is said to have enjoyed a "buttered bun".
Buttock: Whore.
Buttock bell: Coitus.

Cat: Prostitute.
Cauliflower: Vulva.
Clicket: Coitus.
Coffeehouse: Prolonged or interrupted coitus.
Cooler: Woman.
Commodity: Vulva.
Corporal, to mount a, and 4: Onanism (Corporal= thumb; 4 (fingers)=genitals).
Crack: Whore
Crinkums: Syphilis.
Cundum: Condom.

Dock: To copulate.
Doodle: Youth's penis.
Dripper: Gonorrhoea.
Dry bob: Coitus without emission.
Dumb glutton: Vulva.
Dumb watch: Bubo.

Facemaking: Coitus.
Fen: Procuress or prostitute.
Fireship: Syphilitic woman.
Flyer: Extra-marital coitus.
.....: Masturbate.
.....: Copulate.

Games: Whore.
Gap-stopper: Bordel-madam.
Gigg: Vulva.
Giblets, to join: Copulate.
Gingambobs: Testicles.
Goats giggs: Coitus.
Gobble: Lustful woman.

Hat, old: Vulva.
Hooks: Finger.
Horn colick: Priapism.
Huffle: Bestiality.
......: Copulate.

Indorser: Pederast.

Jock or **Jockuncloy:** Copulate.

Kettle drums: Nipples.
Knock: Copulate.

Ladybirds: Whores.
Larking: A lascivious practice that will not bear explanation (sic).

Machine: Condom.
Madge: Vulva.
Madge Culls: Pederasts.
Mantrap: Vulva.
Mettle: Sperm.
Mettle, to fetch: Masturbate.
Molly: Pederast.
Mow: Copulate (Scotch).
Muff: Vulva.

Nigling: Copulate.
Notch: Vulva.
Nub: Coitus.
Nutmegs: Testicles.

Peppered: Syphilitic.
Plug tail: Penis.
........: Penis.
Prigging: Coitus.

Riding St. George: Coitus inversus.
Roger: Penis.
Roger, v.: Copulate.
Running horse or **nag:** Syphilis.

......: Copulate.
Strapping: Coitus.
Stroke, to take a: Copulate.
Strenn: Copulate.
Sunburnt: Infected with gonorrhoea.
Swive: Copulate.

Tallywags or **tarrywags:** Testicles.
Thomas, Man-: Penis
Tiffing: Coitus.
Token: Syphilis.
Tomhup: Copulate.

Wap: Copulate.
Whiffles: Relaxed scrotum.

Whirligigs: Testicles.
Windwind passage, one who uses or navigates the:
Pederast.

The originality and piquancy of the humor in
the above erotic expressions, uncouth and boorish though they may be, cannot be gainsaid. The
essential element of the sexual connotation of a
word is drastically indicated by such a neat met-
aphorical pun as "backgammon player". The
English love for play-on-words has added an
enormous number of ambiguities and equivocations to the English language. The foreigner
must take care in expressing his thoughts lest he
inoffensively commit a breach of good manners
and be ostracized from polite society.

Heinrich Baumann, the talented collector of
London jargon, expressed this fear of equivocal
words in a charming verse in his "Londinismen".
Unfortunately, the poem is untranslatable since
the puns lose all their point:

> Sprich niemals **backside** anstatt **back**,
> Mit Woertchen **bottom** nicht erschreck'.
> Verwechsl' **pot** ja nicht mit **po**;
> Huet' dich zu sagen: **I sh'd think so!**
> In **farther** sprich das **te-age** aus.
> In **sting** ist k dem Ohr ein Graus.
> Zu englischen Ohres Schreck' und Weh'
> Sprich niemals hart das b und g:
> In **cog, frog** und **bug,**
> In **fog, brig** und **brick.**
> Ruf immer **psh!** und niemals **pist!**
> Huet' dich vor **grind, spent, clap** und **kissed!**
> Nie Damen nach ihrem **kitten** frag',
> Nie von ihren **flowers** zu sprechen wag'.
> Wort **purse** mit grosser Vorsicht brauch',
> **"My precious stones"** zweideutig auch!
> **Cock-chafer** bedeutet ein Insekt,
> Doch darin noch was andres steckt.
> Uebersetze stets das deutsche Buettel
> Mit **beadle,** aber nie mit **piddle.**

Verwechsle nimmer **chair** mit **stool**
Hab' acht auf die Woertchen **yard** und **tool!**
Das Woertchen **foot** sprich rasch, nicht **food,**
Doch mit Wort **sheet** dich ja nicht sput'.
Bomb, bum man verschieden prononciert:
Bomb nach oben, **bum** nach unten explodiert.
Wenn eine Dam' vom Hitz ist rot,
So frage niemals: **"Are you hot?"**
Frag' nie, ob sie **"with balls"** gern spiel',
Noch gar, ob **foot-balls** ihr gefiel'.
Ob **nuts** sie lieb', sie auch nicht frag',
Anstatt des **"nut"** stets **"walnut"** sag'.
Ihr **"leg"** bezeichne stets mit **"foot"**.
Den Bauch der **"stomach"** vertreten thut.
Verwechsle **breast, chest, bosom** nie,
Sag' nie, du wohnest in **W. C.!**

3.

Highly Spiced Titles of Erotic Books

LAST peculiarity of English erotica, and one that is not to be found in any other country, is the exceptionally long and highly spiced titles of the majority of the books. We might indeed almost lay down an invariable rule: the longer the title, the trashier the contents. This was especially true of the fifth and sixth decades of the nineteenth century when the unscrupulous publishers tried to tempt their clientele into buying worthless brochures because of flashy and promising titles. As a specimen of such a title we append the following quite characteristic example:

"Yokel's Preceptor: or, More Sprees in London! being a regular and Curious Show-up of all the Rigs and Doings of the Flash Cribs in

this Great Metropolis; Particularly Goodered's
Famous Saloon — Gambling Houses — Female
Hells and Introducing Houses! The Most Fam-
ous, Flash, and Cock-and-Hen Clubs, etc. — A
full Description of the Most Famous Stone-
Thumpers, particularly Elephant Bet, Finnikin
Fan, the Yarmouth Bloater, Flabby Poll, Fair
Eliza, the Black Mott, etc.: And it may be fairly
styled Every Swankey's Book, or the Greenhorn's
Guide Thro' Little Lunnon. Intended as a Warn-
ing to the Inexperienced — Teaching them how
to Secure their Lives and Property during an
Excursion through London, and calculated to
put the Gulpin always upon his guard. — Here
will be fond a Capital Show-Up of the most Infamous Pegging Kens. Bellowsing Rooms. Doss-
ing Hotels. Sharking Fakes. Fencing Cribs.
Fleecing Holes. Gulping Holes. Molly Clubs,
etc. etc. etc. To which is added A Joskin's Vocabulary Of the Various Slang Words now in constant use; the whole being a Moving Picture of
all the New Moves and Artful Dodges practised
at the present day, in all the most notorious Fly-
my Kens and Flash Cribs of London! By which
the Flat is put Awake to all the Plans adopted
to Feather a Green Bird, and let him into the
Most Important Secrets. With a Characteristic
Engraving. Price One Shilling. London: Printed
and Published by H. Smith, 37, Holywell Street,
Strand. Where may be had a Catalogue of a Most
extensive Variety of every choice and Curious
Facetious Work."

This all-inclusive title-page is followed by a
brochure of thirty-one pages in small duodecimo
format!

4.

"Droll Stories" of the Monks

THE honor of producing the first collection of "Droll Stories" belongs, strangely enough, to England. The "Gesta Romanorum" was compiled by many hands very early in the thirteenth century. The oldest manuscript extant dates from the year 1342 and it was first published about 1473 under the title: "Incipiunt Historiae Nobiles collectae ex Gestis Romanorum et quibusdam aliis libris cum applicationibus eorum."

In the one-hundred and fifty-two chapters of this collection there are joined in a bizarre potpourri the literary influences of north and south France, classic, oriental, and Christian theology and literature. The lascivious fabliaux, the uniform declamations of the troubadours, the wonders of the orient, the legends of the saints, the Arabian fantasies and the historical personages of classic times all turn pages on one another. These heterogeneous elements were fused by the monk-compilers by the simple device of subjoining a moral to every tale, and thus transforming it into a Christian or moral lesson.

As a specimen of the style and content of the "Gesta Romanorum" we reproduce the final tale:

ON ADULTERY

A certain king had a lion, a lioness, and a leopard, whom he much delighted in. During the absence of the lion, the lioness was unfaithful, and engaged with the leopard. And that she might prevent her mate's discovery of the crime, she used to wash herself in a fountain adjoining the king's castle. Now the king having often perceived what was going forward, commanded the fountain to be closed. This done, the lioness was unable to cleanse herself; and the lion returning, and ascertaining the injury that had been done him, assumed the place of a judge,—sentenced her to death, and immediately executed the sentence.

APPLICATION

My beloved, the king is our heavenly Father; the lion is Christ, and the lioness the soul. The leopard is the devil, and the fountain is confession, which being closed, death presently follows.

5.

Coarse Obscenity in the Middle Ages

Chaucer's "Canterbury Tales"

"EROTIC literature" in England really begins with the Restoration period. Eroticism was then, for the first time, considered from the standpoint of an art which provided spice, variation, excitement and enhancement to the ordinary joys of every-day love.

This artificial, tendentious emphasis of the sexual element was as foreign to the coarse naturalism of the Middle Ages up to the Shakespearean period as it was to the later prudery which found its roots in the puritanism of Cromwell's Commonwealth. To be sure there was a sufficiency of ribaldry and indecency from Chaucer to Marlowe and Shakespeare, but the obscenity was naive rather than studied. "Prudery was then and for a long time afterwards," says Scherr, "an unknown element." Wharton points to the fact that in the entire period of the Middle Ages not only were the foulest outrages of modesty permitted, but even the most shameful depravity was considered "harmless". The conscious refinement of life first devised new corrupt pleasures, but it also prevented at the same time the colossal monstrosities in the sexual field that were so evident in the Middle Ages. In a word, the "developing civilization" drove debauchery from the public eye to "secret nooks and hidden crannies".

We are therefore not surprised to find in Geoffrey Chaucer, the "first English poet", erotic and indeed, very obscene expressions and situations. The "Canterbury Tales" is especially rich from this viewpoint. A few erotic citations from the "Prologue of the Wife of Bath" will sufficiently demonstrate the natural coarseness of the period. The Wife of Bath expatiates longly and loudly on the divine purposes of the sexual members of humans:

> Tell me also, to what conclusion
> Were membres made of generation,
> And of so parfit wise a wight ywrought?
> Trusteth me wel, they were nat made for nought.
> Glose who so wol, and say bothe up and doun,
> That they were made for purgatioun
> Of urine, and of other thinges smale,
> And eke to know a female from a male:
> And for non other cause? say ye no?
> The experience wot wel it is not so.
> So that the clerkes be not with me wroth,
> I say this, that they maked ben for both,
> This is to sayn, for office, and for ese
> Of engendrure, ther we not God displese.
> Why shuld men elles in hir bookes sette,
> That man shal yelden to his wife hire dette?
> Now wherwith shuld he make his payement,
> If he used his sely instrument?
> Than were they made upon a creature
> To purge urine and eke for engendrure.

In a highly naive fashion the good Wife of Bath, who has buried five husbands, describes her pronounced tastes for the joys of Venus and of Bacchus:

> As helpe me God, I was a lusty on
> And faire, and riche, and yonge, and wel begon:
> And trewely, as min husbondes tolden me,
> I had the best queint that mighte be.
> For certes I am all venerian
> In feling, and my herte is marcian:
> Venus me yave my lust and likerousnesse,
> And Mars yave me my sturdy hardinesse.
> I folwed ay min inclination
> By vertue of my constellation:
> That made me that I coude nat withdraw
> My chambre of Venus from a good felaw.
> Yet have I Martes merke upon my face,
> And also in another privee place.
> For God so wisly be my salvation,
> I loved never by no discretion,
> But ever folwed min appetit,
> All were he shorte, longe, blake, or white,
> I toke no kepe, so that he liked me,
> Howe poure he was, ne eke of what degree.
>
> And I was yonge and ful of ragerie,
> Stibborne and strong, and joly as a pie.
> Tho coude I dancen to an harpe smale,
> And sing ywis as any nightingale,
> Whan I had dronke a draught of swete wine.
> Ne shud he nat have daunted me fro drinke:
> And after wine of Venus most I thinke.
> For al so siker as cold engendreth hayl,
> A likerous mouth most hast a likerous tayl.
> In woman vinolent is no defence,
> This knowen lechours by experience

and even more naively does she tell of her experiences in the bridal bed:

> But in our bed he was so fresh and gay,
> And therwithal he coude so wel me glose,
> Whan that he wolde han my belle chose,
> That, though he had me bet on every bon,
> He could win agen my love anon.

6.

"The Palace of Pleasure"

Rare Collection
of 101 Droll Stories

"THE Palace of Pleasure" (1566) was perhaps the most important repository of erotic plots and inspiration to the Elizabethan dramatists. "The Palace of Pleasure" was written by William Painter (1540-1594), clerk of Queen Elizabeth's Ordnance, who was "an importer rather than a contriver of stories". Painter "beautified and adorned a wealth of pleasant histories and excellent novels" from both ancient and modern literature. "The Palace of Pleasure" contains one-hundred and one tales and histories of varying length and erotic content. Thirty-three stories are derived from classic authors, among them Livy, Aulus Gellius, Plutarch, Aelian, Herodotus, Quintus Curtius and Tacitus. The remaining sixty-eight are drawn from the Southern countries, Italy, France and Spain which were finding such rich harvests in the new literary form of the "novelette". The most famous works of this nature used by Painter were the "Novelle" of Matteo Bandello, "Il Decamerone" of Boccaccio, the "Pecorone" of Giovanni Fiorentino, the "Heptameron" of Queen Margaret of Navarre, the "Notti" of Straparola, and the "Hecatommithi" of Giovanbattista Giraldi Cinthio.

It was the first time that such an abundance of new works and ideas had been brought to the attention of Elizabethan England, and the dramatists found it a veritable thesaurus of literary nuggets. Painter furnished the themes for five of Shakespeare's works, "The Rape of Lucrece", "All's Well that Ends Well", "Timon of Athens", "Coriolanus" and "Romeo and Juliet". Other important Elizabethan dramatists who used "The Palace of Pleausure" were Webster in his "Duchess of Malfi" and "Appius and Virginia", John Marston in his "Wonder of Women" and "The Insatiate Countess", George Peel and many others.

Roger Ascham, the Elizabethan guardian of England's insular virtue, declaimed against "The Palace of Pleasure" in the following wise: "They open, not fond and common ways to vice, but such subtle, cunning, new, and diverse shifts, to carry young wills to vanity, and young wittes to mischief, to teach old bawds new school-points, as the simple head of an Englishman is not able to invent, nor never was heard of in England before."

Painter, on the other hand, saw only the pleasures that might be derived from his adaptations:

"They recreate and refresh wearied minds, fatigued either with painful travel, or with continual care, occasioning them to shun and avoid heaviness of mind, vain fantasies, and idle cogitations. Pleasant so well abroad as at home, to avoid the grief of Winter's night and length of Summer's day, which the travellers on foot may use for a stay to ease their wearied body, and the journeyors on horseback for a chariot or less painful means of travel, instead of a merry companion to shorten the tedious toil of weary ways. Delectable they be (no doubt) for all sorts of men, for the sad, the angry, the choleric, the pleasant, the whole and sick, and for all other with whatsoever passion rising either by nature or use they be affected. The sad shall be discharged of heaviness, the angry and choleric purged, the pleasant maintained in mirth, the whole furnished with disport, and the sick appeased of grief."

How well Painter succeeded in this ambitious program may be determined by the reader from the following charming anecdote in his "Novel of Lais and Demosthenes":

"Phocion, a perepetetic philosopher, in a book which he made, entitled 'Cornucopia', writeth this history of Demosthenes and Lais, the harlot of Corinth, saying: that Lais by reason of her excellent beauty and pleasant favor, demanded for the use of her body, a great sum of money: unto whom was resort of all the rich men of Greece: but she would not admit them to that fact, except they would first give unto her, her demand. The quantity of which sum was exceeding great, whereof rose the proverb, 'Non cuivis homini contingit, adire Corinthum'.

Not every man is able
To go to Corinth's table.

He that travelled to Corinth to Lais, not able to give and bestow that sum upon her, went in vain. To this woman that noble philosopher Demosthenes secretly repaired, praying her to give him leave: but she demanding of him ten thousand denarios (amounting very near to three hundred pounds of our money) astonished at the wantonness of the woman, and discouraged with the greatness of the sum, returned back again, saying: *I come not to buy repentance so dear."*

7.

The Erotic Age
of Shakespeare

CCENTRICITIES, grotesqueries, bizarreries,
the colossus of a maddened passion, the
enormities of love's debaucheries, — all
these satanic elements of love are to be
found in the dramas and poetic reveries of the
erotic age of Shakespeare, in his immediate pred-
ecessors and contemporaries, such as Marlowe,
Greene, Ford, Webster, Massinger and many
others. The "imaginative faculty weighed down
their reasoning". Love became a delirium that
destroyed all with a madman's power, only to
succumb to its own raging germs of mortal failings. All these dramatists were intimate with the
pain and sorrow of love, but knew none of its
joys. Woman became a devil incarnate, as in

Webster's "Vittoria Accoramboni", which was indeed subtitled "The White Devil".

The essence of femininity, it is true, is presented by these dramatists in the "fundamental instinct of feminine fidelity and marital chastity". But these are individualities such as Beaumont and Fletcher's Bianca, Ordella, Arthusa, Juliane, Webster's Duchess of Amalfi and Isabella, Ford's and Greene's Penthea and Dorothea. But "when they love in vain and without hope, neither reason nor life resist; they languish, grow mad, and die", like Shakespeare's Ophelia.

In Beaumont and Fletcher's "The Maid's Tragedy" the forlorn Aspasia:

> Walks discontented, with her watry eyes
> Bent on the earth. The unfrequented woods
> Are her delight; and when she sees a bank
> Stuck full of flowers, she with a sigh will tell
> Her servants what a pretty place it were
> To bury lovers in; and make her maids
> Pluck 'em, and strew her over like a corse.
> She carries with her an infectious grief
> That strikes all her beholders; she will sing
> The mournful'st things that ever ear hath heard,
> And sigh and sing again; and when the rest
> Of our young ladies, in their wanton blood,
> Tell mirthful tales in course, that fill the room
> With laughter, she will with so sad a look
> Bring forth a story of the silent death
> Of some forsaken virgin, which her grief
> Will put in such a phrase, that, ere she end,
> She'll send them weeping one by one away.

"Like a spectre about a tomb, she wanders for ever about the remains of her slain lover, languishes, grows pale, swoons, ends by causing herself to be killed."

Such tender poetic figures are often coarsely joined to scenes of violent murders, strangulations, the slaughters of the battle-field and the grossest debaucheries, which, in turn, the more violently inflame the imagination.

But all the forms and visions of love, pure and profane, common and ideal, tragic and comic, foolish and wise, chaste and debauched, its good and its evil — all are to be seen in perfection in that "masterspirit of all time and clime", the divine Shakespeare.

That unique genius must also be called the first poet of modern love, for none before, and none so well after him, saw and explained the correct relations of love's trinity, its esthetic, sensual and spiritual elements. Shakespeare's love is modern love, in its complete development, and therefore needs no especial analysis for its understanding. Its foundation is passion; purified and ennobled by "a life beyond life".

In general, love in Shakespeare is a "superhuman" passion that mundane reason cannot comprehend within the limitations of its mortal frame; it is beyond good and evil and such bounded measurements of man in his futile clasp for eternity. Love is an ecstacy, a trance, which sweeps all from its path in its consuming frenzy. "Love is my sin," cries Shakespeare, but, equally well, "love is my saviour." In that classically simple sonnet he reveals the motivation of all his works:

> O, know, sweet love, I always write of you,
> And you and love are still my argument;
> So all my best is dressing old words new,
> Spending again what is already spent:
>> For as the sun is daily new and old,
>> So is my love still telling what is told.

But the infinity of his expression is always revealing new and heart-piercing splendor in the irradiation of "love's mad dream". There is no other poet, says Harris in his excellent analysis of the "Women of Shakespeare", who has dared paint with the brush of genius so many different forms of women, and yet, "while the French stocked their stage with masculine heroines, all Shakespeare's heroines are women in the fullest sense of the word".

But Shakespeare did not succeed in baring the heart of human love by pandering to prudes and hypocrites. At all times his vocabulary is bold and forceful. If "vulgar" words are expressive, they are used; if obscenity is needed to bring out his point, he does not use any cheapening euphemism but uses the short, vivid, Anglo-Saxon word. Mrs. Grundy's influence is so extensive in modern times that this work would be instantly interdicted if we quoted the many "obscene" expressions and scenes to be found in his plays. Any complete Shakespearean concordance will show the very frequent use of words and expressions that have been called by one critic "vile, filthy and disgusting", as if such words would drag Shakespeare down from the Olympian heights to the critic's own squalid gutter-thoughts. When Shakespeare puts into Iago's mouth the expression, "the beast with two backs", how infinitely superior does it sound to "coitus".

Shakespeare is a highly realistic observer of all the purely physical phenomena of sexual love. Here is how Iago describes the "lust of the blood":

"Virtue! a fig! 'tis in ourselves that we are thus

or thus. Our bodies are gardens; to the which our wills are gardeners: so that if we plant nettles or sow lettuce, set hyssop and weed up thyme, supply it with one gender of herbs or distract it with many, either to have it sterile with idleness or manured with industry, why, the power and corrigible authority of this lies in our wills. If the balance of our lives had not one scale of reason to poise another of sensuality, the blood and baseness of our natures would conduct us to most preposterous conclusions: but we have reason to cool our raging motions, our carnal stings, our unbittered lusts; whereof I take this, that you call love, to be a sect or scion."

Or, compare the description of an eunuch's emotions in "Antony and Cleopatra":

Cleopatra. Thou, eunuch Mardian!

Mardian. What's your highness' pleasure?

Cleopatra. Not now to hear thee sing; I take no pleasure
In aught an eunuch has: 'tis well for thee,
That, being unseminar'd, thy freer thoughts
May not fly forth of Egypt. Hast thou affections?

Mardian. Yes, gracious madam.

Cleopatra. Indeed!

Mardian. Not in deed, madam; for I can do nothing
But what indeed is honest to be done:
Yet have I fierce affections, and think
What Venus did with Mars.

What genius save Shakespeare would dare close a play, even the merry one of "Twelfth Night or, What You Will", with the highly erotic song of the clown:

When that I was and a little tiny boy,
    With hey, ho, the wind and the rain,
A foolish thing was but a toy,
    For the rain it raineth every day.

But when I came to man's estate,
    With hey, ho, &c.
'Gainst knaves and thieves men shut their gate,
    For the rain, &c.

But when I came, alas! to wive,
    With hey, ho, &c.
By swaggering could I never swive,
    For the rain, &c.

But when I came unto my beds,
    With hey, ho, &c.
With toss-pots still had drunken heads,
    For the rain, &c.

A great while ago the world begun,
    With hey, ho, &c.
But that's all one, our play is done,
    And we'll strive to please you every day.

It would be supererogatory to offer a cursive examination, analysis and biography of Shakespeare when that work has been so splendidly performed by Frank Harris in his many studies on Shakespeare. After centuries of captious criticism, it was Harris who conceived and carried out the only correct method of Shakespearean research: a resurrection of the man Shakespeare from his written words. Strange, that Shakespeare should have been tacitly acknowledged by his own countrymen to be guilty of homosexuality until Harris conclusively proved that there was not a "shred of evidence" to bear this out.

8.

Shakespeare
on Prostitution and
Syphilis

THE magnificence of Shakespeare's observations on the dire results of venereal diseases is usually overlooked by Shakespearean scholars, yet no other poet in world-literature has dared paint the final stages of syphilis with such bold and drastic colors from a master's palette. In "Timon of Athens", the prostitutes Phrynia and Timandra, mistresses to Alcibiades, ask Timon if he has any more gold left. Timon, in his bitterness on the ingratitude of a false world, cries out:

Enough to make a whore forswear her trade,
And to make whores, a bawd. Hold up, you sluts,
Your aprons mountant: you are not oathable;
Although, I know, you'll swear, terribly swear,
Into strong shudders and to heavenly agues,
The immortal gods that hear you: spare your oaths.
I'll trust to your conditions: be whores still;
And he whose pious breath seeks to convert you,
Be strong in whore, allure him, burn him up;
Let your close fire predominate his smoke,
And be no turncoats: yet may your pains, six months,
Be quite contrary: and thatch your poor thin roofs
With burdens of the dead;—some that were hang'd,
No matter:—wear them, betray with them: whore still;
Paint till a horse may mire upon your face:
A pox of wrinkles!

The prostitutes reply:

Well, more gold: what then?
Believe't that we'll do any thing for gold.

Whereupon Timon paints the extent of the ravages they shall cause:

(Until)
Consumptions sow
In hollow bones of man; strike their sharp shins,
And mar men's spurring. Crack the lawyer's voice,
That he may never more false title plead,
Nor sound his quillets shrilly: hoar the flamen,
That scolds against the quality of flesh
And not believes himself: down with the nose,
Down with it flat; take the bridge quite away
Of him that, his particular to forsee,
Smells from the general weal: make curl'd-pate ruffians
    bald;
And let the unscarr'd braggarts of the war
Derive some pain from you: plague all;
That your activity may defeat and quell
The source of all erection. There's more gold:
Do you damn others, and let this damn you,
And ditches grave you all!

Proksch, who has collected the references to syphilis by Shakespeare, states of the above description that "although Shakespeare, does not even mention the name of the disease in this passage, there has been no physician,—nor will there ever be— who has not immediately recognized this three-hundred year-old curse by Timon of Athens as a complete and perfectly correct delineation of syphilis. Exanthema, alopecia, laryngeal affections, osteal diseases, and 'down with the nose, down with it flat';—such a picture can be painted only by the infinite genius of a Shakespeare."

Other allusions to syphilis, in a humorous rather than satirical vein, are to be found in "King Henry the Fourth", Part II (Act I, Scene ii), "King Henry the Fifth" (Act V, Scene i), "Hamlet" (Act V, Scene i), and in "Measure for Measure" (Act I, Scene i).

9.

Sex Life of the Foremost English Rake: The Earl of Rochester

As we previously indicated, the history of the genuinely erotic and obscene literature in England really begins with the Restoration period, when the cult of "sex for sex' sake" domineered over the fields of literature, theatre, art and public morals. After the titanic personages of a Marlowe and a Shakespeare, accompanied by a wealth of brilliant contemporaries, there appeared under the rules of Charles II and James II a flock of erudite scholars and gallant wits who, from Dryden to Durfey, concerned themselves with obscenities and equivocations, flaunting their "coldblooded, shameless and blustering unbridled licentiousness".

"The influence of such writers," says Macau-

lay, "was doubtlessly noxious, yet less noxious
than it would have been had they been less depraved. The poison which they administered
was so strong that it was, in no long time, re-
jected with nausea. None of them understood
the dangerous art of associating images of un-
lawful pleasure with all that is endearing and
ennobling. None of them was aware that a certain decorum is essential even to voluptuousness,
that drapery may be far more alluring than exposure and that the imagination may be far more
powerfully moved by delicate hints which impel
it to exert itself, than by gross descriptions which
it takes passively."

The foremost representative of the Erotic Age
of the Restoration is generally acknowledged by
literary historians to be the notorious "crown-
prince of rakes", John Wilmot, Earl of Rochester, of whom the philosopher Hume said that
"his very name offends a modest ear". And, in
fact, Rochester's claims on posterity are mani-
fold. He was one of the most characteristic phenomena of the Restoration: his short span of life
(he was born on April 10, 1647 and died on July
26, 1680) under the reign of Charles II portrays a true and faithful picture of the wild
passions of England's Age of Debauchery; he
inaugurated a new style of eroticism in his
poems and dramas, that of the "obscene satire"
in which he has never been surpassed or even
equalled for richness and elegance of verse, boldness and coarseness of expression and wit, and
consuming savagery of ribaldry and smut. His
caustic sarcasms spared neither the King nor
his ministers and mistresses, and made him the

most feared man in England. Yet he was recalled to court time and time again for, as Robert Wolseley declares, he was "the delight and wonder of the men, the tender dove and the infatuation of the women". Aphra Behn, the noted authoress, of whom Rochester had a low opinion, nevertheless calls him the "great, the divine Rochester". In an extremely long dirge "On the Death of the Earl of Rochester" she recalls in passionate tones his "beauties" and "divinities".

Dr. Burnet, an intimate friend of Rochester in his last years, contributed "A Character of the Earl of Rochester" to an edition of his works:

"This noble lord appear'd at court with as great advantages as most ever had. He was a graceful and well shap'd person, tall and well made, if not a little too slender. He was exactly well bred, and what by a modest behaviour natural to him, what by a civility become almost as natural, his conversation was easy and obliging.

"He had a strange vivacity of thought and vigour of expression. His wit had a subtilty and sublimity both, that were scarce imitable. His style was clear and strong. When he us'd figures, they were very lively, and yet far enough out of the common road. He had made himself master of the ancient and modern wit, and of the modern French and Italian, as well as the English. He lov'd to talk and write of speculative matters, and did it with so fine a thread, that even those who hated the subjects that his fancy ran upon, yet could not but be charm'd with his way of treating of them. Boileau among the French, and Cowley among the English wits, were those he admired the most. Sometimes other men's thoughts mix'd with his composures; but that flow'd rather from the impressions they made on him when he read them, by which they came to return upon him as his own thoughts, than that he servilely copy'd from any. For few men ever had a bolder height of fancy, more steadily govern'd by judgment, than he had. No wonder a young man so made, and so improv'd, was very acceptable in a court.

"He laid out his wit very freely in libels and satires, in which he had a peculiar talent of mixing his wit with his malice, and fitting both with such apt words, that men were tempted to be pleas'd with them. From thence his composures came to be easily known; for few had such a way of tempering these together as he had. So that when any thing extraordinary that way came out, as a child is father'd sometimes by its resemblance, so was it laid at his door as its parent and author.

"He would often go into the country, and be for some months wholly employ'd in study, or the sallies of his wit, which he came to direct chiefly to satire. And this he often defended to me, by saying, there were some people that could not be kept in order, or admonish'd but in this way.

"For his other studies, they were divided between the comical and witty writings of the ancients and moderns, the Roman authors, and books of physick; which the ill state of health self.

"In his later years, he read books of history more. He took pleasure to disguise himself, as a porter, or as a beggar; sometimes to follow some mean amours, which for the variety of them, he affected. At other times, merely for diversion, he would go about in odd shapes, in which he acted his part so naturally, that even those who were in the secret, and saw him in these shapes, could perceive nothing by which he might be discover'd.

"He dy'd in the three and thirtieth year of his age. Nature had fitted him for great things, and his knowledge and observation qualify'd him to have been one of the most extraordinary men, not only of his nation, but of the age he liv'd in. And I do verily believe, that if God had thought fit to have continu'd him longer in the world, he had been the wonder and delight of all that knew him."

An entirely different portrait from that of the good Bishop Burnet is painted by Taine:

"His manners were those of a lawless and wretched mountebank; his delight was to haunt the stews, to debauch women, to write filthy songs and lewd pamphlets; he spent his time between scandal with the maids of honour, broils with men of letters, the receiving of insults, the giving of blows. By way of playing the gallant, he eloped with his wife before he married her. To make a display of scepticism, he ended by declining a duel, and gained the name of a coward. For five years together he was said to be drunk. The spirit within him failing of a worthy outlet, plunged him into adventures more befitting a clown. Once with the Duke of Buckingham he rented an inn on the Newmarket road, and turned innkeeper, supplying the husbands with drink and defiling their wives. He introduced himself, disguised as an old woman, into the house of a miser, robbed him of his wife, and passed her on to Buckingham. The husband hanged himself; they made very merry over the affair. At another time he disguised himself as a chairman, then as a beggar, and paid court to the gutter-girls. He ended by turning charlatan, astrologer, and vendor of drugs for procuring abortion, in the suburbs. It was the licentiousness of a fervid imagination, which fouled itself as another would have adorned it, which forced its way into lewdness and folly as another would have done into sense and beauty. What can come of love in hands like these? Stendhal said that love is like a dried-up bough cast into a mine; the crystals cover it, spread out into filagree work, and end by converting the worthless stick into a sparkling tuft of the purest diamonds.

"Rochester begins by depriving love of all its adornment, and to make sure of grasping it, converts it into a stick. Every refined sentiment, every fancy; the enchantment, the serene, sublime glow which transforms in a moment this wretched world of ours; the illusion which, uniting all the powers of our being, shows us perfection in a finite creature, and eternal bliss in a transient emotion,—all has vanished; there remains but satiated appetites and palled senses. The worst of it is, that he writes without spirit, and methodically enough. Nothing is more disgusting than obscenity in cold blood. One can endure the obscene works of Giulio Romano, and his Venetian voluptuousness, because in them genius sets off sensuality, and the loveliness of the splendid coloured draperies transforms an orgy into a work of art. We pardon Rabelais, when we have entered into the deep current of manly joy and vigour, with which his feasts abound. We can hold our nose and have done with it, while we follow with admiration, and even sympathy, the torrent of ideas and fancies which flows through his mire. But to see a man trying to be elegant and remaining coarse, endeavouring to paint the sentiments of a navvy in the language of a man of the world, who tries to find a suitable metaphor for every kind of obscenity, who plays the blackguard studiously and deliberately, who, excused neither by character, nor the glow of fancy, nor science, nor genius, degrades a good style of writing to such a work,—it is like a rascal who sets himself to sully a set of gems in a gutter. The end of all is but disgust and sickness. While La Fontaine continues to the last day capable of tenderness and happiness, this man at the age of thirty insults the weaker sex with spiteful malignity:

> When she is young, she whores herself for sport;
> And when she's old, she bawds for her support...
> She is a snare, a shamble, and a stews;
> Her meat and sauce she does for lechery chuse,
> And does in laziness delight the more,
> Because by that she is provoked to whore.
> Ungrateful, treacherous, enviously inclined,
> Wild beasts are tamed, floods easier far confined,
> Than is her stubborn and rebellious mind.
> Her temper so extravagant we find,
> She hates or is impertinently kind.
> Would she be grave, she then looks like a devil,
> And like a fool or whore, when she be civil...
> Contentious, wicked, and not fit to trust,
> And covetous to spend it on her lust.

"What a confession is such a judgment! what

an abstract of life! You see the roisterer dulled at the end of his career, dried up like a mummy, eaten away by ulcers. Amid the choruses, the crude satires, the remembrance of abortive plans, the sullied enjoyments which are heaped up in his wearied brain as in a sink, the fear of damnation is fermenting; he dies a devotee at the age of thirty-three years."

The incident referred to by Taine is graphically described by M. de St. Evremond in a letter to the Duchess of Mazarine:

"The Duke of Buckingham (his boon companion) being at this time under disgrace for things of another nature, they resolv'd to go in search of adventures; among many of which, this was one. There was an old covetous hunks (a term of contempt, applied especially to a miser) in the neighbourhood, who had, notwithstanding his age, got a very pretty young wife. In the poetical age, she had been taken for one of the wood-nymphs. Salmacis was not more charming, nor more fit for the joy. Her husband was as watchful of her as of his money; nor ever trusted her out of his sight, but into the hands of an old, ill-natur'd, ugly, hypocritical sister, who having never experienc'd the joys of love, had the true envy of an old maid to all that were young and handsome. Our noble hosts had no manner of doubt of his accepting a treat, for he had done many; loving a debauch with all his heart, when it cost him nothing, else the most temperate and abstemious man alive; but then they could never prevail with him to bring his wife along with him, notwithstanding they urg'd the presence of so many good wives of the neighbourhood, to

keep her company. All their study was then, how
to charm the dragon that he left behind to guard
the delicious Hesperian fruit, which he could
neither eat himself, nor suffer any other to eat.

"Such difficulties as these, did not use to puz-
zle such inventions. It was therefore agreed, that
my Lord Rochester should be dress'd in woman's
cloaths, and while the husband was engag'd by
my Lord Duke, and his good liquors, he should
go and try his luck with the old hypocrite at
home. He knew that she was a mighty fine lover
of a dram of the bottle, when she could come by
it. With that viaticum he marches, equip'd like
a country lass, to the old miser's house. Much
ado he found means to get sight or speech of the
old woman; but at last he obtained that favour,
when perfect in all the cant of those people, he
began to tell the occasion of his coming, and ban-
tering her, in hopes she would invite him in, but
all in vain; he was admitted no farther than the
porch, with the house-door just ajar. At last, my
Lord, finding no other way, rising up as going
away, pretends himself in a fit, and falls in at the
door. The noise brings the young wife to them,
who with much ado perswades her keeper to
help her into the house in respect to the decorum
of her sex, and the unhappy condition she was in.
The door had not been long shut, but by degrees
he comes to himself, and being set on a chair,
cants a very religious thanksgiving through the
nose for the good old gentlewoman; and begins
to tell how deplorable her hard fortune was to
have such fits which often took her in the street,
and so made her liable to many accidents; but
every now and then, as a relief, took a sip of the

bottle, and recommended it to the old woman, who was sure to drink a hearty dram; and when offer'd the young lass, she would stop the bottle, and say, it was naught for young people, and the like; but it was more to save a larger share for herself.

"My Lord had another bottle qualify'd with a little opium, which would sooner accomplish his desires, and lay the dragon asleep. The next time he drank off the former bottle, and gave the beldam the somniferous liquor, which drinking with greediness enough, she fell fast asleep. My Lord, now fir'd with the presence of the lovely creature, which he had made so near approaches to, was full of eager desires, which made him often change colour, and which made her imagine some return of his fits, and asking the question, my Lord reply'd, That if she would be so charitable to let him lye down on the bed, he should soon recover. The good-natured creature shew'd him the way, and being laid down, and staying by him at his request, he put her in mind of her condition, asking about her husband, whom the young woman painted in his true colours, both up and abed, supposing she had only a woman with her. By her story, he found that a little love would not be disagreeable, opportunity, revenge, and various pleasures concurring. As soon as she had laid herself down by my Lord, pleas'd with his conversation, his Lordship began to kiss her, embrace her, and to proceed farther. She was wonderfully surpriz'd at such addresses from a woman, but was soon made sensible by his Lordship, that he did not provoke without a power of appeasing. In short,

Madam, his Lordship was as happy as he could desire, and as long as he durst stay, for fear of the husband's return, and the keeper's awaking.

"But Phillis was unwilling to part with him, and resolv'd to escape from her prison, where she had neither pleasure nor ease, to one where she promis'd herself abundance of both. My Lord was glad of the opportunity, by which he not only gratify'd himself, but his friend my Lord Duke likewise. However, she took care of some money, having long since resolv'd on a flight, and being acquainted with the old gentleman's hoards, supply'd herself with one hundred and fifty broad-pieces, and march'd off with my Lord to the inn about midnight. They were to pass over three or four fields before they reach'd it, and in the last they were very near falling into the enemy's hands, had he not call'd aloud to him that carry'd the lanthorn; his voice discovering him, our adventurers struck down the field out of the path, and to be the more secure, lay down in the grass. The place, the occasion, and the person that was so near, put his Lordship in mind of renewing his pleasure in sight of his cuckold. The nymph was no longer nice, and easily comply'd with any of his desires. But not to detain your Grace any longer with this story, he had the damsel home, convey'd her up stairs to my Lord Duke's bed, and there having laid her, retir'd with a promise of returning as soon as he could change his cloaths, look after the family, and the like.

"But he having his ends already, sent up my Lord Duke in his place, whom the ignorant and passive nymph bore with equal satisfaction. The

husband coming home, finds his doors open, his
sister asleep, his wife fled, and his money gone.
After raving like a mad-man, he hanged himself. This news was soon spread about the neighbourhood and reached the inn; where both lovers, now as weary of their purchase, as desirous
of it before, adding to her stock as much more,
advise her to retire to London; and there, this
disgrace not being known, she might get another
husband; and that they intended soon to be there
themselves. She follow'd their advice; and so
this adventure ended . . . .

"His amours at court are too well known to
your Grace, to need my repeating of them. Besides, they are mingled too much with the repu-
tations of ladies of quality, to revive them. I cannot omit that affair which my Lord had with the
fine Miss R . . . . . . ts, mistress to the King
(Charles II), whom she left and refus'd, for the
possession of my Lord's person and heart, as she
imagined. But he was soon cloy'd with the enjoyment of any one woman, tho' the fairest in
the world, and forsook her. The lady, after the
first indignation of her passion was over, grew
as indifferent, and considered how she should
retrieve the King's heart. The occasion was luck-
ily given her one morning; while at her window
she was dressing, she saw the King coming by.
She made haste down with her hair about her
ears, and threw herself at his feet, implor'd his
pardon, and vow'd constancy for the future. The
good King, vanquish'd with the sight, took her
up, and protested no man could see her, and not
love, waited on her up to her lodging, and there
compleated the reconciliation."

10.

The Erotic Works of the Earl of Rochester

ROCHESTER'S genius as a satirist is incontrovertible; literary historians incline to agree with Graesse's opinion that Rochester would have become the greatest satirist in English literature had he been spared a few more years of life. Dryden's famous couplet is quite applicable to the Earl of Rochester:

> Whether, inspir'd by some diviner lust,
> His father got him with a greater gust.

And yet Rochester was an apt pupil at the "polite language of society", as the following pretty love-song will attest:

SONG

My dear mistress had a heart
Soft as those kind looks she gave me,
When with love's resistless heart,
And her eyes, she did enslave me.

But her constancy's so weak,
She's so wild, and apt to wander,
That my jealous heart would break,
Should we live one day asunder.

Melting joys about her move,
Killing pleasures, wounding blisses;
She can dress her eyes in love,
And her lips can arm with kisses.

Angels listen when she speaks,
She's my delight, all mankind's wonder;
But my jealous heart would break,
Should we live one day asunder

In a similar vein are the following verses that begin his famous "Mistress Song":

MISTRESS SONG

Why dost thou shade thy lovely face. O why
Does that eclipsing hand of thine deny
The sunshine of the sun's enlivening eye?

Without thy light, what light remains in me?
Thou art my life, my way, my light's in thee:
I live, I move, and by thy beams I see.

To be sure, the number of such effusions of pure love-poetry is but slight in comparison to those of erotic and obscene content, which, in spite of the delicacy and animation of the songs, appear to have been composed in the very state of priapism, or as the result of a physical and moral breakdown from a too strenuously amorous night. The following song affords us an excellent illustration of Rochester's method of transcribing his emotions:

ET CAETERA

A Song

In a dark, silent, shady grove,
Fit for the delights of love,
As on Corinna's breast I panting lay,
My right hand playing with Et Caetera.

A thousand words and am'rous kisses
Prepar'd us both for more substantial blisses;
And thus the hasty moments slipt away,
Lost in the transport of Et Caetera.

She blush'd to see her innocence betray'd,
And the small opposition she had made;
Yet hugg'd me close, and, with a sigh, did say,
Once more, my dear, once more Et Caetera.

But oh! the power to please this nymph, was past;
Too violent a flame can never last;
So we remitted to another day
The prosecution of Et Caetera.

An apparent case of satyriasis appears to have engendered in the poet the following:

THE WISH

Oh! that I could by some new chymick art,
To sperm convert my vitals and my heart,
That at one thrust I might my soul translate,
And in the womb my self regenerate:
There steep'd in lust, nine months I would remain,
Then boldly .... my passage out again.

His striking imagery and fantasy is well seen in:

THE MAIDENHEAD

Have you not in a chimney seen
A sullen faggot wet and green,
How coily it receives the heat,
And at both ends does fume and sweat?
    So fares it with the harmless maid,
When first upon her back she's laid;
But the well-experienc'd dame,
Cracks and rejoices in the flame.

One of the most striking examples of Rochester's power of description is contained in the following apologia of an attack of impotency:

THE DISAPPOINTMENT

Naked she lay, clasp'd in my longing arms,
I fill'd with love, and she all over charms;
Both equally inspir'd with eager fire,
Melting thro' kindness, flaming in desire;
With arms, legs, lips, close clinging to embrace,
She clips me to her breast, and sucks me to her face.
The nimble tongue (love's lesser lightning) play'd
Within my mouth, and to my thoughts convey'd
Swift orders, that I shou'd prepare to throw
The all-dissolving thunderbolt below.

When with a thousand kisses, wand'ring o'er
My panting breast, "And is there then no more?"
She cries. "All this to love and rapture's due;
Must we not pay a debt to pleasure too?"
But I, the most forlorn lost man alive,
To shew my wish'd obedience, vainly strive:
I sigh, alas! and kiss, but cannot swive.
Eager desires confound my first intent;
Succeeding shame does more success prevent,
And rage at last confirms me impotent.

Rochester's self-revealment reaches its apogee in what is probably his best known "sonnet":

THE DEBAUCHEE

I rise at eleven, I dine about two,
I get drunk before sev'n; and the next thing I do,
I send for my whore, when, for fear of a clap,
I .... in her hand, and I spew in her lap;
Then we quarrel and scold, 'till I fall asleep,
When the ...... growing bold, to my pocket does creep;
Then slily she leaves me, and t'revenge the ......,
At once she bereaves me of money and .....
If by chance then I wake, hot-headed and drunk,
What a coil do I make for the loss of my punk?
I storm, and I roar, and I fall in a rage,
And missing my ....., I ...... my page.
Then crop-sick all morning, I rail at my men,
And in bed I lie yawning 'till eleven again.

But Rochester's excellencies are best to be seen in his satires, in which a highly developed caustic and mordant wit assails the follies of his age and the sallies of his enemies. He himself composed a "Defence of Satire", in which he delivers the following judgment on the moral significance of the satire:

IN DEFENCE OF SATIRE

When Shakespeare, Johnson, Fletcher, rul'd the stage,
They took so bold a freedom with the age,
That there was scarce a knave or fool in town,
Of any note, but had their pictures shown.
And (without doubt) tho' some it may offend,
Nothing helps more than satire, to amend
Ill manners, or is trulier virtue's friend.
Princes may laws ordain, priests gravely preach,
But poets more successfully will teach.

His most famous satire is that against marriage, in which he recapitulates, with deadly effect, the excoriations against wives from his other satires:

A SATIRE AGAINST MARRIAGE

Marriage! O Hell and Furies name it not;
Hence, hence, ye holy cheats, a plot, a plot!
Marriage! 'Tis but a licens'd way to sin,
A noose to catch religious woodcocks in;
Or the nick-name of love's malicious fiend,
Begot in hell to persecute mankind.
'Tis the destroyer of our peace and health,
Misspender of our time, our strength, and wealth;
The enemy of valour, wit, mirth, all
That we can virtuous, good, or pleasant call.
By day, 'tis nothing but an endless noise,
By night, the echo of forgotten joys.
Abroad, the sport and wonder of the crowd,
At home, the hourly breach of what they vow'd.
In youth, 'tis opium to our lustful rage,
Which sleeps a while, but wakes again in age;
It heaps on all men much, but useless care,
For with more trouble they less happy are.
Ye Gods! that Man, by his own slavish law,
Should on himself such inconveniences draw!

If he would wiser Nature's Laws obey,
Those chalk him out a far more pleasant way.
When lusty youth and potent wine conspire
To fan the blood into a gen'rous fire,
We must not think the gallant will endure
The puissant issue of his calenture,
Nor always in his single pleasures burn,
Tho' Nature's handmaid sometimes serves the turn.
No, he must have a sprightly youthful wench,
In equal floods of love his flames to quench;
One that will hold him in her clasping arms,
And in that circle all his spirits charms;
That with new motion, and unpractis'd art,
Can raise his soul, and re-insnare his heart,
Hence spring the noble, fortunate, and great
Always begot in passion, and in heat.
But the dull offspring of the marriage-bed,
What is it, but a human piece of lead;
A sottish lump, ingender'd of all ills,
Begot like cats, against their father's wills?
If it be bastardiz'd 'tis doubly spoil'd,
The mother's fear's intail'd upon the child.
Thus, whether illegitimate or not,
Cowards and fools in wedlock are begot.
Let no ennobled soul himself debase
By lawful means to bastardize his race;
But if he must pay Nature's debt in kind,
To check his eager passion, let him find
Some willing female out; what tho' she be
The very dregs and scum of infamy;
Tho' she be Linsey-Woolsey, bawd, or whore,
Close-stool to Venus, Nature's common-shore,
Impudent, foolish, rotten with disease,
The Sunday-crack of suburb-'prentices:
What then? She's better than a wife by half,
And if thou'rt still unmarry'd, thou art safe.
With whores thou can'st but venture; what thou'st lost
May be redeem'd again with care and cost;
But a damn'd wife, by inevitable fate,
Destroys soul, body, credit, and estate.

No less famous is his satire against Charles II,
for which he was banished from the court.
Rochester's audaciousness in ridiculing the King's
impotency is rivalled only by the boldness of
language:

A SATIRE ON THE KING

In the Isle of Great Britain, long since famous known
For breeding the best ...... in Christendom,
There reigns, and there long may he reign and thrive,
The easiest Prince, and best bred man alive;
Him no ambition moves to seek renown,
Like the French fool, to wander up and down,
Starving his subjects, hazarding his crown.
Nor are his desires above his strength,
His scepter and his ..... are of a length;
And she that plays with one, may sway the other,
And make him little wiser than his brother.
I hate all monarchs and the thrones they sit on,
From the Hector of France to the Cully of Britain.
Poor Prince, the ....., like the buffoons at court,
It governs thee, because it makes the sport.
Tho' safety, law, religion, life lay on't,
'Twill break thro' all, to make its way to .....
Restless he rolls about from whore to whore;
A merry monarch, scandalous, and poor.

The following quatrain is even deadlier in its devastating effect:

THE KING'S EPITAPH

Here lies our sovereign Lord the King,
Whose word no man rely'd on;
Who never said a foolish thing,
But never did a wise one.

11.

Discovered Among
Harleian Manuscripts of British Museum

The Greatest Obscene Drama in English Literature: "Sodom"

By the Earl of Rochester

EVEN the boldest of Rochester's obscene lyrics and satires are far surpassed in point of cynicism and sexual revelations by his justly notorious drama, "Sodom", which presents a vivid and faithful picture of the sex life in the Court of Charles II, a Court of Debauchery that specialized in pederasty. "Sodom" is unique in the history of English literature; indeed, there is only one other work in any language that may be compared to it for breadth of imagination and capability of performance: we refer to the "120 Days of Sodom" of the Marquis de Sade, a work of much later composition, and which may well have been inspired by Rochester's drama.

An early imprint of this play is supposed to

read: "SODOM. A PLAY, BY the E. of R. Antwerp; Printed in the Year 1684."

This example was undoubtedly printed in that year; it was in octavo format but appears to have completely disappeared for Fraxi was unable to come across any known copy. He believed that an example of this edition existed in the Heber collection, and that it was burned with other obscene works. Fraxi knew of no other printed edition, but personally saw three manuscripts of "Sodom".

The first manuscript is still in the State Library of Hamburg; the size is small quarto and it contains thirty-nine pages written on both sides. The chirography is poor, careless, and the manuscript swarms with mistakes. It is plainly a copy by one who was not overly familiar with the English language, most probably a German. This example contains five acts and a prologue of one hundred lines, the "dramatis personae", and closes with two epilogues, one spoken by " .... icula", the other by " .... adilla", the latter consisting of ten lines titled "Madame Swivia in Praise of her ...".

The second manuscript is contained in a volume of miscellaneous poetry. This is also written on both sides, but in an excellent calligraphy. Although the text is more accurate than the Hamburg copy, this specimen lacks the title-page, prologue, epilogue, and "dramatis personae", and the play ends with Act Four, where "Bolloxinion" is soundly thrashed.

A third manuscript reads: "Sodom, or The Quintessence of Debauchery. By E. of R. Written for the Royal Company of Whoremasters."

This is to be found in Volume 7312 of the Harleian Manuscripts of the British Museum. There are no imprints, mottoes, or announcements to show that it was printed. It contains five acts, two prologues (one of seventy-two, the other of twenty-nine lines), and two epilogues (the one spoken by "....igratia" contains twenty-nine lines, the other of "....adilla" fifty-one lines, besides the ten lines of "Madame Swivia in Praise of her ...."). The text is superior to the other two manuscripts.

It has been asserted that "Sodom" was actually presented before King Charles II and his court, and also that women were present at this performance. This assertion apparently rests on the following verses from the prologue:

> I do presume there are no women here,
> 'T is too debauch'd for their fair sex I fear,
> Sure they will not in petticoats appear,
> And yet I am informed here's many a ....
> Come for to ease the twitching of ... .,
> Damn'd pocky jades, ... are hot as fire,
> Yet they must see this play t'increase desire.

The true author of this play is unquestionably the Earl of Rochester. For some time the authorship was a moot point, since Rochester had written in mock seriousness an abusive lampoon against the work and its author:

TO THE AUTHOR OF A PLAY CALL'D SODOM

> Tell me, abandon'd miscreant, prithee tell
> What damned power, invok'd and sent from hell
> (If hell were bad enough) did thee inspire
> To write, what fiends, asham'd would blushing hear,
> Hast thou of late embrac'd some succubus,
> And us'd the lewd familiar for a muse.
> Or didst the soul by inch of candle sell,
> To gain the glorious name of pimp to hell?

If so, go, and its vow'd allegiance swear,
Without 'press-money, be its volunteer.
May he who envies thee, deserve thy fate,
Deserve both heaven's and mankind's scorn and hate.
Disgrace to libels! Foil to very shame!
Whom 'tis a scandal to vouchsafe to name.
What foul description's foul enough for thee,
Sunk quite below the reach of infamy?
Thou covet'st to be lewd, but want'st the might,
And art all over devil, but in wit.
Week feeble strainer at mere ribaldry,
Whose muse is impotent to that degree,
It must, like age, be whipt to lechery.
Vile sot, who, clapt with poetry, art . . . . ,
And void'st corruption like a shanker'd . . . . . ,
Like ulcers thy imposthum'd addle brains
Drop into matter, which thy paper stains;
Whence nauseous rhimes by filthy births proceed,
As maggots in some t. . d ingend'ring breed.
Thy muse has got the . . . . , and they ascend,
As in some green-sick girl, at upper end.
Sure nature made, or meant at least to 'ave . . . '.,
Thy tongue a . . . . , thy mouth a . . . . .
How well a D. . . . wou'd that place become,
To gag it up, and make't for ever . . . . . ?
At least it should be frying'd . . . . ,
Or wear some stinking merkin for a beard,
That all from its base converse might be scar'd.
As they a door shut up, and mark'd, beware,
That tells infection and the plague is there.
Thou Moor-Fields author, fit for bawds to quote,
(If bawds themselves with honour safe may do't)
When suburb-'prentice come to hire delight,
And wants incentives to dull appetite.
There punk, perhaps, may thy brave works rehearse,
. . . . the senseless thing with hand and verse,
Which after shall (preferr'd to dressing-box)
Hold turpentine, and med'cines for the pox.
Or (if I may ordain a fate more fit
For thy foul nasty excrements of wit)
May they condemn'd to th' public Jakes be lent,
(For me, I'd fear the piles in vengeance sent,
Shou'd I with them profane my fundament.)
There . . . . . . wiping porters when they . . . . . ,
And so thy book itself turn Sodomite.

A superficial examination of "Sodom" is sufficient to dispel this transparent subterfuge. Even if we had not contemporary evidence as proof of Rochester's authorship, the style, wit, expression, favorite words and phrases, all point unerringly to Rochester. The pederasty against which he ranted so bombastically in the above poem was glorified in "Valentinian", a tragedy which he wrote for the stage and which was presented at the "Theatre Royal":

> 'Tis a soft rogue, this Lycias
> And rightly understood,
> He's worth a thousand women's nicenesses!
> The love of women moves even with their lust,
> Who therefore still are fond, but seldom just:
> Their love is usury, while they pretend,
> To gain the pleasure double which they lend.
> But a dear boy's disinterested flame
> Gives pleasure, and for mere love gathers pain;
> In him alone fondness sincere does prove,
> And the kind tender naked boy is love.

Let us now examine, concisely but completely, the content of this notorious but little-known play. The following characters are the main personages:

DRAMATIS PERSONAE

Bolloxinion	King of Sodom
....igratia	Queen
Picket	Princess
Swivia	Princess
.....anthos	General of the Army
Pockenello	Prince, Colonel, Favorite of the King
Borastus	The Chief of pederasts
Pine	
....adilla Twely	Two noble pimps
Officina Clitoris ....icula	Noble virgins
Flux	Physician to the King
Virtuoso	Court-purveyor of dildoes
Lads, knaves, pimps, and other rascals.	

At the curtain's rise we see an antechamber, the walls of which are covered with immense panels representing all the coital positions in Aretino's "Figurae Veneris". The King is the first to appear on the stage; he is followed by Borastus, Pockenello, Pine and Twely. Bolloxinion then begins:

> Thus, in the zenith of my lust, I reign;
> I eat to swive, and swive to eat again;
> Let other monarchs who their scepter bear
> To keep their subjects less in love than fear
> Be slaves to crowns, my nation shall be free;
> My ..... only shall my sceptre be,
> My laws shall act more pleasure than command,
> And with my ..... I'll govern all the land.

Such liberal pronunciamentos, which announce the complete freedom of sexual relations, unfettered by the slightest law, are befittingly received by the enthusiastic courtiers. Each one wheedles and cajoles the King with flattery and compliments. Thereupon Bolloxinion continues with his "opening speech":

> I do no longer old stale ..... admire,
> The drudgery has worn out my desire.
>
> Borastus, you spend your time I know not how,
> The choice of buggery is wanting now.

The learned pederast, Borastus, thereupon gives the following advice to the King who yearns for such new, untrodden pleasures:

> I would advise you, sire, to make a ....,
> Once more at Pockenello's .... .

The King chooses Pockenello and Twely for his lovers, and issues the following proclamation, which assures all homosexualists and pederasts complete freedom in the satisfaction of their sexual inclinations:

> Henceforth, Borastus, set the nation free,
> Let conscience have its right and liberty.
> I do proclaim that bugg'ry may be us'd
> Through all the land, so .... be not abus'd
> That's the proviso.

Borastus and Pine now leave the stage, Pockenello then reveals to the King that Pine has cohabited with the Queen, and Twely adds that "he swiv'd her in the time of term". Bolloxinion, with his magnanimous disposition, takes no offense at being royally cuckolded, and closes scene and act with the words:

> With crimes of this sort I shall now dispense,
> His .... shall suffer for his ...... offense.

The first and second scenes of the second act take place "in a lovely garden which is embellished by many statues of men and women in various indiscreet attitudes"; in the middle of the garden a woman represents a fountain and is "flowing bold upright". This description appears to be an imitation of Rabelais' "Gargantua", Book One, Chapter Fifty-five: "In the middle of the court there was a splendid fountain of fair alabaster: Upon the top stood the three Graces, with their cornucopias of fecundity; they emitted water at their breasts, mouths, ears, eyes, and other orifices of the body."

To the accompaniment of gentle music and song the queen appears, followed by Officina, Clitoris and ....icula. They bewail the careless slights of the king, but console themselves with the thought that there are far better men than

His Royal Highness. Queen ....igratia declares
that she is not the least jealous, and gladly describes the virility of Buggeranthos in attractive
colors to her court-ladies:

> He has such charms,
> You'd swear you had a stallion in your arms,
> He swives with so much vigour, in a word,
> ... . is as good metal as his sword.

In the third scene the court-ladies make valiant
use of their dildoes, whereupon there follows an
interesting discussion as to the various merits
and qualities of such products. The queen impatiently awaits the arrival of Buggeranthos and
commands ....adilla to while away the time with
an obscene song. The act closes with a dance of
nude men and women, and the resulting orgy of
sexual intercourse between the terpsichorean
participants.

The third act has but little to do with the theme
of the play, since it concerns itself mostly with
the seduction of the young prince by his sister
Swivia. At a second essay by the insatiable Swivia they are surprised by the drunken ....icula
who becomes a zealous partner in their love-
bouts, which end with the removal of the exhausted young prince to his royal bed.

In the first scene of the fourth act we find the
Queen and her general in tender tête-à-tête. She
is enthused at the results of her tests of her new
lover's virility, and continually implores him for
fresh evidence until at last he can no longer
satisfy her desires:

> Love, like war, must have its interval;
> Nature renews that strength by kind repose,
> Which an untimely drudgery would lose.

And he leaves her, "lassata, sed non satiata", (tired but not content) whereupon she delivers a monologue complaining of the mockery of this "sated rake".

The second scene brings back the King, Borastus and Pockenello who speak at great length of the joys of pederasty and compare its superiority to that of normal sexual intercourse. Buggeranthos appears and is asked by the King how the soldiers received his proclamation:

Bolloxinion: How are they pleased with what I did proclaim?
Buggeranthos: They practise it in honour of your name.

Buggeranthos then reports on the pastimes and amusements of the women of the empire:

> Dildoes and dogs with women do prevail,
> I caught one with a cur's bob tail.

He then tells the King in complete detail how a woman, "faute de mieux", was caught with a stallion. Bolloxinion interrupts most gleefully to offer the woman an elephant for the same purpose.

Twely now appears and announces the arrival of an ambassador, whom Tarse-...., King of Gomorrah, has sent him, together with a retinue of forty boys. Bolloxinion is entranced, sends for one of the boys, and immediately withdraws from the scene with him.

The first scene of the fifth act is the most humorous one of the entire play. The young court-ladies bitterly complain to Virtuoso, court-purveyor of dildoes, of the poor quality and inadequacy of his products. They finally succeed in inducing him to substitute his "natural" capabilities for his "artificial" talents.

The last scene, in complete contrast to the former one, is the most tragic of the play. The scene is a "grove of cypresses in the form of a phallus with a banquet-hall". After a sad song by a wandering youth there appear Bolloxinion, Borastus, and Pockenello. Shortly thereafter Flux, the royal physician, enters and paints in the blackest colours the horrible results of the prevailing anarchy in the sexual relations of his subjects. Chancre, gonorrhoea, satyriasis, and so forth, are raging throughout the land in frightful fashion. The queen has succumbed to the fatal love-thrusts of her lovers. The prince has gonorrhoea, the princess likewise, and so forth. The frightened King asks the physician if there is any means of checking this sexual plague, whereupon Flux answers.

> To love and nature all their rights restore,
> .... women, and let bugg'ry be no more,
> It doth the procreative end destroy,
> Which Nature gave with pleasure to enjoy,
> Please her, and she'll be kind, — if you displease,
> She turns into corruption and disease.

But Bolloxinion shudders at the thoughts of a woman in sexual connection. He hesitates to revoke the proclamation. Thereupon the clouds burst asunder, fiery demons appear and disappear. The ghost of .....icula shows itself. Horrible groaning and sighing penetrate the stage as if from the nethermost depths; throughout the stage ghastly figures sway to and fro.

And as a grand finale, they rest on their lusts:

Pockenello: Pox on these rights, I'd rather have a whore.

Bolloxinion: Or ..... rival.

Flux: For heaven's sake no more;
Nature puts on me a prophetic fear,
Behold, the heavens all in flame appear.

Bolloxinion: Let heav'n descend and set the world on fire,
We to some darker cavern will retire.

Fire, brimstone and smoke.

The curtain falls.

12.

Great Erotic Masters of England's Age of Debauchery

OTHER great erotic masters in this age of debauchery pale into insignificance beside the imposing genius of a Rochester. Only the literary historian is interested in the lesser figures of Dorset, Roscommon, Edmund Waller, Buckingham and Otway. But especial attention should be called to the prevalence in this debauched age of women who thought little of attaching their names to highly erotic and even obscene works. We can even speak in this connection of an erotic female trinity: Aphra Behn, Susanna Centlivre, and Mary Manley. The last named wrote "Atalantis", a satiric and indecent description of the England of 1700, somewhat similar in treatment to the cynical poem by Samuel Butler, "Hudibras" (1663-1678), a satire on the Puritans.

We have already alluded to the erotic-frivolous character of the dramatic literature of this age. Not even the work of a Dryden remained free from such influences. But the height of debauchery in dramatic literature was reached by the plays of Wycherley, Congreve, Vanbrugh and Farquhar.

Love to them is a snare, a delusion: Wycherley cries out: "Her love — a whore's, a witch's love! — But what, did she not kiss well sir? I'm sure, I thought her lips — but I must not think of 'em more — but yet they are such I could still kiss, — grow to, — and then tear off with my teeth, grind 'em into mammocks, and spit 'em into her cuckold's face." Lady Flippant is a fair specimen of the morals of the women of the Restoration: "Unfortunate lady that I am! I have left the herd on purpose to be chased, and have wandered this hour here; but the park affords not so much as a satyr for me; and no Burgundy man or drunken scourer will reel my way. The rag-women and cinder women have better luck than I."

Thackeray declares that the Restoration plays awaken sensations that make one feel as if one were present at the leavings of an orgy in Sallust's home in Pompeii. Taine unkindly adds that the Restoration dramatists possessed all the vices they described in their plays. We need not analyze these highly erotic works of the Restorationists for they are readily available to students in all the larger libraries and bookstores.

13.

Famous Erotic Novelists of the Eighteenth Century

HE first half of the eighteenth century is the age of the moralizing and satiric forces that swept literature and is illuminated by the brilliant genius of Defoe, Swift, Richardson, Sterne, Smollett and Fielding.

Daniel Defoe (1663-1731) deserves special mention for his two novels about prostitutes, "Mother Ross", and the more famous "Moll Flanders", the complete title of which follows: "The Fortunes and Misfortunes of the Famous Moll Flanders, etc. who was Born in Newgate, and during a Life of continu'd Variety for Three-score Years, besides her Childhood, was Twelve Year a Whore, five times a Wife (whereof once to her own Brother) Twelve Year a Thief, Eight

Year a Transported Felon in Virginia, at last grew Rich, liv'd Honest and died a Penitent."

Where Swift touches on sex it is only for the purpose of showing its contrary side. He drags, in the literal sense of the word, love into all the muck and filth, as in "A Love-poem from a Physician".

Sterne, especially in the many obscene parts of "Tristam Shandy", entertains the same notion:

"He loves the nude, not from a feeling of the beautiful, and in the manner of painters, not from sensuality and frankness like Fielding, not from a search after pleasure, like Dorat, Boufflers, and all those refined pleasure-seekers, who at the same time were rhyming and enjoying themselves in France. If he goes into dirty places, it is because they are forbidden and not frequented. What he seeks there is singularity and scandal. The allurement of this forbidden fruit is not the fruit, but the prohibition; for he bites by preference where the fruit is withered or worm-eaten. That an epicurean delights in detailing the pretty sins of a pretty woman is nothing wonderful; but that a novelist takes pleasure in watching the bedroom of a musty, fusty old couple, in observing the consequences of the fall of a burning chestnut in a pair of breeches, in detailing the question of Mrs. Wadman on the consequences of wounds in the groin, can only be explained by the aberration of a perverted fancy, which finds its amusement in repugnant ideas, as spoiled palates are pleased by the pungent flavour of moldy cheese."

Taine adds that similar cynicism and "putrid

paronomasia" are to be found in Smollett's and Fielding's novels.

Since all the above mentioned works are well known and readily accessible in complete and unexpurgated editions we shall pass over to a consideration of the famous and rare English classics of eroticism and pornography in the eighteenth century.

14.

Contents of the Greatest Erotic Poem in the English Language: "The Toast"

By Dr. William King

IN the genuinely "erotic literature" of the eighteenth century two works stand out as unique accomplishments of English genius. They are "The Toast" by Dr. William King, considered by many critics to be the foremost erotic poem in the English language, and "Fanny Hill or the Memoirs of a Woman of Pleasure" by John Cleland, acknowledged by all critics to be the greatest novel of its kind in English, if not in the entire realm of world-literature.

"The Toast, an Epic Poem in Four Books" was first published in 1732 under the guise of an English translation by Peregrine O. Donald from the Latin original of Frederick Scheffer. The true author of "The Toast" is Dr. William King, son of the clergyman Peregrine King, headmaster of St. Mary Hall, Oxford. He was born in Stepney, Middlesex, 1685, and died in 1763. King was highly honored by the leading men of his age, especially by his intimate friend Swift, because of his brilliant wit and profound learning. He was a splendid speaker and a polished writer, who was as familiar with the Latin as he was with his native English tongue.

Johnson declares: "I clapped my hands so loudly and longly after Dr. King's speech that they are all wounds." The poet Thomas Warton describes King's resplendent oratorical genius in the following lines of his "Triumph of Isis":

> See, on yon Sage how all attentive stand,
> To catch his darting eye and waving hand.
> Hark! he begins, with all a Tully's art,
> To pour the dictates of a Cato's heart.
> Skill'd to pronounce what noblest thoughts inspire,
> He blends the speaker's with the patriot's fire;
> Bold to conceive, nor timorous to conceal,
> What Britons dare to think, he dares to tell.

On the other hand, there are many opponents who accuse King of discoursing on revolutionary themes and preaching on the delights of debauchery. Churchill in his "Candidate" even doubts the purity of King's Latin:

> King shall arise, and, bursting from the dead,
> Shall hurl his piebald Latin at thy head.

In a poem, "A Satire upon Physicians", King describes himself in the following terms:

In me, ah! pity to behold!
A wretch quite wither'd, weak and old;
Who now has pass'd by heaven's decree,
The dangerous year of sixty-three;
On asses' milk, and caudle fed,
I doddle on my cane to bed,
Of every step I take, afraid;
My coat unbuttoned by my maid.
My memory oft mistaking names,
For G-orge I often think of J-mes;
Am grown so feeble frail a Thing,
I scarce remember who is King!
Th' imperial purple which does wear,
A lawful or a lawless Heir!

"The Toast", itself, is perhaps the strangest and most remarkable erotic work in English literature. Curious enough is the enormous expenditure of patience and learning in attacking a single woman, who moreover is by no means an imposing figure. Stranger yet is the fact that so revolting a satire could be penned by a theologian and principal of a college.

"The Toast" revolves about the work of a Faustian genius who is completely intimate with the world, its woes and its vices, and whose masterful command of the English language is surpassed only by his extraordinary genius in the Latin classics. It is a moot point whether the English verses, the rhymed verses of the alleged Latin original, or even the curious notations in prose, are a more striking product of the phantasy! The entirety of "The Toast" is indeed nothing short of astounding; it is replete with excellent wit and humor, extensive scholarship and erudition, pointed satire and mordant characterization. Sylvain van de Weyer, one of the leading students of English curiosa, states that it is a "poème extraordinaire", and Octave Delepierre agrees to this judgment in even more enthusiastic terms in his "Macaroneana".

The historical antecedents of the poem involve the person of Lady Frances Brudenell, the widowed Countess of Newburgh, who concluded a second marriage in 1699 with Richard, Lord Bellew, an Irish nobleman. The result of this union was a son John, later Lord Bellew. Her second husband died in 1714 and left the "divine Myra" of the later poem in a very precarious position, for the debts of her deceased spouse were considerable. She was forced to borrow money from all quarters, in particular from Sir Thomas Smith, Inspector of the Phoenix Park in Dublin, and uncle of our William King.

After Smith had already advanced large sums of money to Lady Bellew he induced his rich nephew, William King, to take over his rôle. King was "milked" of many thousand pounds sterling by this highly experienced lady, and was unable to recover his money after involved proceedings and trials.

The only revenge to which the talented King had recourse was by the composition of "The Toast", that unique English lampoon, in which he made practical use of his extensive erudition in ascribing the most monstrous and unnatural vices and crimes to the object of his hatred.

The personages of "The Toast" are introduced in an anomalous compound of ancient mythology and modern phantasy as the "dramatis personae" of a poem which is alleged to be the translation of a Latin original, and which in turn is illuminated by an exhaustive commentary! The author uses the transparent pseudonym of Scheffer. The hero and heroine appear in mythological garb. Lady Newburgh is "Myra", a perverse, lecherous, old witch; Sir Thomas Smith, the uncle of the author, figures as an old, unfortunate, passionate "Mars", the "third husband" of the lady. "Myracides" is Lord John Bellew; Lady Allen is "Ali", an accomplice of Myra; "Pam" is Bishop Hort, and he is also addressed as "Hortator Scelerum", an excellent bilingual pun. Many other contemporary personages figure throughout the poem under disguised names.

King plainly began "The Toast" as a vicious satire, but as he himself remarks, "I started in ire and ended in mirth." Early in the poem he was seized with the desire to utilize the framework of "The Toast" as a vehicle for his literary talent, and in this way there arose one of the strangest of classical studies.

In order to acquaint the reader with the nature and style of "The Toast", which is one of the rarest of English works and is even inaccessible to the literary historian, we here include, despite its length, the most characteristic verse, the description of Myra's person, truly a most amazing product from a poet's pen:

There he saw the huge Mass tumble out of her Bed;
Like Bellona's her Stature, the Gorgon's her Head;
Hollow Eyes with a Glare, like the Eyn of an Ox;
And a forehead deep furrow'd, and matted grey Locks;
With a toothless wide Mouth, and a Beard on her Chin,
And a yellow rough Hide in the place of a Skin;
Brawny Shoulders up-rais'd; Cow-Udders; Imp's Teat;
And a pair of bow'd Legs, which were set on Splay Feet.
With the figure the God was surpriz'd and offended,
When he mark'd how these various Defects were amended;
How her back was laid flat with an Iron Machine,
And her breasts were lac'd down, with a sweet Bag between:
How she shaded her Eyes, and the squalid black Beard

Was so smoothly shav'd off, scarce a Bristle appear'd;
How she clear'd the old Ruins, new plaister'd her Face,
And apply'd Red or White, as it suited the Place:
With a set of Wall's Teeth, and a Cap of Dear's Hair,
Like a Virgin she bloom'd, and at sixty seem'd Fair.
Thus you see an old Hulk, many years Weather-beaten,
All the Timbers grown rotten, the Plank all Worm-eaten,
Which the owners, who doom her to make one more Trip,
Scrape and calk, tar and paint, till she seems a new Ship.
But alas! for the Wretches, whose Gods have forgot' 'em,
That are bound to adventure in such a foul Bottom.
Here his Godship (inclin'd to examine the whole,
Which compos'd this odd Creature) look'd into her Soul
He conceiv'd a faint Hope, that within he should find
Hidden Beauties, good Sense, and a virtuous fair Mind:
Which, he knew, for Exteriors would make full Amends,
And enroll her a Toast among Platonic Friends.
But again he was baulk'd:—For a Soul he espy'd
Full of Envy, black Malice, base Leasing, and Pride;
Hypocritical, sordid, vain-glorious, ingrate;
In her Friendships most false, and relentless in Hate.
He beheld, at one View, all the Acts of her Life;
How experienc'd a Miss; how abandon'd a Wife:
Then advancing in Years, all her Wants she supply'd,
By an Art, which the fam'd Messalina ne'er try'd.
Tho' her Gallants were few, or not made to her Mind,
Yet her Joyance was full, if the Jewess was kind.
While the God, that no Room might be left for a Doubt,
Turn'd her upside and down, and then inside and out;
And survey'd all her Parts; many more, than is fit
For the Bard to describe;—but still found himself bit.

This pleasing description of Myra continues
at some length in the same tone until she has
finally made herself decent enough to receive
the onslaughts of her lovers, who appear one
after the other, almost without end:

First approaches majestic the tall Grenadier,
All her Fury the Sight of such Manhood suppress'd;
And a train of soft Passions re-enter her Breast.
She embrac'd the great Soldier; she measur'd his Length;
Into Action she warm'd, and experienc'd his Strength:
Nor so much had false Dalilah's Spouse in his Locks:
Nor the Witch more pleas'd, when she strove in the Box.
Introduc'd in good Order, succeed to the Fight
A mechanic, a Courtier, a Collier, and Knight:
As he finish'd to each she assigned a new Day,
And, extolling his Labours, advanc'd a Week's Pay.

But even this number of men can not satisfy her lecherous yearnings, and she calls for succour in the form of flagellation and tribadism.

> O ma Vie, ma Femme! What a Shape, and a Face!
> Then impatient she rush'd to a closer Embrace.
> Let the rest be untold!—And thus ever forbear,
> Lest thy Numbers, O Scheffer, offend the chaste Fair.

As a sample of the Latin "original" we append the following verse describing the nature of Myra's passionate desires, which has already been given in the above "translation":

> Quos puellulae calores,
> Nuptae vidit quos furores!
> Quae libido, cum vetu-la,
> Inflat tetra et Mascu-la!
> Messalina si certaret,
> Messalinam superaret,
> Mira, Priapeium decus,
> Moechi, moechae, moecha, moechus.
> Quid, quod juvenes protervi?
> Quod suorum rigent nervi?
> Tribadum dum Shylockissa,
> Venere non intermissa,
> Miram patitut, amorum
> Haud indocilis novorum.

15.

The Greatest Erotic Novel in English Literature: "Fanny Hill, or the Memoirs of a Woman of Pleasure"

THE greatest work in both the erotic and pornographic literature in the English tongue — and we feel tempted to say in any language—is unquestionably "Fanny Hill, or the Memoirs of a Woman of Pleasure" (1749) by John Cleland. This most famous erotic novel has been translated into every major language, an achievement not approached by any other modern work. Indeed, there are no less than a dozen different translations in the French language alone, while the Germans possess almost as' many different editions. The magic charm of "Fanny Hill" is universal and, "sui generis", is an unique classic in the annals of literature. We shall therefore discourse at some length on the author and his work.

John Cleland (1707-1789) was the son of Colonel Cleland, the original of "Will Honeycombe", that famous fictive member of the "Spectator's Club", a favorite character of Steele and Addison. The Colonel was a bit of a rake and rapidly disposed of the family fortune. However, he provided an excellent education for his son, John, who was admitted to Westminster College together with Lord Mansfield in 1722. At the death of his father he used the small legacy in obtaining a position as English Counsel to Smyrna. He may there very well have been impregnated with erotic experiences and theories which he developed so masterfully in his notorious works. After returning from Smyrna he departed for East India but almost immediately came into violent conflict with his superiors in Bombay, and was expeditiously returned to England. Lack of money in London soon reduced him to vile straits, prison being not the least of his misfortunes.

In this state of dreadful penury, he was approached by a publisher who commissioned him to write "some kind of erotic novel". "Fanny Hill" was the result. Its immediate fame brought equal notoriety to its author. The book was banned and Cleland was summoned before the Privy Council to answer for his crime. The President of the Privy Council, John, Earl Granville, recognized the intrinsic merit of the work but deplored its publication. On condition that he refrain from writing any similar work Earl Granville provided Cleland with a yearly pension of one hundred pounds sterling. A princely bribe!

Cleland naturally obeyed the terms of his Maecenas and concerned himself mainly with philologic and political publications, with the exceptions of "Memoirs of a Coxcomb", which belongs to the class of frivolous literature, and the "Man of Honour", a kind of literary atonement for his "Memoirs of a Woman of Pleasure". He died at the advanced age of eighty-two years in very pleasant circumstances, thanks to his pension. It is idle to speculate on the possible masterpieces in the vein of "Fanny Hill" that might have flowed from his pen. Indeed, it is doubtful whether Cleland could have repeated his "success". He received only twenty guineas for "Fanny Hill" from the bookseller Griffiths, who earned no less than ten thousand pounds in a short space of years! Almost every civilized country has an erotic work that stands head and shoulders above all others. "Fanny Hill" is preëminently England's own, and one of which she may well be proud, exemplifying as it does the genius of the English language in narrative technique and style.

The plan of the work is so simple, the erotic scenes follow one another so naturally and intelligently, the descriptions are so vivacious and clear, the characters are so truthful and lifelike, that the reader immediately realizes that it is an important classic and not a "dirty book" as censorious smuthounds make it out to be. Indeed, there is scarcely a word or phrase used by Cleland that would shock even the most squeamish of spinsters. It is only because of the puritanical prohibition of descriptions of the most vine law of God, the complete union of two harmonious bodies, that the great majority of English speaking peoples have been deprived of a sane and clear exposition of the sex life as practised in England. That the harm far outweighs the questionable benefits of such a policy is proven by the mute testimony of the divorce courts.

In the very first page Cleland indicates the position he is taking on the standpoint of morals and prudery. Fanny (née Frances) Hill is presumably writing her autobiography at the behest of a noble and fashionable patroness:

"Madame: I sit down to give you an undeniable proof of my considering your desires as indispensable orders. Ungracious then as the task may be, I shall recall to view those scandalous stages of my life out of which I emerged, at length, to the enjoyment of every blessing in the power of love, health, and fortune, to bestow, whilst yet in the flower of youth, and not too late to employ the leisure afforded me by great ease and affluence to cultivate an understanding naturally not a despicable one, and which even amidst the whirl of loose pleasures I had been tossed in, exerted more observation on the characters and manners of the world than is common to those of my unhappy profession, who, looking on all thought or reflection as their capital enemy, keep it at as great a distance as they can, or destroy it without mercy. Hating, as I mortally do, all long unnecessary prefaces, I shall give you good quarter in this, and use no further apology, than to prepare you for seeing the loose part of my life, written with the same liberty that I led it. Truth, stark naked truth, is the word! and

I will not so much as take the pains to bestow the
strip of gauze wrapper on it, but paint situations
such as they actually rose to me in nature, careless
of violating those laws of decency that were never
made for such unreserved intimacies as ours; and
you have too much sense, too much knowledge
of the originals, to sniff prudishly and out of
character at the pictures of them. The greatest
men, those of the first and most leading taste,
will not scruple adorning their private closets
with nudities, though, in compliance with vulgar prejudices they may not think them decent
decorations of the stair-case or saloon. This, and
enough, promised, I go some into my personal
history."

Let us now accompany Fanny Hill in her erotic adventures: Fanny, the daughter of extremely poor parents in a small village near Liverpool,
Lancashire, at the death of her parents leaves
with the Chester Post for London, accompanied
by a certain Esther Davis, a cunning creature,
who callously leaves Fanny in the lurch when
they reach London. Destitute and friendless, she
turns to an employment bureau, where she is
picked up and engaged by an old madam, Mrs.
Brown, who takes her to her "home". The innocent fifteen-year-old country girl naturally has
no suspicions as to the nature of the hands in
which she has fallen, and is sounded out by her
room-mate Phoebe who has been ordered by
Mrs. Brown to remove any "provincial prejudices" of the novice.

Phoebe, however, unable to control herself at
this image of sweet innocence, goes beyond the
letter of her order and introduces Fanny into the

initial practices of tribadism. A few days pass until the madam has found a suitably rich purchaser for Fanny's virginity.

He was "a man rather past three-score, short and ill-made, with a yellow cadaverous hue, great goggling eyes, that stared as if he was strangled; an out-mouth for two more properly tusks than teeth, livid lips, and a breath like a jakes'; then he had a peculiar ghastliness in his grin, that made him perfectly frightful, if not dangerous to women with child; yet, made as he was thus in mock of man, he was so blind to his own staring deformities, as to think himself born for pleasing, and that no woman could see him with impunity, in consequence of which idea he had lavished great sums on such wretches as could gain upon themselves to pretend love to his person, whilst to those who had no art or patience to dissemble the horror it inspired, he behaved even brutally. Impotence, more than necessity, made him seek in vanity the provocative that was wanting to raise him to a pitch of enjoyment, which he too often saw himself baulked of by the failure of his powers; and this always threw him into a fit of rage, which he wreaked, as far as he durst, on the innocent objects of his fit of momentary desire. This then was the monster to which my conscientious benefactress, who had long been his purveyor this way, had doomed me, and sent for me down purposely for his examination. Accordingly she made me stand up before him, turned me round, unpinned my handkerchief, remarked to him the rise and fall, the turn and whiteness of a bosom just beginning to fill: then made me walk, and took even a handle from the rusticity of my charms, in short, she omitted no point of jockeyship, to which he only answered by gracious nods and approbation, whilst he looked goats and monkeys at me, for I sometimes stole a corner glance at him, and encountering his fiery eager stare, looked another way from pure horror and affright, which he, doubtless in character, attributed to nothing more than maiden modesty, or at least the affectation of it."

This precious specimen of manhood has purchased Fanny's virginity for the sum of fifty guineas, but despite Phoebe's blandishments she is unwilling to sacrifice herself so cheaply to so ugly a monster, and resists his passionate attacks so successfully that the old rake gives up in disgust. Fearing his return, she willingly entrusts herself to the care of a handsome young man, a frequent visitor to Mrs. Brown's seraglio. He helps her escape from the house and brings her to his own lodgings where she willingly yields herself to him. Charles, her liberator, is naturally as astonished as he is pleased to find that he has deflowered a veritable virgin instead of a common whore. Their mutual regard rapidly develops into ardent love, and they set up an elegant apartment. Fanny is insanely happy, since Charles is the exact opposite of her would-be deflowerer:

"Oh, could I paint his figure as I see it now, still present to my transported imagination! a whole length of an all-perfect manly beauty in full view. Think of a face without a fault, glowing with all the opening bloom and verdant freshness of an age, in which beauty is of either sex, and which the first down over his upper lip scarce began to distinguish. The parting of the double ruby pout of his lips seemed to exhale an air sweeter and purer than what it drew in; ah, what violence did it not cost me to refrain the so tempted kiss! Then a neck exquisitely turned, graced behind and on the sides with his hair, playing freely in natural ringlets, connected his head to a body of the most perfect form, and of the most vigorous contexture, in which all the strength of manhood was concealed and softened to appearance by the delicacy of his complexion, the smoothness of his skin and the plumpness of his flesh. The platform of his snow white bosom, which was laid out in manly fashion, presented on the vermillion summit of each pap, the idea of a rose about to blow. Nor did his shirt hinder me from observing that symmetry of his limbs, that exactness of shape, in the fall of it towards the loins, where the waist ends and the rounding swell of the hips commences; where the skin, sleek, smooth, and dazzling white; burnishes on the stretch-over firm, plump, ripe flesh, that crimped and ran into dimples at the least pressure, or that the touch could not rest upon, but slid over as on the surface of the most polished ivory. His thighs, finely fashioned and with a florid glossy roundness, gradually tapering away to the knees, seemed pillars worthy to support that beauteous frame."

But their good fortune is not of long duration. Charles' escapade is discovered and he is sent away to one of his father's factories in the South Sea. Fanny, all unknowing, is left to her fate. When her landlady, Mrs. Jones, tells her of

Charles' abduction she falls into a swoon and miscarries. No sooner has she recovered than Mrs. Jones presents her with a bill for her services and graciously informs her that she has found a new friend for her who will pay all her debts. Fanny, reduced to extremity, is forced to give in. Her new protector, although of respectable position and education, is not to Fanny's taste and can not remove Charles' image from her heart. Nevertheless she remains true to him until she discovers him one day in a tender tête-à-tête with her own chambermaid. She immediately resolves to give him tit-for-tat and seduces his own servant, a young lad from the country. They spend a number of pleasant hours together but are inevitably discovered in the act by her protector who dismisses her from his services.

In this defenseless position there appears a notorious madam from Covent Garden, Mrs. Cole, "a middle-aged discreet sort of woman", who has known Fanny for a long time and offers her means and protection. Fanny accepts the offer and takes up new quarters near the house of Mrs. Cole. The establishment of Mrs. Cole affords a pleasant contrast to that of Mrs. Brown. "Decency, modesty and order" are the rule. A respectable shop cloaks the bordel,—for that is its sole business—and the girls, four in number, are pampered and coddled. Under Mrs. Cole's protection and in the pleasant company of girls of her own age and inclinations, Fanny passes a pleasant time until their madam, who feels the weaknesses of oncoming age, decides to retire from her business and to spend the rest of her days peacefully in the country.

"I had, on my separation from Mrs. Cole, taken a pleasant, convenient house at Marlebone, easy to manage for its smallness, which I furnished neatly and modestly. There with a reserve of eight hundred pounds, the fruit of my deference to Mrs. Cole's advice, exclusive of some clothes, jewels and plate, I saw myself in purse for a long time, to wait without impatience for what the chapter of accidents might produce in my favour. Here under the character of a young gentlewoman whose husband had gone to sea, I had laid out such lines of life and conduct, as leaving me at liberty to pursue my desires, bound me nevertheless strictly within the rules of decency and discretion, a course in which you cannot escape observing a true pupil of Mrs. Cole's."

Fortune now favors Fanny. She renders first aid to an old gentleman who has been seized by a choking fit, and, in gratitude, he takes her to his home, adopts her, educates her, leaves his fortune to her and then conveniently dies. So our Fanny becomes a great lady and quite her own mistress. She has everything her heart desires, except Charles, whom she has never forgotten.

Taken by a whim to revisit her birthplace she stops midway at an inn. A sudden storm arises and two horsemen are driven in by the rain. To her infinite joy and delight she recognizes one of the bedraggled figures as none other than her long-lost Charles, who is just returning from his involuntary sea-trip. It is true that fortune has not smiled on Charles, but Fanny has enough for both and places her entire fortune at his disposal. She also renders him a complete account of her life since he was forced to leave her, but Charles does not mind. They are legally married and Fanny becomes a good and virtuous housewife.

"Thus, at length, I got snug into port, where, in the bosom of virtue, I gathered the only incorrupt sweets, where, looking back on the course of vice I had run, and comparing its infamous blandishments with the infinitely superior joys of innocence, I could not help pitying, even in point of taste, those who, immersed in gross sensuality, are insensible to the delicate charms of virtue, than which, even pleasure has not a greater enemy. Thus temperance makes men lords over those pleasures that intemperance enslaves them to; the one, parent of health, vigour, fertility, cheerfulness, and every other desirable good of life; the other, of diseases, debility, barrenness, self-loathing, with only every evil incident to human nature.

"You laugh, perhaps, at this tail-piece of morality, extracted from me by the force of truth, resulting from compared experiences; you think it, no doubt, out of place; possibly too, you may look on it as the paltry finesse of one who seeks to mask a devotee to vice under a rag of a veil, impudently smuggled from the shrine of Virtue; just as if one was to fancy one's self completely disguised at a masquerade, with no other change of dress than turning one's shoes into slippers; or, as if a writer should think to shield a treasonable libel, by concluding it with a formal prayer for the king. But, independent of my flattering myself that you have a juster opinion of my sense and sincerity, give me leave to represent to you, that such a supposition is even more injurious to Virtue than to me, since consistently with candour and good nature, it can have no foundation but in the falsest of fears, that its pleasures cannot stand in comparison with those of Vice; but let truth dare to hold up in its most alluring light, then mark, how spurious, how low of taste, how comparatively inferior its joys are to those which Virtue gives sanction to, and whose sentiments are not above making even a sauce for the senses, but a sauce of the highest relish, whilst Vices are the harpies that infect and foul the feast.

"The paths of Vice are sometimes strewed with roses, but then they are forever infamous for many a canker-worm; those of Virtue are strewed with roses purely, and those eternally unfading roses. If you do me justice then, you will esteem me perfectly consistent in the incense I burn to Virtue. If I have painted Vice in all its gayest colours, if I have decked it with flowers, it has been solely in order to make the worthier, the solemner sacrifice of it to Virtue."

An interesting annotation on the literary difficulties of an eroticist is also to be found in "Fanny Hill":

"I imagined, indeed, that you would have been cloyed and tired with uniformity of adventures and expressions, inseparable from a subject of this sort, whose bottom, or ground-work being, in the nature of things eternally one and the same, whatever variety of forms and modes the situations are susceptible of, there is no escaping a repetition of near the same images, the same figures, the same expressions, with this further

inconvenience added to the disgust it creates,
that the words joys, ardours, transports, extasies,
and the rest of those pathetic terms so congenial
to, so received in the practice of pleasure, flat-
ten and lose much of their due spirit and energy, by the frequency they indispensably recur
with, in a narration of which that practice pro-
fessedly composes the whole basis."

16.

First English Work
on Tribadism

THE first English work, or rather brochure, on tribadism is dated 1752 and bears the characteristically long title: "The surprising adventures of a female husband, containing the whimsical amours, curious incidents, and diabolical tricks of Miss M. Hamilton, alias Minister Bentley, alias Doctor O'Keefe, alias Mrs. Knight, the Midwife, &c., who married three wives! and lived with each some time undiscovered, for which acts she was tried at the summer Sessions in the county of Somerset, in the year 1752, found guilty, and whipped several times, in four market towns, and afterwards imprisoned six months: notwithstanding which, on the evening of her first day of her exposure, she attempted to bribe the gaoler to procure her a

fine young girl to gratify her monstrous and unnatural propensity."

There is a fine folding frontispiece signed by
Cruikshank which represents one of the whippings of this extraordinary English tribade, who
was born, peculiarly enough, in the Isle of Man,
in 1721. She is represented as a slight, youthful-
looking person, with short, curly hair, blue
breeches and topboots, but being stripped to the
waist, the artist has been careful to draw a fine
feminine bosom. She is standing with her arms
above her head, fixed in the pillory, and a fat
executioner is drawing blood from her back with
a large cat-o'-nine tails.

The heroine in question seems to have been
debauched when young by a neighbor, Anne
Johnson: "And transactions pretty generally
took place which decency forbids us to explain,
suffice it to say, curious and gratifying machinery of delicate composition were (sic) in great
request."

Miss Hamilton then left for Bristol with
Anne, the latter marrying a real man. Mary
Hamilton was absent at Bath at the time and
wrote the following characteristic epistle:

My dear Miss Johnson,

*I have had extraordinary pleasure
since I have been here, and fared well in
my double capacity. I have been to the Theatre five times, twice as a woman, and thrice
as a man, and one night, in the former character, throwing out a bait, I was picked up
by an army officer, who was pretty mellow;*

*he took me home with him and treated me
with a good supper and wine, we slept together, and in the morning he expressed
himself highly gratified, and at breakfast,
presented me with a five pound note.*

*Three nights out of five, I succeeded
in picking up and taking home some young
girl, and after practising the usual game,
they promised to secrecy, sold them some of
my wares at a high price, who brought me
a lot of customers, and took off all my stock
—but with no one have I ever enjoyed half
the pleasure as with my dear Johnson, whom
I long to be with again, therefore expect
me in a day or two.*

Yours, etc.

M. Hamilton

One of her adventures consisted in masquer-
ading in the garb of a doctor and marrying a
young woman "who had the green sickness".
"The doctor and her wife lived together about
a fortnight without the least doubt being conceived either by the wife, or any other person,
of the doctor's being as much a man as he appeared; but women will gossip, and one morning, the doctor having drunk too freely over
night, slept rather soundly and longer than usual, and was at length awakened by the curiosity
of his wife, who was crying and sobbing as if
her heart would break; on perceiving which,
says she, my dear, what, what, is the matter?
what have I done to make you so uneasy? tell
me, pray do tell!! Done, says she, amidst many

sobs, have you not married and ruined me, a poor young girl, when you have not—have not the essentials of a man?"

The horrified girl leaves her, and Mary Hamilton is off again and finds fresh victims, until she is finally found out and sentenced: "to be publicly and severely whipped four several times, in four market towns, and to be imprisoned for six months. These whippings were accordingly inflicted, and indeed so severely, that many persons who had more regard to beauty than to justice, could not refrain from exerting some pity for her when they saw so lovely a skin sacrificed with rods, and to such a degree that her back was almost flayed. Yet, astonishing to tell, so little effect had the smart of the punishment upon her that on the evening of the very same day she had suffered the first Whipping, she endeavored to bribe the gaoler to procure her a young girl to gratify her most monstrous and unnatural propensities, having artfully secreted some of her indescribable Machinery."

Mary Hamilton afterwards set up as a midwife, still carrying on her old practices, and died about three years afterwards, aged thirty-seven, "leaving behind her a trunk nearly full of her diabolical machinery, and a recipe for the green sickness".

17.

"The Pleasures of Love"

very rare and interesting work that appeared shortly after Cleland's "Memoirs of a Woman of Pleasure" is the anonymously written "The Pleasures of Love. Containing a Variety of Entertaining Particulars and Curiosities, in the Cabinet of Venus." The frontispiece represents a portly young lady in bed, drawing the curtain to one side so that four naked legs can be seen peeping from under the bedcover. Upon the curtain are written the words: "The Pleasures of Love, 1775." A modern reprint of this scarce work has the title "The Adventures of a Rake".

"The Pleasures of Love" is a kind of autobiography told by the hero, the son of a rich man, who emphasizes the value of his undertaking in these words: "There is no man in the world, no matter how insignificant, whose truthfully written autobiography would not be interesting, at least to some degree. The stupidities of our own life and those in which we were betrayed by others will always afford material for serious consideration. Innocent stupidities will always be the most interesting and the depravity, when correctly told, will frighten others from the same path."

The gallant hero is sent by his uncle to the country where he promptly falls in love with the farmer's daughter, even to the point of marrying her. Since such a union is repugnant to both families, the enamoured youth escapes with his dear Betsy. His uncle follows him and forces him to return, despite the fact that the youth has prevailed over the girl and she has granted him her boon. The youth is bound over to the study of law in London. The unrest caused by such labor, augmented by the sorrow at the loss of his mistress, causes the youth to give way to the extremest debaucheries. His father accidentally meets him in the pursuit of such pleasures, pays his debts, sends him to a new teacher, and forgives his sins. But the hero is no longer satisfied with an honorable life, falls back into his old dissolute habits, is reduced to penury, and must take a position in the country as servant to a lady. Soon after his arrival he is made aware that his services are to be of a very personal and intimate nature. Since she is a woman in the full flower of life he gladly performs such services and becomes her personal "major-domo". The cook and servant girl are also willing recipients of his services so that his virility is in constant use. The lady finally has to send to London for a new chambermaid and, to our hero's great surprise and delight, it turns out to be none other than his beloved Betsy, for whom he had sought so long in vain. Betsy brings with her a newspaper in which he discovers also that his father has died and has left him his fortune. He marries Betsy and returns home with her, when, for the third time, they discover that she is not the daughter of a farmer but of a very rich man and possesses no less than twenty thousand pounds in her own name.

Despite the poverty of the tale, "The Pleasures of Love" is historically important because it mentions by name important London bordels in which the hero has sown his wild oats. There is also an interlude in which the hero establishes his sexual prowess with two London prostitutes, who in gratitude disclose many interesting pleasures to him.

18.

Textbooks
on the English Art
of Love

The Peculiar English Mania
for Deflowering Virgins

VERY country has its famous textbook on the art of love. India has the "Kamasutra" of Vatsyayana, Rome the "Ars Amandi" of Ovid, Persia the "Scheikh Nefzaui", France the "120 Journées de Sodome" of the Marquis de Sade. England, too, has "The Battles of Venus".

The complete title of this very scarce work, a "rara rarissima", is as follows: "The Battles of Venus. A descriptive Dissertation on the Various Modes of Enjoyment: Comprising Philosophical Discussions of the most interesting and affecting Questions. Demonstrative that the loosest Thoughts and Sensations may be conveyed without an Expression verging on Immodesty" (1760). According to some collectors of curiosa this work appeared much later; at any rate, a reprint in 1860 bears the following, slightly changed title: "The Battles of Venus, a Descriptive Dissertation of the Various Modes of Enjoyment of the Female Sex, as practised in different Countries, with some curious Information on the Resources of Lust, Lechery, and Licentiousness, to Revive the Drooping Faculties and Strengthen the Voluptuous and Exhausted."

The following couplet also appears on the title-page:

Wine, Women, Warmth, against our lives combine,
But what is Life without Warmth, Women and Wine.

This brochure is written in a very interesting style, eschewing unnecessary coarseness. The various coital positions are completely discussed, with the reasons for and against, the best time of the year, hour and day, etc. The author also shows a decided preference for the natural positions rather than the artificial ones of Aretino.

"The Battles of Venus" is especially interesting to us for its excellent excursis on the vast extent of the mania for defloration among Englishmen. Inasmuch as this is vitally important to an understanding of the sex life in England we shall digest the main facts on this "English vice".

This brutal feature of the sex life is to be seen at its greatest extent in England. The Englishmen seem to have a violently biased taste for virgins. "Forty years ago a 'virgo intacta' brought

no less than fifty pounds, today a virgin is pro-
curable for one-tenth that amount. There are physicians who provide virginities, and specialists
who train girls in the simulation of such desirable objects. One individual, alone, used seventy
virgins a year, and wanted to increase his quota
to one hundred !" This defloration mania attacked
all classes of society, from the highest to the
lowest.

The ordinary *preference* for virginity in unmarried girls, according to Westermarck, "partly
springs from a feeling akin to jealousy towards
women who have had previous connections with
other men, partly from the warm response a man
expects from a woman whose appetite he is the
first to gratify, and largely from an instinctive
appreciation of female coyness".

The explanation of the English *mania* for virginity is usually found in the general coarseness,
brutality and grossness of the Englishman in his
sexual expression. The real reason, we believe,
is more profound and psychologically grounded.
To an Englishman, as Arnold Bennett would
often say, "the best is good enough". He must
have something which can be had only once and
by one party, and so distinguish himself from all
others. This is true of the virginity of a girl,
which enchants the Englishman as being unique
and select.

The author of "The Battles of Venus" extolls
and describes in full detail the delights of defloration; he holds, however, that the taste for
virgins is an acquired one, but that it is nevertheless the acme of sexual pleasure. "Is the prevailing lust of enjoying feminine 'cherries' a

command of nature to ensure posterity, or is it a refinement of rakes and an artifice of impotent society? I, for my part, prefer to believe in the latter two causes. Every man, I think, can recall those glorious days of his youth when all his thoughts and desires were turned to Woman, and not to Virginity. The object of his fervid phantasy is pure pleasure, and one pretty woman is just as good as another in this regard. Indeed, it is problematic whether a youth, not initiated into the secrets of Venus, does not even prefer an experienced woman to a shy and chaste virgin. For it is no different with male novices: they are just as timid, trembling, and fearful as the virgin miss. The artifices of a highly perfected courtesan are really necessary for the arousing of the youth's virility, which would be dampened by an inexperienced lassie. Modesty inculcated in the youth by breeding and custom robs the youth of the major portion of his powers and makes him extremely self conscious during the love-bout.

"It is the oldsters who have the necessary experience and imagination to appreciate the extraordinary charms of a girl who has never known the love of any man, or so the deflowerer deludes himself. How his imagination is titillated, his veins enflamed, his body pulsating with new or refreshened vigour, truly, the virgin is the only fit mate for an Englishman!" The author then gives explicit information on the sadistic delights encountered in defloration. Flagellation is also often used as an added excitant.

A natural result of such madness for the enjoyment of "untouched fruit" led to the establishment of bordels stocked only by children. This trade reached its greatest development in the last two decades of the nineteenth century. Talbot informed Ryan: " 'There are dens of vice among us, in which boys as well as girls are abused in the most horrible fashion. He mentioned localities which of course cannot be printed. These most infamous and horrible dens, are partly supplied by children and young persons, who are observed gazing at the windows of the improper printshops . . . . as much as ten pounds was expended to secure one boy."

In 1885 a reform movement started by the "Pall Mall Gazette" disclosed a complete system of procuring, ensuring, and despatching of girls and young women to the bordels and wealthy libertines of London and the suburbs. This "mad hunt for fresh stock" naturally brought about a tremendous increase in the numbers of panders and procuresses. The English authorities, both past and present, prefer to whittle away at the results of this pernicious system instead of making a systematic attack on the initial psychological cause of this "English mania".

Mention should also be made of the infamous "Horn Book". The complete title reads: "How to Raise Love, or Modern Studies in the Science of Stroking. The Horn Book. A Girl's Guide to the Knowledge of Good and Evil" (1901). This is an English imitation of the "Figurae Veneris" and consists of a pornographic description of the various coital positions. This is the work most often reprinted in modern times, both in England and America, but since its literary merit is nil, and since it throws no light on the sex life in England, we shall not examine this wretched product any further.

19.

"New Attalantis", Escapades of the English Aristocracy

AN extremely scarce work, replete with interesting disclosures on the sexual escapades of aristocratic folk, appeared in 1762 under the title of "New Attalantis", a collection of five original tales, each purporting to give a true account of the dreadful state of the morals of the day.

The exact title of this collection reads: "New Attalantis For the Year 1762: Being A Select Portion of Secret History; Containing Many Facts, Strange! but True!"

> The godly dame who fleshly failing damns
> Scolds with her maid, or with her chaplain crams;
> Would you enjoy soft nights and solid dinners
> Faith, gallants, board with saints and bed with sinners.

—Pope.

The work contains the following tales:

1. *The Amours of Lady Lucian.*
2. *The Loves of Henry and Emma.*
3. *The History of the Countess of B.*
4. *A Private Anecdote in the Fashionable World.*
5. *The Royal Rake: or the Adventures of Prince Yorick.*

In the first tale, "The Amours of Lady Lucian", we discover that "this young lady was not pretty, for she had a Dutch physique, was very corpulent, with common features, and a tolerable complexion that was due more to the perfumer than to nature. She lived in a state of virginity so long that she could count her number of years by the teeth in her mouth. But when I say that she lived in a virginal state, it does not mean more than to say that she was unmarried. For, apart from the actual intercourse with the male sex, it is well known that French manufacturers sell more than one instrument to alleviate the stringencies of celibacy in womankind.

"A pious and learned nobleman, by name Lord Lucian, bombarded her with politics, poesy, and religion (in which three he was equally conversant) so successfully that he soon conquered the fortress. But see, scarce three minutes of the honeymoon had slipped by, when his mind was taken up with the notion, not of fulfilling the rites of Hymen, but of again arising and transcribing one of the letters of St. Paul the Apostle. This took up so much of his thoughts and time that he was unable to find any leisure for the important business at hand."

The next and the following night pass in the very same manner until the bride can no longer endure her husband's neglect. She reproaches him in a bitter scene, demanding from him the "real thing" instead of "sweet verse", but is unable to obtain any satisfaction from the confirmed and incorrigible poetaster. She now lays bare her heart to Madame Rouge, the "embodied idea of pimpess and smuggler", who declares herself ready to aid her. But Lady Lucian shrinks from the results of illegitimate sexual intercourse, so the madam proposes to her a castrate since "these creatures, are very easy to handle. It flatters their pride for a woman to take notice of them."

The procuress arranges a rendezvous between Lady Lucian and the singer Signor Squalini, upon whom she had already cast a beaming eye from her box. He satisfies her in every respect so perfectly that she confers upon him the position of personal "music-master". But her husband surprises her one day during a "music-lesson". The separation of the couple follows and Lady Lucian now "has full opportunity to enjoy the society of her dear castrato without molestation". Squalini, however, soon tires of his "musical instrument" and seeks "new strings for his bow". Lady Lucian finds comfort in the arms of another castrated singer, and the tale ends with the lady usurping her cuckolded husband's role and writing a long poem "In Praise of My Castrato".

The second tale, "Henry and Emma", describes the love of Emma, the daughter of Albertus, and

Henry, the husband of the pretty Priscilla.
Emma, too, is not free, for she is engaged to be
married to Nauticus. The two lovers escape to
the continent, where their further adventures are
described. The story is told in a dry, philosophic
manner and is interesting only in an excursus
which discusses the prevalence of masturbation
among young Englishwomen.

The third tale, "The History of the Countess
of B.", opens with a highly realistic and brutal
account of the defloration of the young Countess
of B. by her husband. This revolting procedure
was demanded by the countess of her unwilling
husband! She soon drives her husband to an early
end by overtaxing his sexual powers. This English Messalina then casts her eyes about for a
successor and fastens her heart upon a Squire
Bullrudery, whom she had accidentally espied
in an embarrassing posture, and mistakenly imagines to be a man of great strength and promise.
Soon after the wedding she is disagreeably surprised to find that he has fooled her by means of
a French artificial member. Enraged, she refuses
to grant him his conjugal rights, and calls in an
eighteen-year-old footman. The tale ends with
the exhaustion of all the footmen in the neigh-
borhood.

A somewhat similar surprise of a woman at
the sight of masculine nudities forms the dramatic climax of the fourth tale of the "New Attalantis" and bears the title: "A Private Anecdote
in the Fashionable World". The pretty Melessa,
wife of a respectable gentleman on the island
Angola, has been carrying on a love-affair for
some time with the young rake Hyppolitus. He,

however, is weary of her—a young opera-dancer has captivated him — and he begs his friend, Colonel Bevil, to free him from his burdensome duties. One day, as Melessa hurried to visit her beloved Hyppolitus, — "immediately after she had dined; she scarce allowed herself time to eat, so much more valuable in her sense were the pleasures of love" — she at once entered her lover's bedroom. Because of the midday heat the shades had been drawn and the room was somewhat dark. There she spies sleeping in a bed of roses a youth in a very seductive posture. Although she cannot make out the exact features she supposes him to be her lover. The burning kisses with which she covers her Hyppolitus awakens the denuded youth, and he arrogates to himself all the rights of her lover. Melessa is quickly aware of the deception but is so satisfied with the colonel that "she bestowed upon him what she before, in her own opinion, had bestowed upon Hyppolitus". As the reader no doubt has surmised, Hyppolitus now breaks in on the embarrassed couple and swears never to pardon the faithless Melessa for such outrageous conduct.

The fifth tale, "The Royal Rake: or the Adventures of Prince Yorick", describes the extravaganzas of a company of noblemen, among them a Prince Yorick, in the vicinity of Drury Lane. These good Englishmen seize hold of some passing girls, pick up all the street-walkers, and repair to a tavern, where they order the servants to go out on the streets and procure as many more girls as they can. Finally the barroom is as packed as the foyer of a theatre at a first night, and no

more girls can get in. Then each nobleman se-
lects his favorite, the remainder being sent "to
Mother Bodgy to tell them all about it". After
they have satisfied themselves they leave for a
fashionable bordel where the virginity of a robust country girl is offered for twenty guineas.
The Prince Charming, who draws this virginal
prize, pays the money, and sends her home to
her parents in the same virginal condition in
which he found her.

20.

"Memoirs of a Man of Pleasure":
The "Masculine 'Fanny Hill'"

IN 1769 there appeared an erotic work entitled "The History of the Human Heart, or the Adventures of a Young Gentleman", but it is far better known to collectors under the more apposite title of a later reprint (1827), "Memoirs of a Man of Pleasure; or the Amours, Intrigues, and Adventures of Sir Charles Manly". The author has attempted to imitate the style and art of Cleland, substituting a man for a woman as his fictive protagonist. For this reason the work has often been called "the masculine 'Fanny Hill' ".

The "Memoirs of a Man of Pleasure" begins with a description of the conception and delivery scenes quite à la Tristam Shandy, except that the author throws in for good measure a complete discussion of the various theories of procreation. Our hero's precocious lust for the fair sex is explained by a kind of "maternal impression" (pregnancy shock). His mother had suddenly been seized by an uncontrollable passion for her cousin who was sleeping in the same room with her during the period of pregnancy. Hence Charles Manly is not at fault for having inherited such perverse longings and at the age of twelve has already seduced his fair young cousin of the opposite sex. When time reveals this precocious feat, his parents send him to a friend of theirs for "treatment" and then send him abroad under the care of a tutor. His preceptor, however, exhorts him to a further study of libertinism and introduces him to a company of gay young bloods. Numerous love-adventures are now recounted. They are of the usual sort, their sole claim to distinction being the improbability of the vaunted sexual prowess of our hero. Charles finally seduces, marries, and abandons a young lady of good breeding. She does not despair but follows the wake of his revelries. She at last encounters him at the "psychological moment" and the "Memoirs of a Man of Pleasure" ends with the moral precept: "Adeline combined conjugal love with so much tenderness that she was able to claim the full-hearted devotion of the once so lustful Charles, who freely declared that one blissful hour with her was worth more than all those sinful scenes in which he had dissipated so much money, time, health, and years."

21.

"The Fruit=Shop"

The Most Humorous English Erotic Classic

ONE of the most famous works of this period is now practically unobtainable, although it is an English classic of wit and humor. We refer to "The Fruit-Shop" which appeared in two volumes in 1765. The title-page consists of a very curious engraving which purports to represent an actual scene in a private garden. Before an oriental temple there stands a tree in the form of a phallus; two cupids embrace this image and, joining hands and feet, imitate the exterior of the female genitals. A man, who is leaning against an old and feeble ass, led by a boy, points dramatically to the tree. The man represents that "imposing personality" to which the book is dedicated. But the author inveighs against the person in a violent tirade.

He is none other than the author of "Tristam Shandy". The work derives its title from the "fruit-shop", which the author considers the essential nature of a woman. There is an allegorical investigation of that part of the feminine structure which serves for fecundation and the reception of fruit. The author seeks especially to imitate the style of Swift and Sterne, and although he never reaches the height of sarcastic irony and wit of these geniuses, there are many instances of excellent humor and satire on his contemporaries.

Of the four parts of this work the first discusses Paradise, its probable position, its class of inmates, the various pleasures at the disposal of its inmates, etc., until the erotic novelty wears off and the reader becomes impatiently bored.

The second part reports on what actually happened after the "original sin": the discovery of the fig leaf, its use as a device for titillation, and so on, leading up to the "desserts that may be found in the fruit-shop".

The third part contains a survey of the "unwearied passion for the fruit-shop" among the Romans, beginning with Jupiter and concluding with Julius Caesar. There are no new facts, but the mythology is treated with such scant respect that the reader thinks the more highly of his own sex life. This is reminiscent of William King's couplet:

The Roman rants of heroes, gods and love,
The Briton purely paints the Art of Love.

The fourth and last part contains the most

curious observations of all; in particular, the chapter on conception, celibacy and flagellation as a "roundabout way to heaven". A monk preaches that in flagellation the humblest and most pleasing manner to God transforms the greatest part of the body to the basest, and the basest to the greatest. "In which situation they might be sure of receiving, anon, animating impressions and missionary irradiations, if they were destined to figure among the elect."

The theme of "The Fruit-Shop" is woman as a source of pleasure and propagation of mankind. Those persons, celibates, onanists and pederasts, who scorn or misuse the divine powers at their command, are sharply reproved and taken to task for their derelictions and aberrations.

In the "Appendix" and the "Notes" at the end of the second volume there is a long description of the "fruit-shop in St. James Street", where "matters never proceed further in this chaste domain than to a kiss or a feel, transiently and with the greatest decorum".

22.

Love Life of John Wilkes, the "Ugly Casanova"

His Notorious "Essay on Woman", An Obscene Parody of Pope's "Essay on Man"

NEXT to William King's "The Toast", the most prominent satiric eroticum of the eighteenth century is undoubtedly Wilkes' "Essay on Woman", an obscene parody of Pope's classic "Essay on Man".

John Wilkes was born on October 17, 1727 in St. John's Street, Clerkenwell, London, and died on December 26, 1797 in his house in Grosvenor Square. He was the son of a rich distiller, received a liberal education, travelled abroad, married a lady of fortune, became a colonel of the militia, and finally entered politics. He became notorious for his attack on the king in the famous forty-fifth issue of his periodical, the "North Briton"; he was prosecuted, outlawed and ex-

cluded from the House of Commons till he had
been four times re-elected for Middlesex.

Although he, himself, was a rake and libertine, his public life was free from arrogance and
avariciousness. He was a dutiful father and was
idolized by his daughter. His manners were those
of a perfect gentleman and, despite his ugliness,
he had astounding success with the fair sex. He
is said to have boasted that he could "with an
hour's start, compete with the handsomest man
agoing for the favours of a beautiful woman —
and win". He is supposed to have often won this
wager! The magnetic attractions that he had for
women were said to consist in his sparkling con-
versational talents and a certain peculiar physical odor, not unlike that of the Gypsies.

"Wilkes," says Macaulay in his essay on the
Earl of Chatham, "was a man of taste, reading,
and engaging manners. His sprightly conversation was the delight of green-rooms and taverns,
and pleased even grave hearers when he was sufficiently under restraint to abstain from detailing the particulars of his amours, and from break-
ing jests on the New Testament."

A characteristic anecdote about Wilkes, which
reveals in drastic fashion his moral unscrupu-
lousness, is contained in the "City Biography"
for 1800. Wilkes was also a man of great pru-
dence and discretion in his sexual debaucheries.
He once asked Sir Fletcher Norton for his legal
advice on how he could avoid a criminal action
for seduction if he were to take into his domicile
a certain young girl from the home of her parents. Sir Fletcher, the prototype of the modern
unethical lawyer, advised his client that he could

"get around the face of the law" by hiring the girl as an "upper servant" and giving her double wages, "extra pay", with the natural understanding that "more than ordinary services" would be required of her. Wilkes took up the cunning suggestion and actually engaged the girl as combined "fille de joie" and servant for twenty pounds yearly. It is also characteristic of Wilkes that he swore "by my goddess Venus" that lawyer and knave are identical!

Wilkes' appearance, his long, skinny figure, his decidedly ugly countenance, heightened by his squinting eyes, made him a favorite object for caricature. We need but recall Hogarth's famous portrait, a gross caricature, yet one which Wilkes took in good spirits. In an epigram of the age we read:

Says John Wilkes to a lady, pray name if you can,
Of all your acquaintance the handsomest man.
The lady replied if you'd have me speak true,
He's the handsomest man that's the most unlike you.

* * *

The notorious work of Wilkes, "An Essay on Woman", was printed by himself on a small press in an edition numbering only twelve copies! No known example of this first edition is extant. The earliest edition we have is dated 1763 with the following title: "An Essay on Woman; By Pego Borewell Esq.; With Notes by Rogerus Cunaeus, Vigerus Mutoniatus, etc. And A Commentary by the Rev. Dr. Warburton. Inscribed to Miss Fanny Murray."

This small volume of thirty pages contains the following:

The "Essay on Woman" contains ninety-four lines and begins with the words:

Awake my Fanny! Leave all meaner things;
This morn shall prove what rapture swiving brings!
Let us (since life can little more supply
Than just a few good . . . ., and then we die)
Expatiate free.

It concludes no less stirringly:

Hope humbly then clean Girls; nor vainly soar
But . . . . the . . . . at hand, and God adore.
What future . . . . . . he gives not thee to know,
But gives that . . . . to be thy Blessing now.

The "Universal Prayer" is annotated and consists of thirteen stanzas, each of four lines. The opening and closing stanzas follow:

Mother of all! in every age,
In ev'ry Clime ador'd,
By Saint, by Savage, and by Sage,
If modest, or if whor'd.

To thee whose . . . . thro'out all space,
This dying World supplies,
One Chorus let all Beings raise!
All . . . . . . in rev'rence rise.

Similarly cynical is the short conversation, consisting of eighteen lines of the "Dying Lover to his . . . .".

"Veni Creator; or the Maid's Prayer" consists of fifteen stanzas of unequal length. The beginning reads:

> Creator Pego, by whose Aid,
> Thy humble Suppliant was made.

It concludes:

> Immortal Honour, endless Fame,
> Almighty Pego! to thy Name;
> And equal Adoration be
> Paid to the neighbouring Pair with Thee,
> Thrice blessed Glorious Trinity.

At this late date we can scarcely conceive the immense furor that this parody caused through the entire realm of England. The Houses of Parliament were ablaze with debates and attacks on the "Essay on Woman". All the prominent men in England took sides on the question of whether the work was an obscene blasphemy, and one for which the author should be heavily punished. Action was brought against Wilkes but there was no definite proof of the authorship and he was finally released. The "Essay on Woman" was more than a nine days' literary sensation; it became a national problem. The literature on this subject is very extensive, as is the enormous number of imitations of the "Essay on Woman". We refer the interested reader for further information to Pisanus Fraxi's "Index Librorum Prohibitorum", which we shall discuss in a later section.

We cannot however refrain from mentioning

one of the best of the imitations of Wilkes' parody. It is also called "An Essay on Woman", and is dated 1763. It consists of an "Invocation", two "Cantos", a "Conclusion" and an "Epilogue." Canto I begins:

> But to our purpose, Invocation — — — stop!
> Now recollect the theme I meant to write on,
> My ever faithful and obedient muse.
> O it is Woman! lovely! beauteous Woman!
> Say, what is Woman? what? what is she not?
> Life of this world! the cordial of existence!
> The grot of bliss! the alcove of delight!
> The turret head is on a column propt,
> Exceeding those from parian marbles rais'd;
> Its wondrous flexures charm a lover's eye.
> But a more charming object strikes our view;
> O! the red-rose-tipt globes on her white breast,
> That rise and fall alternate! sweet vicissitude!
> To them a lover's heart beats sympathy,
> His fond soul gazing thro' enraptur'd eyes,
> And ev'ry fibre throbbing for enjoyment;
> Essay on Woman instantly to make:
> Essay on Woman be this Poem nam'd.
> Down o'er the velvet plain, Abd-o-men call'd,
> The hand slides, glowing, to the zone of bliss—
> Stop hand, stop muse, nor farther now proceed,
> But, from th' extreme below, resume thy plan.
> On foot that's small, not large she stands erect.
> Neat moulded legs shoot upwards to the knee;
> Whence (cones invers'd) the thighs alluring swell,
> Plump instruments in amorous debate,
> With pow'rs re-active fraught, when close imping'd
> To bound resilient, and give Quid pro Quo.

23.

George Alexander Stevens: "The Adventures of a Speculist"

ONE of the most interesting writers on the manners and customs of the eighteenth century is George Alexander Stevens, who ran the gamut of experiences not a whit less adventurous and exciting than those of his fictive heroes. He was born in London in 1720 and died in Biggleswade, Bedfordshire, on September 6, 1784. Although of a lovable character he was a rascally ne'er-do-well, and combined the trades of itinerant actor, poet, dramatist and lecturer. His learned friend Sparks nevertheless stated that he was the best student of Greek in all England. Almost always in want, at times in prison, he passed through all the extremities of fortune and pleasure as well as destitution and misery. At all times he managed somehow or other to "soak himself in the wildest debaucheries and lowest company". He had a lively wit and an exceptionally intelligent comprehension of the psychology of persons which, sadly enough, he was unable to use for his own edification.

Stevens is best known for his discovering a new curious art of theatrical representation, the so-called "Lecture Upon Heads", which he introduced in April 1764 in the Haymarket Theatre. He was greeted with great acclaim and is said to have realized the enormous sum of ten thousand pounds for his performances and sale of lecture rights to Lee Lewis. Whatever the sum was, he ran through it quickly enough in travel and riotous adventures. His performance seems trite enough now but it was then a sensation. It consisted of a great number of lifelike busts made of pasteboard and animated by the voice, gestures and movements of Stevens. Almost every member of society was represented in this collection and Stevens had such a gift for mimicry that he transformed the subject into a living person.

These lectures were collected in a book which sold extremely well. The copy in our possession appeared in 1799 and bears the following title: "A Lecture on Heads by Geo. Alex. Stevens, with Additions by Mr. Pilon; as delivered by Mr. Charles Lee Lewes. To which is added An Essay on Satire. With twenty-four heads by Nesbit, from designs by Thurston".

Among the many excellent descriptions of London types around 1770, the following deserve especial mention: the effeminate or "Master Jackey", the virago, the prostitute, the president of a feminine debating club, the old virgin. As a specimen of Stevens' method of representation we submit the following on the last named "head":

"When they become superannuated, they set up for suitors, they ogle through spectacles, and sing love songs to ladies with catarrhs by way of symphonies, and they address a young lady with 'Come, my dear, I'll put on my spectacles and pin your hankkerchief for you; I'll sing you a love song':

> How can you, lovely Nancy, (Laughs aloud)
> How droll to hear the dotards aping youth,
> And tale of love's delight without a tooth!
>   (Gives the head off).

Stevens did not balk at painting the wretchedness of his own life. In his poem "The Repentant Libertine" (1751) he gives the following sketch of his "career":

> By chance condemn'd to wander from my birth
> An erring exile o'er the face of earth;
> Wild through the world of vice,—licentious race!
> I've started folly, and enjoy'd the chase:
> Pleas'd with each passion, I pursued their aim,
> Cheer'd the gay pack, and grasp'd the guilty game;
> Till youth, till health, fame, fortune, are no more.
> Too late I feel the thought-corroding pain
> Of sharp remembrance and severe disdain:
> Each painted pleasure its avenger breeds,
> Sorrow's sad train to Riot's troop succeeds;
> Slow-wasting Sickness steals on swift debauch;
> Contempt on Pride, pale Want on waste approach.

More complete autobiographical revelations are to be found in that famous English classic, "The Adventures of a Speculist; or, a Journey through London. Compiled from Papers written by George Alexander Stevens (author of

'A Lecture upon Heads') with his Life, a Preface, Corrections, and Notes, by the Editor. Exhibiting a Picture of the Manners, Fashions, Amusements, etc. of the Metropolis at the Middle of the Eighteenth Century: and including Several Fugitive Pieces of Humour, by the Same Author, now first collected and published. In Two Volumes" (1787).

The "Adventures of a Speculist" is one of the most important source works for a study of the social and sexual life in London about the period of 1760. Says Fraxi: "A more truthful and striking picture of London life during the middle of the 18th century it would be difficult to find; and who knew it better than Stevens, a regular man-about-town, and constant frequenter of its most doubtful haunts!"

The "Speculist" begins his rounds in the City, then visits Fleet Prison, Exchange Alley, Jonathan's Hospital and Bedlam Hospital, which he describes with piercing wit; his characters are plainly taken from life and run from doddering lords to bestial pimps. His friend Flight, whom he accompanies, hands over to him a manuscript, "Authentic Life of a Woman of the Town" (forming the major part of "The Adventures of a Speculist"), in which he states: "The Adventures have been actually experienced and the observations are all truthful. They provide a splendid supplement to your own observations so that you can now form an authentic opinion on the moral degeneration of mankind." There then follow humorous and interesting sketches on the taverns and "night-clubs" and their frequenters. The most interesting descriptions are of such clubs as the "Jolly Dog's", the "Damn'd High Fellows", the "Momus Court" in White Horse, Fetter Lane, also Covent Garden, "as it was and now is", and the infamous bordels run by Jenny Douglas and Bob Derry.

Stevens is also the author of five plays, a few poems, and a novel "The History of Tom Fool" (1760). He is the author of two rare small collections "The Humours of London, A choice Collection of Songs", and "Songs, Comic and Satirical". Stevens' talents should have served him to a far better end than his wretched mode of existence. As Davis remarks in his "Olio": "Stevens could keep an auditorium entranced for four full hours with his brilliant recitations and lectures." Stevens is one of the many sadly neglected figures in the history of English literature and deserves better shrift at the hands of the critics.

24.

"The Pupil of Pleasure": Samuel Johnson Pratt

literary turncoat of almost as many variegated colors as Stevens was the "pupil
of pleasure", Samuel Johnson Pratt. He
was born in St. Ives, Huntingdonshire,
on December 25, 1749, and died in Birmingham
on October 4, 1814. He wrote under the pseudonym, Courtney Melmoth, derived from the
name of his mistress, the famous Mrs. Melmoth.
He was an actor, poet, bookseller, lecturer and
author of many novels and essays, in fact, "a
very voluminous gentleman who had no scru-
ples, however, about being supported by his mistress".

Pratt here interests us as the author of "The
Pupil of Pleasure: or, The New System Illustrated. Inscribed to Mrs. Eugenia Stanhope, ed-

itor of Lord Chesterfield's Letters. By Courtney Melmoth. Versatile Ingenium. Two Volumes" (1776).

The "Pupil of Pleasure", although it deals
principally with the theory, art and practice of
seduction, has basically a moral motivation. The
work confutes the maxims of Lord Chesterfield
and tries to prove that his precepts exert a depraved influence on the youth. Sedley, a handsome and wealthy young man-about-town, soaked
in the letters of Chesterfield, visits Buxton where
he promptly succeeds in seducing two respectably married young ladies, Harriet Homespun
and Fanny Mortimer. His rascality is finally
unearthed and he is killed by the cuckolded
husband of Mrs. Mortimer.

The above story is told in a series of one hundred and eleven letters by various persons, mainly by Sedley and his friend Thornton. Although
"The Pupil of Pleasure" is of unmistakable originality it is written in a tasteless style of affected sentimentality that makes it completely un-
suitable to modern temper. A point worthy of
note is the complete absence of all obscene descriptions and "dirty" words, despite the fact
that the tale centers about the seduction of wom-
en by a master "pupil of pleasure".

25.

"The Mysteries of Venus or Lessons of Love"

HE famous work by Octave Mirabeau, "Journal d'une Femme de Chambre", was inspired by a French translation in 1786, "Memoires d'une Femme de Chambre", of an English original which appeared in the seventies or eighties of the eighteenth century. There is no known copy extant of this edition but Gay believes that the original English title was "The Waiting Woman, or the Galantries of the Times". It is now better known as "The Mysteries of Venus or Lessons of Love: exemplified in the amatory Life and Adventures of Kitty Pry" (1830).

This edition is also noteworthy for the inclusion of an excellent erotic poem:

Wishes unknown to fill her breast began;
Through every vein the glowing transport ran!
Now in his vigorous grasp, half-won, she pants
Struggles, denies—yet in denying grants.
White, like the wanton tendrils of the vine,
Their limbs in eager amorous folds entwine.
Breast joined to breast, caressing and caressed,
Of all but love's last fondest bliss possessed;
That to indulge did Nature give command,
And grown impetuous does full joy demand:
Then sunk the maid in her adorer's arms—
No more a maid—she yields up all her charms!
Half-pleas'd, half-pain'd, she sighs and smiles by turns
And whilst she bleeds for what has hurt her, burns:
Her lover clasps the murmuring, melting fair,
And both each rapture of possession share.

The chambermaid, Kitty Pry, declares in the introduction: "The curiosity of a chambermaid is proverbial. And it was so in my case. Curiosity, not necessity nor inclination, caused me to seek out such a position, and lest I be accused of hiding my talents in such low positions I have decided to make public my 'discoveries' for the edification and entertainment of all mankind."

Kitty spies about all the houses in which she is employed and ferrets out all the secrets and intrigues of her employer. In this way we obtain a complete, though caustic, picture of the sex life of all classes of society. The authoress does not, of course, forget to include her own erotic adventures, but her heart is not in them. She prefers to "peep" at the escapades of others. A true English voyeur!

The book is not badly written, and although every chapter contains a highly indecent episode obscene words are avoided in their description.

26.

Secret Pornologic Clubs in England

RANCE is notorious for its secret sex clubs; England is not far behind in its pornologic clubs. We even have literal accounts of two such infamous pornologic clubs in printed form. The title of the first reads: "The Phoenix of Sodom or the Vere Coterie, Being an Exhibition of the Gambols Practised by the Ancient Lechers of Sodom and Gomorrah, embellished and improved with the Modern Refinements in Sodomitical Practices, by the members of the Vere Street Coterie of detestable memory" (1813).

This "sex house" was most luxuriously constructed and furnished: each lady-member even had a separate dressing-room! The religious ceremony of marriage is travestied for each couple, who simulate a private wedding-night and then join the company in a general orgy. The members of the club were mostly prominent personages in the "high life" of London society and were known to one another by an obscene nickname. Meetings of this pornologic club usually took place on Sunday and other solemn holidays and lasted all night and morning.

The existence of this club could not be hidden from the police, but it was not banned until close and prolonged observance of the house conclusively proved the performance of "filthy acts", principally that of pederasty. The house was formally closed by the authorities in July 1810 and less prominent members were taken into custody. Twenty-three women-members, who were unable to present any evidence of their standing in society, were condemned to prison for a term of one to three years.

The solemnities of the initiation-rites of such sex-clubs is described in detail in "The Merry Order of St. Bridget. Personal Recollections of the Use of the Rod" (dated 1857, but first appeared in 1869). The novice is presented to the members of this flagellation club and the following ritual then takes place:

"'Are you prepared to serve the Merry Order to the best of your power, and to assist, as bidden by your mistress, in the ceremonies thereof?'

"'I am.'

"'And do you bind yourself never to reveal aught that you see, hear, or do in this room, on peril of losing your place without character?'

" 'I do.'

" 'Do you know the object of the Merry Order?'

" 'I do.'

" 'Detail it.'

"Again prompted, I replied, 'The wholesome and pleasant discipline of the rod, to be enforced by its members one upon another during their social meetings in this room.'

" 'Have you ever been whipped?'

" 'I have.'

" 'Do you promise to submit to such flagellation as the Merry Order shall ordain for you without rebellion or murmuring thereat?'

" 'I do.'

" 'Prepare her.'

"I heard more tittering when this order was given, and I could feel that Mrs. D........ was shaking with suppressed laughter as she obeyed the command, and took off my peignoir. She pinned up the petticoats and chemise to my shoulders, and then, my dear, I knew what was coming. Then some one else took hold of one of my hands, and Mrs. D........ the other, and waited the word of command.

" 'Advance.'

"They led me forward, and at the first step a stinging blow from a birch fell on my hips from one side, then from the other, till I had gone the length of the room. I screamed and struggled, but it was all in vain; my guides held me tight, and by the time they stopped I could only sob and writhe.

"Then came the command, 'Kneel down,' and I knelt in front of the square ottoman; the ladies held my hands across it, and Lady C........ came down from her dais and whipped me till I hardly knew where I was. Then they made me stand up, and her ladyship said,

" 'Ladies of the Order of St. Bridget, do you receive Margaret Anson as a member and servitor sworn to do your bidding?'

" 'We do,' said those who were not laughing.

" 'Let me see,' was the next order, and at the word one lady let my clothes drop, and the other took the bandage from my eyes. I was so smarting from the whipping I had received, that I could see nothing for a while, and Mrs. D........ took me by the arm and led me to the bottom of the room again.

"Every lady held a rod in her hand, made of lithe and strong twigs, tied up with ribbons that corresponded with the colours of her dress. On the ottoman over which I had knelt to receive my final castigation lay two more rods.

" 'Margaret Anson, approach,' said Lady C.... once more, and I went timidly forward, wondering whether any more whipping was in store for me.

" 'Kneel down.'

"I knelt and she presented me with a rod, and informed me that I was now a servitor of the Merry Order of St. Bridget — allowed to join their ceremonies, and bound to do their bidding; and then I was made to go and stand at the bottom of the room ready to do to the next comer as the ladies had done to me."

27.

Sixteen Famous Erotic and Obscene Works:

1780 = 1860

LIMITATIONS of space do not allow more than a description and short analysis of other famous erotic and obscene works in this transitional period in the history of erotic literature, which was marking time until the appearance of Edward Sellon. The most important works in this era are as follows:

1. *The Woman of Pleasure's Pocket Companion* (1830, original edition: 1787). This contains six erotic but not indecent tales, some of them rather humorous. One of the stories, *The Modern Susanna and the Two Elders,* is a translation from *Les Bijoux du Petit Neveu de d'Arétin* (1791).

2. *Dialogue between a Woman and a Virgin* (1786). This dialogue, based on various sources, has the following content: Volupta, who has "initiated" many a maiden, describes to Lydia, a young virgin, the delights of sexual intercourse, and her own enchantment at the loss of her maidenhead. Mr. Do Little, an impotent old rake, appears and is relieved of one hundred pounds for a few minutes of dallying with Lydia. After he leaves, Charles, a powerful young man and acquaintance of the two girls, enters the scene and completes the work of defloration on Lydia to her complete satisfaction.

3. *The Voluptarian Museum: or, History of Sir Henry Loveall. In a Tour through England, Ireland, Scotland, and Wales* (1790 ?). *Sir Henry Loveall* is light, entertaining and not too obscenely written. It is supposed to be the work of a "man of fashion, of gallantry, and of adventurous daring" and contains many scenes of flagellation. The book is noteworthy for the complete absence of perverse and unnatural sex acts.

4. *A Cabinet of Amorous Curiosities. In Three Tales. Highly calculated to please the Votaries of Venus. Tale I.—The Village Bull. Tale II.—Memoirs of a Feather-Bed. Tale III.—Adventures of a Droll One; or the Broke Open Casket* (1786). These three tales all treat of the same theme, the defloration of the various heroines. In the first tale this fate is the lot of two fresh country girls who are bringing a cow to a bull. In the second, Julia, the proud daughter of a country gentleman, is seduced by Alexander, a London fop. In the third, a quack-doc-

tor completes the bloody deed on an innocent
girl by the pretext that he is going to show how
he carried out the same medical procedure on
her grandmother!

5. *The Cabinet of Fancy, or Bon Ton of the
Day; A Whimsical, Comical, Friendly, Agree-
able Composition; Intended to please All, and
offend None; suitable to amuse Morning, Noon
and Night, writte* (sic) *and compiled by Tim-
othy Tickle-Pitcher* (1790).

> *With songs, and strange extravagancies
> He tries to tickle all your fancies.*

An amusing collection of short pieces, both prose
and poetry, stories, anecdotes, epigrams, songs,
etc. Erotic, but not indecent.

6. *The Bed-Fellows: or Young Misses Man-
uel* (sic). *In Six Confidential Dialogues between Two Budding Beauties, who have just
fledged their teens. Adapted to the capacity of
every loving virgin who has wit enough in her
little finger to know the value of the rest. Printed and Published on Mons Veneris: and may
be had by all who seek it there* (1820). This is
a well written book, but does not deviate from
the usual pattern of such obscene works. Lucy
and Kate tell one another of their erotic adventures as they undress every night and go to bed.
Their first seductions are told in the greatest of
detail, and their lascivious conversations are interrupted only by tribadic practices.

7. *The Modern Rake; or the Life and Adventures of Sir Edward Walford: Containing*

*a Curious and Voluptuous History of his lus-
cious intrigues, with numerous women of fashion, his laughable faux pas, feats of gallantry,
debauchery, dissipation and concubinism! His
numerous rapes, seductions, and amatory scrapes.
Memoirs of the Beautiful Courtezans with whom
he lived; with some Ticklish Songs, Anecdotes,
Poetry, etc.* (1824). The book describes, as is
amply indicated by the title, the erotic adventures of a young rake in France, Spain and England, until his conversion by a fortunate marriage. There is in addition an autobiography of a
French courtesan, and mention is made of many
erotic and obscene works.

8. *The Amorous Intrigues and Adventures
of Don Ferdinand and Donna Marie. Ferdinand's Intrigue with the Innkeeper's Wife. Cata-
line's Amour with Ferdinand. Donna Marie's
Intrigue. Curious Adventures of the Duke &
Duchess of Storza* (1820-1830). The title sufficiently indicates the nature of the contents. The
"Faublas" motif is also used: a boy dressed as a
girl is the constant bed-companion of Donna
Marie.

9. *The Seducing Cardinal, or, Isabella Peto.
A Tale founded on Facts* (1830). The seducing
cardinal" is "John Peter Caraffa, afterwards
Pope Paul III" (this assertion is untrue for
Paul III was a Farnese and no Caraffa; a Giovanni Pietro Caraffa also mentioned in the work
never existed). Isabella Peto is an orphan of
eighteen years at the point of marrying Signor
Antonio Lucca. The cardinal is madly in love
with her and has her thrown into the inquisition-

prison. The price of her release is the loss of her virginity. A week after her marriage with Lucca, the latter is called away to Candia, and the cardinal renews his intimacy with Isabella. She later departs for Candia where her husband is killed by the Turks. Isabella becomes an inmate in a Turkish harem and is well looked after. Caraffa accidently visits the Sultan, sees Isabella and transfers her to his own harem in a private convent. The book is extremely obscene.

10.   *The Lustful Turk. A History Founded on Facts, Containing An interesting Narrative of the cruel fate of the two Young English Ladies, named Silvia Carey, and Emily Barlow. Fully explaining how Emily Barlow, and her servant, Eliza Gibbs, on their passage to India, were taken prisoners by an Algerine Pirate, and made a present of to the Dey of Algiers; who, on the very night of their arrival debauched Emily. — Containing also, every particular of the artful plans laid by the Dey, to get possession of the person of Silvia Carey, etc. with the particulars of her becoming a victim to his libidinous desires. Which Recital is also interspersed with the Histories of several other Ladies confined in the Dey's Harem. One of which gives an account of the horrid practices then carrying on in several French and Italian convents by a society of Monks, established at Algiers, under pretence of redeeming Christian slaves; but who, in reality, Carried on an infamous traffic in Young Girls. — Also an account of the sufferings of Eliza Gibbs, from the flogging propensities of the Bey of Tunis. With many other curious circumstances, until the reduction of Algiers*

by Lord Exmouth; by which means these par-
ticulars became known. — *The whole compiled*
from the Original Letters, by permission of one
of the sufferers (1828). The title satisfactorily
and sufficiently conveys the impression of the
highly passionate scenes contained therein.

11.   *Scenes in the Seraglio. By the Author of*
"The Lusty (sic) *Turk"* (1820-1830). This book
has often been reprinted and may well have been
written by the author of "The Lustful Turk".
Adelaide, a young Sicilian beauty, is abducted
by a corsair who has fallen in love with her. But
his avariciousness dispels his passion as he discovers that Adelaide is a real virgin and he de-
termines to fetch a high price for her virginity.
He therefore forces her to submit to his embraces
and to stay by his side as he satisfies his aroused
passion with a countess, whom he has also kid-
napped. He then brings his victim to Constantinople where he sells her to the Sultan Achmed.
The Sultan treats Adelaide with the greatest
courtesy and refinement until she voluntarily
offers to appease his passion. The work ends in a
blissful harem-orgy.

12.   *Memoirs of Rosa Bellefille; or, A De-*
licious Banquet of Amorous Delights! Dedicated
to the Goddess of Voluptuous Pleasure, and her
soul-enamoured votaries (1828). This is a drawn-
out and rather boring tale. Rosa, a young girl
of markedly developed erotic temperament, tells
of her various affairs. She runs away from school
and literally throws herself into the hands of
every young man she encounters on the street.
She is also supported by many lovers, but leaves

them one by one, as soon as she finds out that she is surfeited with him, or that he cannot equal her own salacity. She finally becomes a common prostitute and takes up quarters in Drury Lane.

13. *The Favourite of Venus; or, Secrets of My Note-Book: Explained in the Life of a Votary of Pleasure. By Theresa Berkley* (1820-1830). A rather poor description of the love affairs of a young shipping-clerk with prostitutes and mistresses, to whom he presents gifts stolen from the shop.

14. *How to Make Love, or The Art of Making Love in more ways than one, exemplified in a series of Letters between two Cousins* (1823). A supplement to the above reads: *How to Raise Love, or the Art of Raising Love in more ways than one, etc.* (1829). The correspondents and main participants in "How to Raise Love" are the two cousins Stella and Theresa, Gabriele, a friend of Theresa, and her pupils Lalette, Charles, later the husband of Stella, Theresa's brother and a school-friend Friedrich. It is impossible to give a short sketch of this work for the intricate relationships defy a cursory analysis. This group of friends of mutual passions describe in their letters the affairs they have had since they last met one another. The book is not badly written, and coarse words and expressions are avoided.

15. *The Adventures, Intrigues and Amours of a Lady's Maid! Written by Herself* (1822). A sequel reads: *The Life of Miss Louisa Selby, Being the Second Part of the Adventures, etc.*

(1822). These two works describe the love career of Louisa Selby, the natural daughter of a country parson, by whom she was incestuously seduced, and then marketed by her pimping mother. She later becomes a maid to various mistresses, among them a tribade, is thereafter enclosed in an Italian convent, experiences further erotic adventures in Naples, falls in the hands of lecherous brigands, and finally marries a widowed English preacher.

16. *The Ladies' Tell Tale; or, Decameron of Pleasure. A Recollection of Amorous Tales, as related by a party of young friends to one another* (Five Volumes, 1830). This has been reprinted many times in varying editions and titles. The last complete edition was in 1865. The subtitle, *Decameron of Pleasure,* refers to the framework of the plot: a pornologic club of ladies and gentlemen who relate their most exciting adventures which are then collected by the feminine president. For the major part they refer to the first seduction which, both male and female agree, was the most exciting of all. The titles of the individual tales follow:

Vol. I, Tale 1. *Little Miss Curious's Tale.*
2. *The Young Gentleman's Tale.*
3. *The Young Lady's Tale.*
Vol. II, Tale 4. *The Traveller's Tale.*
5. *The Amateur Artist's Tale.*
6. *The Student in Art's Tale.*

We have given in full the individual titles of "The Ladies' Tell Tale" because they represent types that are found time and time again in erotic and obscene literature, not only in England but in all countries. For, as the reader by now has discovered, there is a definite tradition in erotic writings, the same as in any other class of literature. This point will be discussed more fully in the chapters on modern English erotic literature.

28.

Secret Sex Life of Lord Byron

"Lord Byron's" Suppressed Works

THE romantic figure of Lord Byron, tinged with his slight erotic poetry, could not help but gain him the notoriety and name of a Don Juan. Yet Byron was more "loved than loving"; his genius, beauty and passion made him a target for the amorous emotions of the ladies and thus gave him an unearned reputation of a Don Juan par excellence. No other literary figure has been "honored" by so many scandalous biographies, for example, "The Loves of Byron", his "Intrigues with Celebrated Women", "Amours of Lord Byron", "Private Intrigues of Lord Byron", "Private Life of Lord Byron", "The Secret Affairs of Lord Byron", etc., etc.

This plethora of erotic biographies was augmented the more by Lady Byron's notorious action against him for divorce. One of the grounds was "a hideous practice of incest with his half-sister, Mrs. Augusta Leigh" of which he was accused by the crusading Mrs. Harriet Beecher Stowe, author of "Uncle Tom's Cabin". The other ground was "an even more hideous practice which cannot be named".

This unmentionable action was pederasty, which was commonly ascribed to Lord Byron. Recent biographers deny the truth of either of these charges but that did not prevent Byron's less reputable colleagues from bursting into poetry on his "secret vices and strange sex life". Two poems appeared in 1865-1866 purporting to be by Lord Byron, himself, settling the question of his sex life once and for all. The first poem is titled: "Don Leon; A Poem by the late Lord Byron, Author of Childe Harold, Don Juan, etc., etc. And forming Part of the Private Journal of his Lordship, supposed to have been entirely destroyed by Thos. Moore". The title-page includes the following lines:

> Pardon, dear Tom, these thoughts on days gone by;
> Me men revile, and thou must justify.
> Yet in my bosom apprehensions rise,
> (For brother poets have their jealousies)
> Lest under false pretences thou should'st turn
> A faithless friend, and these confessions burn.

This poem is an enthusiastic apologia for pederasty. "Lord Byron" describes his many pederastic love affairs, and explains and defends the practice of pederasty. The cause for his marital conflict with his wife is given in the following lines:

That time it was, as we in parlance wiled
Away the hours, my wife was big with child.
Her waist which looked so taper when a maid
Like some swol'n butt its bellying orb displayed,
And love, chagrined, beheld his favourite cell
From mounds opposing scarce accessible.
"Look, Bell," I cried: "yon moon, which just now rose
Will be the ninth; and your parturient throes
May soon Lucina's dainty hand require
To make a nurse of thee, of me a sire.
I burn to press thee, but I fear to try,
Lest like incubus my weight should lie;
Lest, from the close encounter we should doom
Thy quickening foetus to an early tomb.
Thy size repels me, whilst thy charms invite;
Then, say, how celebrate the marriage rite?
Learn'd Galen, Celsus, and Hippocrates,
Have held it good, in knotty points like these,
Lest mischief from too rude assaults should come,
To copulate ex more pecudum.
What sayst thou, dearest? Do not cry me nay;
We cannot err where science shows the way."

Ah, fatal hour! for thence my sorrows date:
Thence sprung the source of her undying hate.
Fiends from her breast the sacred secret wrung,
Then called me monster; and, with evil tongue,
Mysterious tales of false Satanic art
Devised, and forced us evermore to part.

The second poem is titled: "The Great Secret Revealed! Suppressed Poem by Lord Byron, never before published, Leon to Annabella. Lord Byron to Lady Byron, An epistle explaining the Real Cause of Eternal Separation, And Justifying the Practice which led to it. Forming the most Curious Passage in the Secret History of the Noble Poet, Influencing the Whole of his Future Career, etc." There is first quoted the statement by Lushington, Lady Byron's advocate: "Lady Byron can never return to her husband. He has given her cause for separation which can never be disclosed. Her womanly

modesty forbids further intercourse with him."
The cause for the separation is described in
the following lines, which are quite decently
worded:

> Oh, lovely woman! by your Maker's hand
> For man's delight and solace wisely planned.
> Thankless is she who nature's bounty mocks,
> Nor gives Love entrance whereso'er he knocks.
>
> Matrons of Rome, held ye yourselves disgraced
> In yielding to your husband's wayward taste?
> Ah, no!—By tender complaisance ye reign'd:
> No wife of wounded modesty complained.

Naturally, Lord Byron never set hand to either
of these two poems. Equally false is the ascription to him of an erotic poem, "Forbidden Fruit.
A Description of the First Coition Between
Adam and Eve". This work, however, is not
badly done and we quote the concluding passage:

> Ah! who shall paint the raptures they first knew
>   Beneath that spreading canopy of blue.
> While in the pride of their full strength and youth,
>   They tasted sweetly of the cup of truth,
> And found that joy then to man unknown—
>   A priceless boon which he might call his own.
> And this pure bliss which in the garden came
>   Still thrills as sweetly through each mortal frame.
> And each new couple on their marriage bed,
>   When husband takes his young wife's maidenhead,
> Repeats again the same old pleasure o'er
>   And finds in love a never failing store,
> When to her husband she gives up the gem
>   The sweetest jewel in love's diadem.
> Hark to the mutt'rings that are heard afar,
>   As nature feels an elemental war;
> Thunder is rolling now along the skies
>   The vivid lightnings blind their fearless eyes,
> The winds speed onward with a shrieking blast,
>   And deep with gloom the skies are overcast;
> While from the clouds the pelting rains descend
>   And with the storm the war of wild beasts blend.

Each brute feels all its instinct wildly stirred
    While in the air is heard the screaming bird.
In one wild shriek a thousand tongues give vent
    To the deep passion the world has sent.
Now storm and darkness settled o'er the land
    And the blue sea comes bellowing on the sand;
The massive trees before the whirlwind rock,
    The earth now trembles with the earthquake shocks.
The earth is shrouded with the midnight gloom
    For man has heard from God his doom.
No more the fruits of Eden's fruitful soil
    His sweat shall moisten all he earns by toil;
While Eve in anguish shall to life give birth
    And leave an heritage of woe on earth.
God made them pure, but out of worldly dust
    And from the clay they gathered all its lust.
From that sweet scene within the grove began
    All the long sorrows that have tortured man,
Until the trump of Gabriel gives us peace
    Those woes entailed on earth shall never cease.

Lord Byron has also been accused by Moll of being a confirmed homosexualist, but there is little or no evidence to support this view beyond his practice of sexual intercourse "a retro" with his wife, and perhaps some of the gallant ladies who could not refuse an expressed desire of their "Love's Favorite".

In passing, we would also like to mention that a pornographic novel named "Flossie" is often attributed to Algernon Charles Swinburne, but there is no reason to believe that this is true. The complete title of this work reads: "Flossie, a Venus of fifteen, by one who knew this charming goddess and worshipped at her shrine. Printed at Carnopolis for the delectation of the Amorous and the Instruction of the Amateurs". The reason for the ascription probably rests on the erotic nature of many of Swinburne's poems, as well as the author's confessed admiration for the works of the Marquis de Sade.

29.

Edward Sellon: Mad Escapades of the English Casanova

MONG the vast number of erotic and pornographic works that flooded England in the latter half of the nineteenth century, those of the famous anthropologist Edward Sellon deserve especial mention. In Sellon we have perhaps the only pornographist in the nineteenth century whose work can be compared with that of John Cleland, in point of style, literary and cultural significance.

Edward Sellon (1818-1866) was a spirited epicurean who reeled from appetite to pleasure and from pleasure to appetite, not because of "gross sensuality but from higher motives". In this and many other respects he was a true Casanova, the only differences being the absence of the latter's optimistic viewpoint and religiousness, for Sellon died a confirmed atheist. Sellon has described his own life in a highly erotic work:

"The Ups and Downs of Life. A Fragment.

All the world's a stage
And all the men and women merely players;
They have their exits and their entrances,
And one man in his time plays many parts.

—As you like it, act 2, scene VII.

(Subtitle) My Life: The Beginning and the End. A Veritable History" (1867).

Sellon's father was moderately well-to-do and had decided to have his son take up a military career when he suddenly died, leaving Sellon to fulfill his wishes. At the age of sixteen he was accepted as a cadet and departed for Portsmouth. He then spent ten long years in India and was made a captain at the age of twenty-six. The greatest part of his erotic autobiography is his description of his stay in India and his many love affairs with European and native women. He emphatically declares that the Hindu women are eminently superior to the English, French, German and Polish girls of all classes, for these latter cannot even hope to compare with the "salacious, succulent houris of the far East". Moreover the Hindu girls "understand in perfection all the arts and wiles of love, are capable of gratifying any tasters, and in face and figure they are unsurpassed by any women in the world".

At his return to England he discovered that his mother wished to marry him off to "a young lady of considerable personal attractions", and also an heiress of twenty-five thousand pounds of landed property. He yielded to her wish and passed the winter of 1814 in Paris with his precious bride. But at his return to England he was unpleasantly surprised to find that his wife's property brought her only four hundred pounds a year in rentals. His mother-in-law also informed him that he would have to live in a pretty but small cottage in Devonshire which she had already arranged for them. With violent reproaches he left his wife and joined his mother in Bruton Street, London. During this two-year separation from his wife he comforted himself in the arms of a "dear girl" whom he was maintaining in a small suburban village. A reconciliation then followed and his wife joined him at his mother's home.

Everything went well the first month, but unfortunately one of his mother's servants was a sweet little girl, the daughter of a merchant, who resembled a servant girl neither in breeding nor manners. Shortly before the return of his wife Sellon had seduced this young girl of fourteen and was now facing the difficulty of retaining his little mistress without being discovered by his wife.

Discovery followed only too soon. One Sunday morning, after returning from church, his wife found little Emma's hat on her bed. Her husband had pleaded a headache and had not arisen until she left the house. There then followed a turbulent scene of jealousy in which our hero remained cool and refused to give his wife any satisfactory explanation. The enraged wife naturally lost control of her emotions and gave the faithless husband a mighty box on the right cheek. "I quietly threw away the stub of my cigar on the hearth-grate, firmly grasped both her arms and pressed her into a chair. Now, you little devil, I said, you will sit here, I assure you on my honour, I will hold you firmly in this fashion until you humbly beg my pardon for the vulgar insult you have given me."

Despite a violent fight and desperate bitings on the part of the embittered wife Sellon succeeded, after many exhausting hours, in taming this unreasonable woman, but only after he had lost much blood from her sharp bites. Immediately after her apology he fell to the floor unconscious and the services of a physician were necessary for the binding of his wounds. But his wife was so well cured of her jealousy that she quietly, even smilingly, endured Emma's sitting on his bed, eating with them in common, and even usurping her rightful place in the marital bed after dinner! This did not prevent Augusta from receiving her share of conjugal blessings the same night. Little wonder that the net result of such a sexual performance was a breakdown of Sellon's health which lasted for a full month, during which period he was nursed by his wife and his mother. After his convalescence he left with his wife for Hastings. Emma had been left behind, but an earlier mistress appeared to plague him and was the cause of another break with his wife.

His mother now suffered the loss of her entire fortune and Sellon had to seek means of support. He became a postilion under an assumed name and for two years drove the post to Cambridge. This gave him the opportunity of successfully embarking on the career of a "riding Casanova". Sellon lost count of his many love affairs. He then established a fencing academy in London. Here his wife again sought him out and pleaded with him to resume his rightful place as her husband. "The gods alone know how many times I've been untrue to her since we last separated six years ago."

They obtained a small pretty home not far from Winchester, Hampshire, where they carried on "veritable erotic orgies" with one another, resulting in a three-year period of faithfulness by Sellon. From this "golden dream" he was rudely awakened by the pregnancy of his wife which, at one blow, drove away his passion for her, especially since his wife now gave all her tendernesses to the expected offspring.

Sellon abruptly left for London, "indulging in every kind of debauchery". His wife again sought him out and was successful in bringing him back to Hampshire but this picture of domestic fortune lasted only a short time. His wife caught him one day taking a group of schoolgirls into the forest to play "hide-and-seek".

"After this escapade, I could no longer remain in Hampshire, so packed my portmanteau, and was once more a gentleman at large in London." Here the book closes with the following note, allegedly written by the publisher, but actually by the author himself. "The story breaks off suddenly at this point, and so far as it can be determined it seems as if the author died shortly thereafter. At any rate, he was never seen again, either living or dead, by his many acquaintances."

The truth is that Edward Sellon, on April 1, 1866 in Webb's Hotel, No. 219-220, Piccadilly (later the Criterion Restaurant), mortally shot himself. His friends persuaded the newspapers to refrain from mentioning this unfortunate end of a talented man. Sellon, before committing suicide, had written to a friend and informed him of his determination. But the letter came late the following morning when all was over. In the letter was found the following poem dedicated to a woman who was in love with him and had wished to help him when he had fallen in want.

NO MORE!

No more shall mine arms entwine
Those beauteous charms of thine,
Or the ambrosial nectar sip
Of that delicious coral lip—
　　　　　No more.

No more shall those heavenly charms
Fill the vacuum of these arms;
No more embraces, wanton kisses,
Nor life, nor love, Venus blisses—
　　　　　No more.

The glance of love, the heaving breast
To my bosom so fondly prest,
The rapturous sigh, the amorous pant,
I shall look for, long for, want
　　　　　No more.

For I am in the cold earth laid,
In the tomb of blood I've made.
Mine eyes are glassy, cold and dim
Adieu my love, and think of him
　　　　　No more.

Vivat lingam.
Non Resurgam.

With this melancholic swan-song of eroticism there ended the life of a man who was certainly destined for a far better fate. Sellon died unrepentant and still believing firmly in atheism and the truth of the motto with which he closed the above poem. The hiatus which falls between the abrupt end of the autobiography and the equally abrupt end of his own life is filled by a letter dated March 4, 1866 and addressed to the same friend whom he had informed of his suicidal intent. In this letter Sellon tells in a very humorous fashion how he accompanied a friend and his bride on a honeymoon trip to Vienna, how he cuckolded the bridegroom on the trip, and how, shortly before they arrived in Vienna, he was forced to engage in a solemn fist-fight with the groom because of his friendly services to the bride. Sellon's money quickly vanished in Vienna in riotous living and he was forced to return to London.

* * *

But before we discuss the other erotic works of Sellon we should like to pay tribute to the important services he rendered to anthropology. He acquainted the intelligent public with many unknown facts on Hindu culture and civilization. A good number of his important lectures are contained in the "Transactions of the London Anthropological Society". Even in his first mildly erotic novel, "Herbert Breakspear, A Legend of the Mahratta War" (1848), he gives a graphic picture of the real Hindu life. Further anthropological contributions of Sellon are: "Monolithic Temples of India", a translation of the "Gita-Radhica-Krishna". and "Annotations on the Sacred Writings of the Hindus", which is especially rich in interesting information on religious prostitution in India.

The transition to real erotic writings is provided by "Selections from The Decameron of Giovanni Boccaccio. Including all the Passages hitherto suppressed" (1865), an Italian translation by Sellon, now excessively rare.

In his last few years of life, Sellon, probably driven by debt, wrote some erotic works for the publisher William Dugdale, but they are of the better kind in regard to their literary value. The first work of this nature is "The New Epicurean; or, The Delights of Sex, Facetiously and Philosophically Considered, in Graphic Letters Addressed to Young Ladies of Quality" (1865).

In "The New Epicurean" Sellon has described in the person of Sir Charles a character and a mode of living after his own tastes. In the preface Sir Charles tells us: "I am a man who, after crossing the Rubicon of youth, has attained that age where passion demands a more stimulating diet than is to be found in the arms of painted courtesans." In furthering his quest Sir Charles has rented a suburban villa, the high surrounding walls effectively concealing this idyllic location from the eyes of prying neighbors. The villa is surrounded by a true English park with splendid shady walks, alcoves, grottos, fountains, beautifully laid out flower-beds, a statue of Venus in white marble in the center of rosebushes, a statue of Priapus at each end of the shady paths, sometimes as an Indian Bacchus, or as feminine and delicate as Antinous, or provided with hermaphroditic armor. In the carefully kept ponds swarm gold and silvery colored fish.

The interior of the villa is decorated with studied elegance entirely in the style of Louis XV; Watteau's foremost paintings adorn the stately walls; a select library of the finest erotic and pornographic works takes up a separate room; gilded furnishings, silken coverlets, and rose-colored Venetian rouleaux all combine in impressing the spectator with the sense of tasteful splendor.

In this Elysium Sir Charles revels in all conceivable sexual orgies. He has an especial predilection for immature girls who are furnished by a headmistress of a finishing school in his possession. Sir Charles is indeed married, but Lady Cecily does not disturb his debauchings; she even takes a leading part in the more imposing orgies, and has a private page at her disposal.

Nevertheless the work has a rather tragic dénouement. Cecily, without the knowledge of her husband, has concluded an affair with her cousin Lord William. Sir Charles surprises them in the very act. A duel takes place immediately between the two men and both are wounded, though not seriously. Lady Cecily enters a convent and takes the veil. Sir Charles sells his villa and returns to his estate in Herfordshire, bringing with him Phoebe and Chloe, his servants, Daphnis, the page of Cecily, and the steward Jukes.

The work then closes with the following statement by Sir Charles: "Having lived every day of my life, as the saying is, you will readily suppose that I cannot perform the feats of Venus I once indulged in, but two or three blooming little girls, who pass for the sisters and cousins of Phoebe and Chloe, serve to amuse me by their playfulness, and tumbling about showing their beauties, sometimes stir my sluggish blood into a thrill." In other words, Sir Charles must now content himself with serving Venus only as a voyeur. "The New Epicurean" is even more lascivious than the works of de Sade but lacks the latter's delight in cruelty. The book is cast in the form of intimate letters to various women and has a good many autobiographical sketches.

Further self-revelations are also to be found in a later erotic work of Sellon, "Phoebe Kissagen; or, the Remarkable Adventures, Schemes, Wiles, and Devilries of Une macquerelle, being a sequel to the 'New Epicurean', etc." (1866).

Sir Toby:—"Do'st thou think that because thou art virtuous there shall be no more cakes and ale?"—

Clown:—"Yes! by St. Anne, and ginger shall be hot i' the mouth too!"—

—Twelfth Night; or What you will.

Sellon sent the publisher Dugdale another erotic tale, since he did not think "Phoebe Kissagen" was long enough for a separate book. Its title was "Scenes in the Life of a Young Man, a narrative of amorous exploits", but it was not included or printed.

"Phoebe Kissagen" is written in the style of eighteenth century French erotica and consists of letters addressed to a Lady G.... R. The work begins with an account of the death of Sir Charles who was taken down with a stroke in the act of intercourse with his favorite concubine, Phoebe. Chloe and Phoebe each receive a legacy of three thousand pounds with which they return to London and purchase a bordel in Leicester Fields. All the rooms in the bordel have secret peepholes by which the madam can see everything that is going on without the suspicion of the performers. The description of such various scenes takes up the major part of the work. The remainder of the work consists of "bagnio correspondence", that is, letters which Phoebe has received from her many male and female clients and in which their peculiar passions and perversions are brought to light. Phoebe finally falls in love with a young lad who calls himself Captain Jackson, gambler and duelist. He marries her, lays waste to her fortune, infects her with syphilis, and then abandons her. Broken-hearted Phoebe leaves London and spends the rest of her days in a quiet village.

Sellon also wrote three other erotic works which exist in manuscript form only. We should also mention the fact that Sellon was an accomplished artist and contributed obscene illustrations to all his work. Although not of the highest standards the pictures are excellent accomplishments for an amateur.

Strangely enough, Sellon has found few imitators. This may well be due to the circumstances that his works betray the taste of a well educated man, of too high a literary standard for the average Englishman, and because his erotica is not flavored with sufficient scenes of flagellation. The sole imitation of Sellon's autobiography is the fragmentary "Private Recreations, or The

Ups and Down of Life. By one who has been beyond the scenes, and taken part in the performance" (1879). Lord L., a lecherous nobleman, has two mistresses, Lottie and Sue, who entertain him by telling spicy stories of their lives. Lord L. in turn delights them with a demonstration of obscene photographs and pictures. The stories are the usual run and deal mainly with the loss of virginity.

30.

"The Amatory Experiences of a Surgeon"

"THE Amatory Experiences of a Surgeon" deserves especial mention mainly because of its false ascription to John Cleland, author of "Fanny Hill". It was in reality written by a certain James Campbell and was published for the first time in 1871.

The work begins with the following interesting introduction: "Not all the glowing descriptions of amatory writers, nor the inspired breath of passion itself, can truly, and in sufficient degree estimate the force of those desires, and the intoxicating delirium of that enjoyment in which the softer sex plays so important a part, and in the gratification of which it relishes a more than equal degree of pleasure.

"Were I to cover these pages with descriptions

of the most seductive or lascivious scenes, I should fail to realize its full effect.

"Language stops short of the reality. No words, however passionate, however glowing, could transport the bosom, and enthral the frame, like the one magic soul-dissolving sensation, experienced by lovers in the celebration of these mystic rites; but if my readers will follow me, while I tell them of some of my amatory experiences, their own feelings may perhaps enable them to sympathise with mine, and thus by analogy, enjoy again some of the most sensual and moving incidents in their own careers."

Campbell then begins the story of "his life": "To say that I was born of respectable parents would, in the full acceptation of the words, be false. My mother was of that disgraced and neglected race, a discarded mistress; my father, a nobleman of the first rank, while still a young man, full of the fiery vices of youth, had caught her eye, his handsome form and noble bearing won her simple love.

"The old story followed. He seduced her, kept her awhile to be his toy, and at length, grown tired of her society, threw her off as a plaything of which he was weary. She died, but he lived on to break the heart of many other innocent creatures.

"Whatever may have been his errors, among his redeeming points must be reckoned his care of his illegitimate child. After my mother's death I was sent to a boarding school, and at the age of fourteen had grown a tall, well-made and genteel looking youth.

"It is needless to say, that it was here, in the

society of other lads, many of whom were my seniors, that I was first made acquainted with all that is necessary for men to know in a theoretical point of view; of practice with the opposite sex, I knew nothing, but my ardent imagination pictured extasies, which fell but little short of the reality, and which was further assisted in its expanded ideas by the scenes we boys enacted among ourselves. All that we could do we did, and we gave each other as much amusement, as we knew how to adminsiter."

In due time he received his diploma from the Royal College of Surgeons, settled in a small practice at the village near which his parental patron had his principal estate, and thanks to his father's patronage became the fashionable doctor of the district. At this point his "amatory experiences" begin. His first liaison is with his father's mistress, whom he purposely seduces so that he may thus revenge his mother. But he cannot continue the affair after he surprises her with a "strapping six-foot butler". He then finds consolation in the arms of a desirable young virgin and does away with the fruit of the union by criminal abortion. The story then degenerates into a series of seductions of his feminine patients, particularly very young girls. The work also contains some interesting obiter dicto and an exceedingly high judgment of the works of the Marquis de Sade.

This reads as follows: "If the quintessence of sexual excitement and glowing scenes that beggar description can be productive of sufficient effect to produce such a result, even to the author himself, this rare and fearful work is certainly the one capable of doing so. The wonderful descriptions it contains, the fiercely exciting scenes it depicts, and the exhibition of so many varied means of producing the acme of enjoyment, render it no less valuable for its deep effectual influence over the passions than for its deep philosophy and wonderful power of reasoning which stamp it as the work of a genius of extraordinary talent."

We wonder what Campbell would have thought of the "120 Days of Sodom, or the School for Libertinage" if that masterpiece of the Marquis de Sade had been known in his day?

31.

"My Secret Life"
An Encyclopaedia of Fornication

IN 1888 a wealthy old Londoner had privately printed in a limited edition of six copies for his own amusement a voluminous manuscript of his sex life, theories, practices, etc. This work appeared in no less than eleven volumes, totalling approximately four thousand large-sized pages!

It is impossible to give even a short notion of the contents: the titles of the chapters would fill half a book. The extensiveness of the work may be gathered from the fact that there are two hundred and twenty-two subheadings to the subject "copulation" in the index! each being a different principle or practice of that art.

The author evidently kept complete accounts of his daily sex life which ran through every class of woman, from a princess down to the lowest street-walker. His main pleasure consisted in seeking out such adventures without regard to station or calling. The language is exceptionally free, even for an obscene work, but the author nevertheless refuses to make any remarks on his married life, or certain of his mistresses for whom he had some degree of affection. The book then is motivated by lust and is accordingly pure pornography. The literary merit is slight, if any; the work reads more like a series of rapid jottings, hastily transcribed into simple English, not neglecting the use of the commonest and grossest expressions.

We shall therefore indicate, in brief, the nature of one of the innumerable amours of the author. This healthy and wealthy Englishman forms the acquaintance of a retired officer of the French army in Paris, who introduces him to his wife, an attractive lady. The old soldier frequently talks about women and while in one of his customary inebriated states lets out that he once heard of a female who had connection with twelve men in an hour. Pressed by the author of "My Secret Life", he gradually betrays a deep mystery, for the victim of this lustful dozen is no other than the woman who passes as his wife, for he has never legally married her.

This disclosure excites the salacious desire of his listener, and he immediately attacks the officer's mistress, who soon gives way to him, as she had threatened her babbling paramour that if he ever exposed her past to a stranger, that man should have her.

32.

"Raped on the Railway,
Social Studies
of the Century"

HIS "sociological study" is dated 1894 with the complete title: "Raped on the Railway, Social Studies of the Century. A true story of a lady who was first ravished and then flagellated on the Scotch Express." An unusual attraction of this work is the illustrated cover, where a "gentleman" is seen trying to violate a most comely young lady in a dressing gown, or rather the remnants of one, for that garment has been half torn off her gleaming shoulders, exposing her breasts above, and showing her stockings and drawers below.

The hero, Brandon, is a painter with a very sensual wife; he therefore violently takes advantage of a lady in a first-class compartment of a Scotch express. But her brother-in-law happens to be in the same train with some friends, and getting into the carriage, he suspects her of having willingly given way to the fascinating stranger. They fall upon Brandon and bind him, forcing him to be an eye-witness to a terrible flagellation inflicted upon his victim. Later, the avenging brother-in-law tries to rape her, and that is the episode so graphically shown on the cover.

Brandon is pleased with his trifling punishment and returns home to his faithless wife; they have a variety of the most erotic adventures together, in which corporal punishment plays a conspicuous part, and the lustful Mrs. Brandon finally dies of nymphomania.

After her death, the husband leaves for the Transvaal and takes service in the field where he becomes friends with a captain, who, being mortally wounded, confides to him a message to his wife. Brandon, on returning to England, seeks out his comrade's widow and is astounded to find it is the woman he had raped on the Scotch Express. In his letter, the dying man tells her that she cannot do better than marry Brandon, and she takes the advice of her dead husband.

This curious work is notable for the refreshing picturesqueness of expression, a change from the deadening monotony of the usual pornographic books.

33.

The "Ideal Love" Between Two Immortal English Poets:

Oscar Wilde and Lord Douglas

OWARDS the end of the nineteenth century there burst across the English firmament a startling case that was to mark the last death-stand of Victorian puritanism. The "ideal love affair" of two of the foremost English poets was dragged through the mire of the criminal court. All England, with but a few notable exceptions, seemed to unite in heaping venom on the heads of Oscar Wilde and Lord Douglas.

This famous case is still fresh in the public's mind. Who can forget Wilde's stirring defence of his actions during the trial: "The 'love' that dare not speak its name in this century is such a great affection of an older for a younger man as there was between David and Jonathan, such as Plato made the very base of his philosophy and such as you find in the sonnets of Michael-angelo and Shakespeare—a deep spiritual affection that is as pure as it is perfect, and dictates great works of art like those of Shakespeare and Michaelangelo . . . It is beautiful; it is fine; it is the noblest form of affection. It is intellectual, and it repeatedly exists between an elder and younger man, when the elder man has intellect, and the younger man has all the joy, hope and glamour of life. That it should be so the world does not understand. It mocks at it and sometimes puts one into the pillory for it."

Harris, in his magnificent "Oscar Wilde and His Confessions", has left an immortal memorial of the life of a genius whose only fault was sensual indulgence and one for which he was signally punished and martyrized by inhuman English judges (Wilde was tried in 1895, served two years in prison, and died in Paris in 1900). Harris quotes verbatim an unique conversation he had with Wilde, after the latter was released from prison, on the vices and virtues of homosexuality. In this brilliant Socratic dialogue Wilde defends and Harris attacks the practice of male homosexual love.

"Don't talk to me of the other sex," he cried with distaste in voice and manner. "First of all in beauty there is no comparison between a boy and a girl. Think of the enormous, fat hips which every sculptor has to tone down, and make lighter, and the great udder breasts which the artist has to make small and round and firm, and then picture the exquisite slim line of a boy's figure. No one who loves beauty can hesitate for a moment. The Greeks knew that; they had a sense of plastic beauty, and they understood that there is no comparison."

"You must not say that," I replied; "you are going too far; the Venus of Milo is as fine as any Apollo, in sheer beauty; the flowing curves appeal to me more than your weedy lines."

"Perhaps they do, Frank," he retorted, "but you must see that the boy is far more beautiful. It is your sex-instinct, your sinful sex-instinct which prevents your worshipping the higher form of beauty. Height and length of limb give distinction; slightness gives grace; women are squat. You must admit that the boy's figure is more beautiful; the appeal it makes far higher, more spiritual."

"Six of one and half-dozen of the other," I barked. "Your sculptor knows it is just as hard to find an ideal boy's figure as an ideal girls; and if he has to modify the most perfect girl's figure, he has to modify the most perfect boy's figure as well. If he refines the girl's breasts and hips he has to pad down the boy's ribs and tone down the great staring knee-bones and the unlovely large ankles; but please go on, I enjoy your special pleading and your romantic passion interests me; though you have not yet come to the romance, let alone the passion."

"Oh, Frank," he cried, "the story is full of romance; every meeting was an event in

my life. You have no idea how intelligent
he is; every evening we spent together he
was different; he had grown, developed. I
lent him books and he read them, and his
mind opened from week to week like a flower, till in a short time, a few months, he became an exquisite companion and disciple.
Frank, no girl grows like that; they have no
minds, and what intelligence they have is all
given to wretched vanities, and personal
jealousies. There is no intellectual companionship possible with them. They want to
talk of dress, and not of ideas, and how persons look and not what they are. How can
you have the flower of romance without a
brotherhood of soul?"

"Now you have talked about romance
and companionship," I went on, "but can
you really feel passion?"

"Frank, what a silly question. Do you remember how Socrates says he felt when the
chlamys blew aside and showed him the
limbs of Charmides? Don't you remember
how the blood throbbed in his veins and
how he grew blind with desire, a scene more
magical than the passionate love-lines of
Sappho? There is no other passion to be
compared with it. A woman's passion is de-
grading. She is continually tempting you.
She wants your desire as a satisfaction for
her vanity more than anything else, and her
vanity is insatiable if her desire is weak,
and so she continually tempts you to excess,
and then blames you for the physical satiety

and disgust which she herself has created. With a boy there is no vanity in the matter, no jealousy, and therefore none of the tempting, not a tenth part of the coarseness; and consequently desire is always fresh and keen. Oh, Frank, believe me, you don't know what a great romantic passion is."

"What you say only shows how little you know about women," I replied. " If you explained all this to the girl who loves you, she would see it at once, and her tenderness would grow with her self-abnegation; we all grow by giving. If the woman cares more than the man for caresses and kindness, it is because she feels more tenderness, and is capable of intenser devotion."

"You are unpardonable," he cried, "unpardonable, and in your soul you know that all the weight of the argument is on my side. In your soul you must know it. What is the food of passion, Frank, but beauty, beauty alone, beauty always, and in beauty of form and vigour of life there is no comparison. If you loved beauty as intensely as I do, you would feel as I feel. It is beauty which gives me joy, makes me drunk as with wine, blind with insatiable desire . . . . "

34.

"Ulysses", the Anatomy of Humanity

An Epoch=Making American Court Decision

AMES JOYCE'S "Ulysses" (1922) is neither an erotic nor pornographic work. Its suppression is due to the limited use of certain common and sometimes vulgar expressions which were essential to the author's thesis. That this, in itself, should make a book obscene is absurd, and, indeed, has so been found in one of the wisest decisions of modern times. Judge Woolsey of the Federal District Court of the United States in deciding that "Ulysses" was not motivated by any pornographic desire on the part of the author, declared:

It is because Joyce has been loyal to his technique and has not funked its necessary implications, but has honestly attempted to tell fully what his characters think about, that he has been the subject of so many attacks and that his purpose has been so often misunderstood and misrepresented. For his attempt sincerely and honestly to realize his objective has required him incidentally to use certain words which are generally considered dirty words and has led at times to what many think is a too poignant preoccupation with sex in the thoughts of his characters.

The words which are criticized as dirty are old Saxon words known to almost all men and, I venture, to many women, and are such words as would be naturally and habitually used, I believe, by the types of folk whose life, physical and mental, Joyce is seeking to describe. In respect of the recurrent emergence of the theme of sex in the mind of his characters, it must always be remembered that his locale was Celtic and his season Spring.

Whether or not one enjoys such a technique as Joyce uses is a matter of taste on which disagreement or argument is futile, but to subject that technique to the standards of some other technique seems to me to be little short of absurd.

Accordingly, I hold that 'Ulysses' is a sincere and honest book and I think that the criticisms of it are entirely disposed of by its rationale.

"Ulysses" is divided into three parts. The first concerns the morbid reflections of Stephen

Dedalus, the artist. The second concerns Leopold Bloom, an advertizing solicitor. This section takes up the greatest portion of "Ulysses" and follows Bloom's every action, even the most private ones, in the course of twenty-four hours. The third section describes the homeward pilgrimage of Stephen Dedalus and Leopold Bloom. The work ends with a remarkable soliloquy by Mrs. Bloom in the privacy of her bedroom.

The difficulty in reading Joyce is due to the use of different techniques for each separate episode or purpose. According to Smith: "Every method Joyce brings to his work is patently for the purpose of analyzing the stream of consciousness, of tracing it, so far as possible, to its source; for unmasking all the hidden fears and hopes, shames and prides over which respectability has hung the etiolated fig-leaves, and concerning which cowardice has created its canting camouflage."

That such a literary method may sometimes lead to absurdities and incongruities is apparent. Yet the total effect upon the intelligent reader is one of ordered purposiveness, rather than one of diffused madness. A quotation from Mrs. Bloom's soliloquy will bring out this point:

> . . . no thats no way for him has he no manners nor no refinement nor no nothing in his nature slapping us behind like that on my bottom because I didnt call him Hugh the ignoramus that doesnt know poetry from a cabbage thats what you get for not keeping them in their proper place

pulling off his shoes and trousers there on
the chair before me so barefaced without
even asking permission and standing out that
vulgar way in the half of a shirt they wear
to be admired like a priest or a butcher or
those old hypocrites in the time of Julius
Caesar of course hes right enough in his
way to pass the time as a joke sure you
might as well be in bed with what with a
lion God Im sure hed have something better to say for himself an old Lion would O
well I suppose its because they were so
plump and tempting in my short petticoat
he couldnt resist they excite myself sometimes its well for men all the amount of
pleasure they get off a womans body were
so round and white for them always I wished I was one myself for a change . . . .

35.

"My Life and Loves" by Frank Harris

Greatest Erotic Autobiography in the World

His First Completed Manuscript on Art and Technique of Love

EVEN if Frank Harris had not written his famous "My Life and Loves" he would still have been recognized as among the foremost modern English writers. But with the publication of this work in 1922 (Vol. II in 1925, Vols. III and IV in 1927), Harris took his rightful place among the great writers of all time in the history of world-literature.

On the one hand, "My Life and Loves" presents a perfectly rounded picture of the sex life in England and America on a scale never before attempted; on the other hand, it reveals the personality of a masterspirit in a confessional that no other man in history has dared to unfold. Yet the few who have the mind to understand the profundity of a man's genius will the more appreciate the frank life's-blood apparent in every page of "My Life and Loves".

No work in modern times has brought forth such vituperative condemnation as well as ecstatic praise. Judge Levy declares that "My Life and Loves" is " not only obviously and unquestionably obscene, lewd, lascivious and indecent, but it is filthy, disgusting and utterly revolting". Upton Sinclair finds it necessary to add: "I think it is the vilest book I have ever laid eyes on. I think it is absolutely inexcusable. I regard the book as a poisonous one." Such words, however, are meant to frighten babes and sniffling hypocrites. Obviously, "My Life and Loves" is not written for them, nor even for a "purified renegade" such as Sinclair, but for those who have wit enough to understand the self-revealment of a colossus who strode across this puny world. We need not here marshal an army of ardent supporters and admirers of Harris, such as Mencken and Shaw, who describe "My Life and Loves" as "a great human document" and "an English classic in the greatest Shakespearean manner". Let us rather examine the work itself and see what the author attempted and what he actually accomplished.

In the preface to Vol. I, Harris writes:

There are two main traditions of English writing: the one of perfect liberty, that of Chaucer and Shakespeare, completely outspoken, with a certain liking for lascivious details and witty smut, a man's speech; the other emasculated more and more by Puritanism and since the French Revolution, gelded to tamest propriety; for that upheaval brought the illiterate middle-class to power and insured the domination of girl-readers. Under Victoria, English prose literally became half childish, as in stories of "Little Mary", or at best provincial, as anyone may see who cares to compare the influence of Dickens, Thackeray and Reade in the world with the influence of Balzac, Flaubert and Zola.

Foreign masterpieces such as "Les Contes Drolatiques" and "L'Assommoir" were destroyed in London as obscene by a magistrate's order; even the Bible and Shakespeare were expurgated and all books dolled up to the prim decorum of the English Sunday-School. And America with unbecoming humility worsened the disgraceful, brainless example.

All my life I have rebelled against this old maid's canon of deportment, and my revolt has grown stronger with advancing years.

In the "Foreword" to "The Man Shakespeare" I tried to show how the Puritanism that had gone out of our morals had gone into the language, enfeebling English thought and impoverishing English speech.

At long last I am going back to the old English tradition. I am determined to tell the truth about my pilgrimage through this world, the whole truth and nothing but the truth, about myself and others, and I shall try to be at least as kindly to others as to myself.

I intend to tell what life has taught me, and if I begin at the A. B. C. of love, it is because I was brought up in Britain and the United States; I shall not stop there.

Of course I know the publication of such a book will at once justify the worst that my enemies have said about me. For forty years now I have championed nearly all the unpopular causes, and have thus made many enemies; now they will all be able to gratify their malice while taking credit for prevision. In itself the book is sure to disgust the "unco guid" and the mediocrities of every kind who have always been unfriendly to me. I have no doubt, too, that many sincere lovers of literature who would be willing to accept such license as ordinary French writers use, will condemn me for going beyond this limit. Yet there are many reasons why I should use perfect freedom in this last book.

First of all, I made hideous blunders early in life and saw worse blunders made by other youths, out of sheer ignorance; I want to warn the young and impressionable against the shoals and hidden reefs of life's ocean and chart, so to speak, at the very beginning of the voyage when the danger is greatest, the "unpath'd waters".

On the other hand I have missed indescribable pleasures because the power to enjoy and to give delight is keenest early in life, while the understanding both of how to give and how to receive pleasure comes much later, when the faculties are already on the decline.

I used to illustrate the absurdity of our present system of educating the young by a quaint simile. "When training me to shoot", I said, "my earthly father gave me a little single-barrelled gun, and when he saw that I had learned the mechanism and could be trusted, he gave me a double-barrelled shot-gun. After some years I came into possession of a magazine gun which could shoot half a dozen times if necessary without reloading, my efficiency increasing with my knowledge.

My Creator, or Heavenly Father, on the other hand, when I was wholly without experience and had only just entered my teens, gave me, so to speak, a magazine gun of sex, and hardly had I learned its use and enjoyment when he took it away from me forever, and gave me in its place a double-barrelled gun: after a few years, he took that away and gave me a single-barrelled gun with which I was forced to content myself for the best part of my life.

Towards the end the old single-barrel began to show signs of wear and age: sometimes it would go off too soon, sometimes it missed fire and shamed me, do what I would.

I want to teach youths how to use their magazine gun of sex so that it may last for years, and when they come to the double-barrel, how to take such care that the good weapon will do them liege service right into their fifties, and the single-barrel will then give them pleasure up to three score years and ten.

It is the first duty of every individual to develop all his faculties of body, mind and spirit as completely and harmoniously as possible; but it is a still higher duty for each of us to develop our special faculty to the uttermost consistent with health; for only by so doing shall we attain to the highest self-consciousness or be able to repay our debt to humanity. No Anglo Saxon, so far as I know, has ever advocated this ideal or dreamed of regarding it as a duty. In fact, no teacher so far has even thought of helping men and women to find out the particular power which constitutes their essence and inbeing and justifies their existence. And so nine men and women out of ten go through life without realizing their own special nature: they cannot lose their souls, for they have never found them.

For every son of Adam, for every daughter of Eve, this is the supreme defeat, the final disaster. Yet no one, so far as I know, has ever warned of the danger or spoken of this ideal.

That's why I love this book in spite of all its shortcomings and all its faults: it is the first book ever written to glorify the body and its passionate desires and the soul as well and its sacred, climbing sympathies.

Give and forgive, I always say, is the supreme lesson of life.

I only wish I had begun the book five years ago, before I had been half drowned in the brackish flood of old age and become conscious of failing memory; but notwithstanding this handicap, I have tried to write the book I have always wanted to read, the first chapter in the Bible of Humanity.

Hearken to good counsel:

"Live out your whole free life, while yet on earth,
Seize the quick Present, prize your one sure boon:
Though brief, each day a golden sun has birth;
Though dim, the night is gemmed with stars and
    moon."

Frank Harris was born on Feburary 14, 1855 in Ireland. His father, a lieutenant in the navy, was rarely home and consequently had little to do with the boy's education. At the age of four Frank first showed his precociousness:

"I used to get up in the night with my sister Annie, four years my senior, and go foraging for bread and jam or sugar. One morning about daybreak I stole into the nurse's room and saw a man beside her in bed, a man with a red moustache. I drew my sister in and she too saw him. We crept out again without waking them. My only emotion was surprise, but next day the nurse denied me sugar on my bread and butter and I said 'I'll tell' — I don't know why: I had then no inkling of modern journalism.

" 'Tell what?' she asked.

" 'There was a man in your bed,' I replied, 'last night.'

"'Hush, hush!' she said, and gave me the sugar.

"After that I found all I had to do was to say, 'I'll tell!' to get whatever I wanted. My sister even wished to know one day what I had to tell, but I would not say. I distinctly remember my feeling of superiority over her because she had not sense enough to exploit the sugar mine."

At the age of five he was sent with his sister to a girl's boarding school and experienced his first sexual delight at the touch of the spindly legs of the girls. But Frank was poor at arithmetic and was so badly treated by the headmistress that he was removed to Belfast to stay with his elder brother.

Here he remained until he was ten years old, becoming "a healthy, strong, little animal without an ache or pain or trace of thought". Upon his return home to Carrickfergus his sisters, Nita and Chrissie, showed him their budding breasts and had him judge which were prettier, but Frank "learned nothing from this happening". It was his school-companions who initiated him into the elementary mysteries of sex and taught him the practice of masturbation.

In grammar school, Harris discovered his remarkable genius for visualization as well as his "extraordinary verbal memory" which was to stand him in such good stead in later life. His fellow students completed his sexual education:

"The fags, too, being young and weak, were very often brutally treated just for fun. On Sunday mornings in summer, for instance, we had an hour longer in bed. I was one of the half-dozen juniors in the big bedroom; there were two older boys in it, one at each end, presumably to keep order; but in reality to teach lechery and corrupt their younger favorites. If the mothers of England knew what goes on in the dormitories of these boarding-schools throughout England, they would all be closed, from Eton and Harrow upwards or downwards, in a day. If English fathers even had brains enough to understand that the fires of sex need no stoking in boyhood, they too would protect their sons from the foul abuse."

It was not until the age of thirteen that Frank attempted any degree of intimacy with a girl, and this episode fixed his tastes for life and kept him from his school-boy vices of pederasty and masturbation. "That kissing and caressing a girl could inculcate self-restraint is not taught by our spiritual guides and masters; but it is nevertheless true." The failure of a bold attempt at the seduction of a French governess caused this fourteen-year-old to fall back to onanism. But his distaste for the practice was so violent that he forcibly restrained his instinct by tying strong whipcord about his member. An effective but drastic remedy!

"Such experiences made the routine of school-life almost intolerable" to Harris. He forced himself to study because he had to win a scholarship if he hoped to escape to America, the land of every Irishman's dream at this time. By dint of perseverance he gained the mathematical prize of fifteen pounds, took the train for Liverpool on the pretense of returning home, paid four pounds for a steerage passage to New York, and this precocious fifteen-year-old was soon actually on a ship bound for America. The voyage was delightful for he made a rapid conquest of Jessie, the daughter of the ship's chief engineer.

A boy resourceful enough to come to America may be counted on to make his way without much difficulty. But an immediate job at five dollars a day! This work, however, was most dangerous and consisted in working under water in the iron caissons of the Brooklyn Bridge. Harris has described the excruciating tortures of the "bends" in his greatest novel, "The Bomb". The proud worker now resumed his intimacy with Jessie and consummated his first genuine sexual intercourse. With two hundred dollars saved, an opportunity to work in Chicago as a night-clerk in a hotel was offered to Harris through a friend, and off he went, heedless of the ties he left behind him. His first round with American life was over. He was adventuring in wider fields.

Harris made rapid advancement in the hotel profession in Chicago, but when three cattlemen invited him to join them "on the open trail", his adventure-lust overcame him and off he went to the Rio Grande! Since his adventures have been published in a separate volume, "My Reminiscences as a Cowboy", we need but add that this venture brought him the profitable share of five thousand dollars, making the young man feel like a veritable Croesus for a short time.

He returned to Chicago in time to witness the Great Fire of 1871 and then went back to the trail. The arrival and establishment of his older brother in Lawrence. Kansas. as a real-estate agent caused Harris to give up his cowpunching and join him. A fortunate meeting with Professor Byron C. Smith of the State University determined his course in life. He enrolled as a special student in the junior class of the university. His studies, however, did not interfere with his many love-adventures in Lawrence. In due time he studied law, was admitted to practice, and was well on the way to a comfortable success when, as ever, he suddenly decided to pursue his further education in Europe instead of "grubbing away at law in Kansas".

Paris was naturally his first stop, but both sexual and mental over-excitement caused him to return to England, where he was a while Professor of English at Brighton College. When the Russian-Turkish war broke out in the summer of 1877 Harris immediately obtained a position as a correspondent and left for Moscow. At the end of the war, Heidelberg revived the wanderlust of Harris and once again he resumed an academic course at the university. His hot blood involved him in a fight, six weeks in jail, and expulsion from Heidelberg. Harris then went to Goettingen to continue his studies for three semesters. Athens and Rome next engaged his attention: then from Athens to Constantinople to Vienna to Italy and back to Ireland. Harris now felt that his "Lehrjahre" were over and he settled down in London to pursue the career of a "man-of-letters".

The usual hard struggle of a beginning writer followed, but once Harris gained a foothold his rise was meteoric. At the age of twenty-eight he became the editor of the "Evening News", tripled the circulation and was well on the way to financial success. It was about this period that Harris met and fell in love for the first time with an American beauty, Laura Clapton. Insane with jealousy because of a fancied indiscretion on her part, he quarrelled violently with her. Harris deliberately wed a rich widow, a Mrs. Clayton, when he discovered that Laura had left for the continent with a rich suitor in her train. Such a state of affairs could not last. After a year of married life, Harris returned to Laura and separated from his wife. Somewhat before this period, Harris assumed the editorship of "The Fortnightly Review" and gathered under its banner the foremost genius of England: Matthew Arnold, Swinburne, Wells, etc. But it was not until he edited his own magazine, "The Saturday Review" that he reached the full height of his intellectual powers.

Harris' autobiography virtually ends with the turn of the century, although there are frequent references to the last three decades of his life in which he pursued a chequered career as man-of-letters and journalist. He wrote a concluding volume to "My Life and Loves", but it probably will not appear for some time since many of the personages he discusses intimately are still living.

Frank Harris died in Nice on August 26, 1931 at the age of seventy-five. The world that had denied him recognition as a master in his lifetime now burst into enthusiastic praise of the man and his work. It was ever the way of the world to scorn the living and extol the dead genius. But Harris was beyond such petty tri-

umphs. He could comfort himself with his magnificent last words: "In the sun-haze of exquisite memories I, too, like a god, look upon the
world and say it was all 'good'."

But such a cursory summation cannot even
give a faint notion of the wealth of imagery and
power of characterization that flows so easily
from the graphic pen of Harris. All the men of
genius of the latter third of the nineteenth century as well as the first two decades of the twen-
tieth century are visualized in "My Life and
Loves" in clear-cut portraits that glisten with
the brilliance of polished gems: Whitman, Em-
erson, Carlyle, Ruskin, Maupassant, Zola, Ro-
din, Turgenieff, Wilde, Whistler, not to mention all the other great personages, both past as
well as present, Shakespeare, Jesus, Heine, and
so many others, that "My Life and Loves" seems
to be a complete guide to the immortal genius
of all time. Who can forget the stirring revelations of the true sex life of Shakespeare, Maupassant, Carlyle?

And this is "the vilest book" ever published!

In the beginning of the first volume Harris
writes that it would take him six or seven years
at least before he would know whether the book
was "life-worthy", yet at the end of the fourth
volume—fully aware of his own stature and that
of the puny criticism of infantile prudes—he
cries out defiantly to the Levys and Sinclairs:

> But after all what does death matter? It
> is hideous and terrible if you will; but few
> can tell when the curtain will fall and the
> play for them be finished. And meanwhile

one's work remains. A. B. and C. look at it and shrug indifferent shoulders and the years pass by and one seems forgotten. Suddenly some one comes who is interested: 'Strange,' he says, 'how did this work escape praise?' And he begins to praise it, and others follow him, wondering where this new teacher should be placed.

Sometimes, as in the case of Shakespeare, the recognition has to wait three hundred years. What matter? It was a century before anyone dreamed of placing Heine with Goethe: what do the years matter? Sooner or later we are judged by our peers and the judgment is unchangeable. I wait for my peers, welcoming them.

'He has written naughty passages,' says one, and my friend replies, 'so did Shakespeare in *Hamlet* and with less provocation.' 'His life is the fullest ever lived,' says my disciple, and they all realize that a supreme word has been spoken and that such a man is among the great forever.

And yet we have given but a bare notion of the striking eroticism of Harris: the free and untrammeled mind and power that knows no puritanical restraints. We can here give only a brief excerpt from a typical sex-adventure of Frank Harris, but one of the dozens that scintillate thoughout "My Life and Loves":

> I must now tell the greatest amatory experience of my life. I had made a great deal of money with Hooley, and was besides tormented with the wish to complete at any cost my book on Shakespeare.

I had done some chapters in "The Saturday Review"; and Shaw among others had praised them highly. It was and is my belief that Shakespeare has been misseen and misunderstood by all the commentators. Ordinary men are always accustomed to make their gods in their own image, and so the English had formed a Shakespeare who loved his wife and yet was a pederast; who had made money at his business, and retired to enjoy his leisure as a country gentleman in the village of Stratford after living through the bitter despair of "Timon", and the madness of "Lear": "O, let me not be mad, Sweet Heaven . . . I would not be mad!"

The only particle of truth in the fancy portrait has been contributed by Tyler, who, inspired by Wordsworth's saying that in the sonnets Shakespeare "unlocked his heart", proved that the sonnets showed that Shakespeare, about 1506, had fallen in love with a maid-of-honor named Mary Fitton and had been in love with her, as he said himself, about 1600, for three years. I came to Tyler's aid by proving that this episode had been dragged into three different plays of the same period, and I went on to show that this love episode had practically been the great love of Shakespeare's life, and had lasted from 1506 to 1608. I proved also that though he disliked his wife, he was perfectly normal; that his fortune rested on the gift of Lord Southampton to him of a thousand pounds when he came of age in 1596; and that so far from having increased his wealth and been a prudent husbandman, he had never cared for "rascal counters" and died leaving barely one year's income; probably after the drinking-bout of tradition in which he had drunk perhaps a little too much, for, to use his own words, he had "poor unhappy brains for drinking": a too highly powered ship for the frail hull! Does he not talk in "The Tempest" of walking to "still his beating mind"?

All this and more I wanted to set forth; but was it possible to bring such a totally new conception of Shakespeare into life, and so to prove it that it would be accepted. I hated the English climate in the winter, and so I set off in an October fog for the Riviera; and I don't know why, but I went through Nice to San Remo. At San Remo, the hotel life quickly tired me, and I went about looking for a villa. I discovered a beautiful villa with views over both the mountains and the sea and a great garden; but alas, it was for sale and not for hire, the gardener told me.

This gardener deserves a word or two of description. He was a rather small man, perhaps forty-five or fifty years of age, a slight, strong figure with an extraordinarily handsome head set off by quite white moustaches — the suggestion of age being completely contradicted by the clearness of the skin and the brightness of his eyes. Ten thousand pounds was wanted for the villa; but the gardener told me that if I bought it, I could always sell it for as much as I paid for it or more. I took this assertion with a grain of salt, but the end of it was that the gardener amused me so much that I bought the villa and went to live in it.

I ordered my days at once for work; and for the first week or two did work ten or twelve hours a day, but one memorable afternoon I came upon the gardener, whom I had taken into my service, reading Dante, if you please, in the garden. I had a talk with him and found that he knew not only Dante, but Ariosto, and Leopardi, and Carducci, and was a real student of Italian literature. I passed a great afternoon with him, and resolved whenever I was tired in the future to come out and talk with him.

Two or three days afterwards I was overworked again, and I went out to him and he said: "You know, when I saw you at first, I thought we should have a great time together here; that you would love life and love; and here you are writing, writing, writing, morning, noon and night — wearing yourself out without any care for beauty or for pleasure."

"I like both," I said, "but I came here to work; still, I shouldn't mind having some distractions if they were possible, but what is possible here?"

"Everything," he replied, "I have been putting myself in your place: if I were rich, wouldn't I enjoy myself in this villa!"

"What would you do?" I asked.

"Well," he said, "I would give prizes for the prettiest girls, say one hundred francs for the first; fifty francs for the second; and twenty-five as consolation prizes if five or six girls came."

"What good would that do," I asked, "you wouldn't get young girls that way, and you certainly wouldn't get their love."

"Wouldn't I!" he cried, "first of all, in order to see who was the prettiest, they would have to strip, wouldn't they? and the girl who is once naked before you, is not apt to refuse you anything."

I had come to a sort of impasse in my work; I saw that the whole assumption that Shakespeare had been a boy lover, drawn from the sonnets, was probably false, but since Hallam it was held by every one in England, and every one, too, in Germany, so prone are men always to believe the worst, especially of their betters — the great leaders of humanity.

Heinemann, the publisher, had asked me for my book on Shakespeare before I left England, but as soon as I wrote him that I was going to disprove Shakespeare's abnormal tastes, he told me that he had found every authority in England was against me and therefore he dared not publish my book. Just when I was making up my mind to set forth my conviction, came this proposal of my gardener. I had worked very hard for years on "The Saturday Review" and in South

Africa, and I thought I deserved a little recreation, so I said to the gardener, "Go to it; I don't want any scandal, but if you can get the girls through the prizes, I will put up the money cheerfully and will invite you to play Master of Ceremonies."

"This is Tuesday," he said, "I think next Sunday would be about the best day."

"As you please," I replied.

On Sunday, having given a congé to my cook and waiting-maid, I walked about to await my new guests, the cook having laid out a good déjeuner with champagne on the table in the dining-room. About eleven o'clock a couple of girls fluttered in, and my gardener conducted them into two bedrooms and told them to make themselves pretty and we would all lunch at half past twelve. In half an hour five girls were assembled. He put them all into different rooms and went from room to room telling them that they must undress and get ready for inspection. There was much giggling and some exclamations, but apparently no revolt. In ten minutes he came to me and asked me, was I ready for the inspection?

"Certainly," I said; and we went to the first room. A girl's head looked out from under the clothes: she had got into bed. But my gardener knew better than to humor her: he went over and threw down the bed clothes, and there she was completely nude. "Stand up, stand up," he said, "you are worth looking at!"

And indeed she was. Nothing loath, she stood on the bed as directed and lent herself to the examination. She was a very pretty girl of twenty-one; and at length to encourage her, he took her in his arms and kissed her. I followed suit and found her flesh perfectly firm and everything all right except that her feet were rather dirty; whereupon my gardener said, "That's easily remedied." We promised her a prize and told her that we would return when she washed and put on her clothes and made herself as pretty as possible; and he led me into the next room.

The girl in this one was sitting on the bed, half dressed, but she was very slight and much younger, and evidently very much excited because she glowered at us as if she hated us. The moment we came into the room she went for the gardener telling him that if she had known it was required to be naked, she wouldn't have come near us. The gardener kissed her at once and told her not to be frightened; that she was pretty sure of winning a prize, and she need not undress. And we went on to the third room.

There I had one of the surprises of my life: a girl stood on the rug near the bed with the color coming and going in her cheeks; she was in her shirt but with her dress held round her hips. She, too, said she didn't want to strip — she would rather go home.

"But nothing has happened to you," said the gardener, "surely a couple of men to admire you isn't going to make you angry; and that frown doesn't suit your loveliness at all."

In two or three minutes the wily Italian had dissipated her anger and she began to smile, and suddenly shrugging her shoulders she put down the dress and then at once stood up at his request, trying to laugh. She had one of the loveliest figures and faces that I ever saw in my life. Her breasts were small, but beautifully rounded and strangely firm; her hips, too, and bottom were as firm as marble, but a little slight. Her face was lit up with a pair of great hazel eyes and her mouth, though a little large was perfectly formed; her smile won me. I told the gardener that I didn't want to see any more girls, that I was quite content: and he encouraged me to kiss and talk to her while he went into the next room to see the next applicant.

As soon as the gardener left the room, my beauty, whose name was Flora, began questioning me: "Why did you choose me? You are the owner, aren't you?" I could only nod. I had sense enough to say, "partly for your beauty; but also because I like you, your ways, your courage."

"But," she went on, "real liking does not grow as quickly as that, or just by the view of a body and legs."

"Pardon me," I rejoined, "but passion, desire in a man comes first: it's for the woman to transform it into enduring affection. You like me a little because I admire and desire you; it's for me by kindness and sympathy to turn that liking into love; so kiss me and don't let us waste time arguing. Can you kiss?"

"Of course I can," she said, "every one can!"

"That's not true," I retorted, "the majority of virgins can't kiss at all, and I believe you're a virgin."

"I am," she replied; "but you'll not find many in this crowd."

"Kiss me," I went on, taking her in my arms and kissing her till I found response in hot lips. As she used her tongue, she asked roguishly, "Well, Sir, can I kiss?"

"Yes," I replied; "and now I'll kiss you."

Suddenly she started up and danced round me in her fascinating nudity, "shall I have a prize?"

"The first," I cried.

" 'Carissimo mio,' " and she kissed me a dozen times, "I'll be whatever you want and cover you with love."

Our talk had gone on for perhaps half an hour when a knock came at the door, and the gardener came in to find us both quite happy and, I think, intimately pleased with each other. He said, "The other two you had better see, or they will be disappointed, but I think you have picked the prettiest."

"I am quite content," I replied, "to rest on your approval of them." But my self-willed beauty said, "Let us go and see them; I will go with

you;" and we went into the next room, said a few
flattering things, and went on to the fifth room
where there was a girl who said she wouldn't
undress. "At any rate," said the gardener, "the
matter is settled; we can all go in and have lunch
and then my master will give the prizes."

We had a great lunch, all helping each other
and ourselves, and when the champagne was
opened every one seemed to enjoy the feast infinitely. But when the prize-giving came, I was
ashamed, hating to give one less than the other,
so I called the gardener to one side and told him
my reluctance. "Nothing easier," he said, "I have
made you out to be a great English Lord. Go into
that bedroom on the right and I will send them
in one by one. If I were you, I would give the two
first prizes and I will give the consolation stakes."

"Splendid," I said, "but give me a reasonable
half hour before sending in the second one." Flora
came in and got her first prize, kissed me and
offered herself to my desire. Then for some reason or other a good idea came into my head.

I put up my hands: "That's for later, I hope,"
I exclaimed, "it means affection, and you don't
care for me yet; perhaps you will with time, and
if you don't I'll forgive you. There's no compul-
sion here."

"How good of you," she exclaimed, "just for
saying that I want to kiss you, 'caro mio' (you
dear)" and she threw her arms round my neck
and gave me a long kiss.

Naturally I improved the occasion, and turned
the kiss into an embrace as I put my arms
round her and kissed her, she kissed me passion-
ately in return: " 'carissimo mio'," she murmured
and hid her glowing cheek on my neck. While she
was putting her dress in order before the glass,
she began talking quickly: "You know, I hope
this isn't the only time. I want to come back without any prize, for I like you and you have been
kind to me. I was frightened at first — you must

forget all that; you will, won't you? 'Cuore mio'; I'll find new love names for you;" and she did.

"But why did you want to see us all naked," she went on; "we're all alike, aren't we?"

"No, indeed," I cried, "you are all different."

"But you can't love one because her breasts are smaller than another's. No woman would care for such a thing. I love your voice and what you say and your eyes, but not your legs. Fancy!" and she laughed aloud.

Finally she said, "When may I come again? — soon, please!"

"Surely," I replied, "when will you come? I want your photograph."

"Any day you like," Flora said. And we fixed the meeting for Tuesday. She went off delighted.

The next girl who came in was the young girl, the second we saw, who had not undressed and who had declared that she wouldn't have come if she had known the conditions. At once she said to me: "I don't mind undressing for you: I know you now;" and in a trice she had pulled her things off: she was very pretty. I afterwards photographed her in the swing in the garden. But she was nothing astonishing, just a very pretty and well-made girl of sixteen. Her name she told me was Yolande; she lived with an aunt.

When I gave her the second prize of seventy-five francs, she said, "You are giving me the second prize; if I had been nicer you perhaps would have given me the first."

Her frankness amused me. "Does it make much difference to you, the difference between seventy-five and one hundred francs?"

She nodded her head: "It will make a difference to my dress," she said, "I want pretty under-things" — and she curled up her nose.

"Well," I replied, "say nothing about it, and take another twenty-five francs." At once she threw her arms around my neck and kissed me and then, "May I come back?"

"Sure, sure," I replied.

"May I bring some one else?"

"Anyone you please," I said.

That is about all I remember of the first séance except that the beauty, Flora, whom I have tried to describe, did not leave the villa till long after dinner.

When I talked with my gardener of the event afterwards, he told me that he had preferred the youngest of all, whom I had not seen. "Clara," he said, "was the prettiest of the lot." As I told him I thought her too thin for beauty and too young to be mentally attractive, he promised to show me her nudity the next Sunday. I wanted to know about the next Sunday — "Will you be able to get three or four new girls?"

"Good God," he exclaimed, "twenty, if you like! These girls will whisper it all about and you may be sure you will have an ever increasing number. This villa is going to get a good name if you continue!"

"I will continue weekly," I said, "but if there are likely to be more girls, I might bring a friend over from Monte Carlo who happens to be there and who is really an English Lord."

"By all means," he said, "the more, the merrier."

Accordingly I sent a telegram to my friend, Ernest — asking him to come and spend a happy week end with me. In due time he came. And it was well that he did come, for the second week showed me that the gardener was wiser and knew his country people better than I did: at least twenty girls came to win prizes, girls of all ages from fifteen to thirty. My gardener proposed that he should weed them out to six or seven, giving them consolation prizes without stripping them. Both Ernest and I were quite content, but we wanted to see his choice, and we were astonished by the ability with which he made his selection: practically we had to agree with him. Twelve or fourteen girls were sent home with twenty-five francs each, without any further attempt at discrimination; and our inspection began without making me waver in my allegiance to Flora.

It was in these first weeks at San Remo that I discovered that the body was not so important in love or in passion as the mind and character. I had not the slightest desire to leave my beauty for any of the newer queens; and I didn't want her to strip even for Ernest's inspection although she was willing to. But I had become her lover now, and love desires exclusive possession.

The third meeting had a new termination. Another young Englishman, named George—, a friend of Ernest, had fallen in love with one the week before. We had the three queens, as we called them, to dinner, as well as to lunch. After dinner the gardener appeared with one, and declared that if our girls would strip, he would show that his was the prettiest of the lot. None of the three girls minded: they were all willing, so we had another contest; but we resolved to give the winner of this contest two hundred francs. I don't believe that the famous choice of Paris with the three queens of Heaven before him ever showed such beauties. I must try to describe them. Of two of them I have photographs, which I must not reproduce; and the third, my queen, I have already described. It is for my readers to use their imagination. And I cannot even give the photo of the gardener's choice for she wasn't a bit more than fourteen years of age. When we made fun of him about this, he said philosophically, "I am older than you men, and I have noticed that the older we get the younger we like the girls." On this we all burst out laughing.

One day Ernest and George went to Monte Carlo and brought over two more friends. The gardener was overjoyed, for as the girls increased, so his tips increased, and his amusement, too, I think. But from now on, our Sundays occasionally developed into orgies; that is, we wandered about, selecting now this and now that girl instead of remaining faithful to the queens, but usually as soon as the newcomers went away we returned to our old allegiances. But from the outset I limited my time for amusement to two days a week: Wednesdays and Sundays; all the other days I spent working.

I shall never forget one occasion when we all went down bathing in a state of nature — half a dozen girls and four men. After the bath we all came up and lay about on the grass and soon the lovely girl forms seduced the men, and the scene turned to embracing, which the beauty and abandon of the girls made memorable.

This life continued for five or six weeks, till one Thursday I was interrupted by the gardener, who came and asked me to come down to see a cousin of Clara's, Adrianna. I found a very lovely girl with reddish fair hair and gray eyes: quite different in looks from the ordinary Italian. I could reproduce the likeness of her that a painter-friend, Rousselet, developed later from a photograph. But she was certainly one of the most beautiful beings I have ever seen in my life, and curiously enough she seemed at first as sweet and sympathetic and passionate as she was lovely. I took to her at once and, strange to say, even Flora liked her. She told us she was an orphan and seemed always grateful for any kindness: when Flora told her she liked her and was not jealous, "How could you be jealous?" said Adrianna, "you are too lovely to know what envy means." Flora kissed her saying: "My dear, I don't know whether it is wisdom in you or goodness, but you are certainly wonderful."

We had been at these games more than half the summer when Ernest proposed we should vary the procedure by letting the girls select their favorites. No sooner proposed than done. We gave them prizes and asked them to apportion them: at once they established one purse and gave us all an equal prize; but they determined, too, who was the first favorite, and who the second, and so on.

I had no reason to complain of the result; but I was at a loss to know why I was chosen so frequently: was it due to a hint of the gardener or simply to the fact that I was known to be the owner of the villa? I never could quite determine; but I was chosen so often that the game became monotonous, and when I was left out Ernest was the winner, though George was far better looking than either of us, and at least ten years younger.

Two "expurgated" editions of "My Life and Loves" should be mentioned, lest students of all fields—for all will find much of value in this unique work—be confused by garbled texts. The first volume appeared in 1927, the sex life of Harris being excised by some vandal; the second appeared in 1931 in a sub-rosa edition. This time, the "clean parts" of all four volumes were cleverly expunged by an equally conscienceless vandal who inserted connecting paragraphs so that the book might seem to be an organic whole. This "expurgated" edition appeared under the title "My Love Life".

Yet it is no small tribute to the genius of Frank Harris that his work transcends such deletions and still paints the brave, irrepressible "heart's blood of a masterspirit".

We are fortunate enough to have in our possession an original unpublished manuscript by Frank Harris setting forth his sexual philosophy at the age of seventy! Because of its excellent recapitulation of his experiences in the "art of love and seduction" we have reproduced it in

full. This marks the first appearance of this
completed unique manuscript in any printed
work.

"Whose love is stronger — a man's or a
woman's?" It depends on the man and on the
woman. A general statement on such a matter
seems to me absurd. Usually the passion in a man
cloaks his affection, whereas the woman conceals
her passion, if she feels any, and puts her affection to show. Later they both get disillusioned;
the man ceases to make love and the woman
leaves off trying to please; but the man is accustomed in the struggle of life to many disappoint-
ments, and so tries to make the best of matters,
while the woman is by nature more patient, and
a community of interests and children often form
a sufficient practical tie.

"Should a woman show her love?" To some
men "Yes," to others "Not over much." It is much
more important for her to show admiration for
the man, of his strength and virility, if it's a lover
she wants; of his generosity and greatness of
heart, if it's money she's after, and so on. A slowly
growing admiration often expressed by the wife
for the husband is warranted to make an almost
ideal husband of the ordinary man, and, to tell
the truth, the same method of flattery by the husband will keep a cat charitable, a coquette constant, or an extravagant hen-hussy a careful
housewife from twenty till forty, when custom becomes character. Our vanity is the instrument to
play on.

"Is it possible to love more than one person
at the same time?" Surely; but not in the same
degree and hardly for the same qualities. It
should be sufficient for the wife to know that her
husband holds her dearest; passing infidelities
she should try not to see and accustom herself to
disdain, while the husband should teach himself
to admire his wife's weird vanities and interest

himself in all her costumings and feminine achievements as if they were of primary importance, as indeed they are to her.

"Love at first sight — does it often occur?" Of course it does; most frequently in young people, especially young men. Sometimes love begins in pity on the part of the man; sometimes in woman in admiration of a man's imperious strength of character; in fact in a thousand ways. But love only endures when both husband and wife have some brains and are resolved to get the best out of each other and so flatter each other in private and play up to each other in public like well-graced actors on a stage. The husband who exposes any shortcomings in his wife before a third person is as much a fool as the wife who fails to flatter her husband when he comes home late with a lame excuse. She should accept the danger signal and redouble her praising.

"Are love marriages the best?" The Germanic nations think they are: the Latins believe in establishing a family on secure well-being and so seek an equality of fortune instead of a superiority in looks. In this regard the Germanic instinct is the truer and deeper. Even the prudish English have a proverb "as beautiful as a love child" while even the Italians and French admit a greater vigor in the children of a love-union. Love should be the foundation of the house; money may put on some extra stories, or at least a roof.

"Can a plain woman be loved as much as a pretty one?" Often much more; but she must play the game so much the better, and in order to do that, be perfectly conscious of the fact that she is plain. The truth is, all humans love those who admire them, or at least tell them so constantly, and so keep them pleased with themselves. The woman who imagines that a constant tenderness and loving kindness is an enduring bond is apt to get left, as a man who believes when he keeps up a good establishment and gives his wife

a large allowance for pin-money he has ensured
her faithful affection.

"Can any love last for ever?" It can last as long
as we last and grow stronger to the end. There
is no passion in man or woman that endures like
vanity, for it grows with our growth in intellect
or spirit or achievement, and if any power in us
weakens and dies out, vanity immediately transfers its tendrill-roots to some other quality and
throws its head up defiantly twice as high because its shrinking base has made it insecure.
Women are fond of explaining a happy marriage
by endowing the wife with "sex-attraction" or
"magnetism" or some piffle of that sort to con-
ceal want of thought. The man wins the girl by
"close attendance and attention" as old Chaucer
knew, and by telling her she's an angel and lovely
and wise, and loses her by treating her as an ordinary person: the wife, if she's wise, in the early
days, begins to flatter the husband, and if she
keeps it up, he'll soon discover super-excellencies
in her again. VANITAS VANITATUM!

36.

"Lady Chatterley's Lover"

Supreme Modern Work Ennobling Sex Passion

"LADY CHATTERLEY'S LOVER" (1928) is a genuine erotic novel, perhaps the finest of its kind, not only in England but in modern literature. But this magnificent work by D. H. Lawrence is peculiarly insular in quality: it portrays the sex life and sex act as practised in England with a richness and poignancy that indelibly stamps it as an English classic in the most exalted of literary traditions. The coldness, brutality and grossness of the English in sexual intercourse are bitterly criticized by Lawrence. Krutch, however, errs in damning Lawrence's "persistent preoccupation with various sexual abnormalities". For Lawrence was interested not in abnormality but normality; his "preoccupation" with variations of the sex act is an entirely different matter, and represents the sexuality of a healthy, normal human.

Lawrence has expressed himself very pertinently on the subject of normality and obscenity in the introduction to the Paris edition of his chef d'oeuvre:

"English publishers urge me to make an expurgated edition, promising large returns, perhaps even a little bucket, one of those children's sea-side pails!—and insisting that I should show the public that here is a fine novel, apart from all 'purple' and all 'words'. So I begin to be tempted and start in to expurgate. But impossible! I might as well try to clip my own nose into shape with scissors. The book bleeds.

"And in spite of all antagonism, I put forth this novel as an honest, healthy book, necessary for us to-day. The words that shock so much at first don't shock at all after a while. Is this because the mind is depraved by habit? Not a bit. It is that the words merely shock the eye, they never shocked the mind at all. People without minds may go on being shocked, but they don't matter. People with minds realize that they aren't shocked, and never really were: and they experience a sense of relief.

"And that is the whole point. We are today, as human beings, evolved and cultured far beyond the taboos which are inherent in our culture. This is a very important fact to realize. Probably, to the Crusaders, mere words were potent and evocative to a degree we can't realize. The evocative power of the so-called obscene words must have been very dangerous to the dim-minded, obscure, violent natures of the

Middle Ages, and perhaps are still too strong for slow-minded, half-evoked lower natures to-day. But real culture makes us give to a word only those mental and imaginative reactions which belong to the mind, and saves us from violent and indiscriminate physical reactions which may wreck social decency. In the past, man was too weak-minded, or crude-minded, to contemplate his own physical body and phys-ical functions, without getting all messed up with physical reactions that overpowered him. It is no longer so. Culture and civilization have taught us to separate the reactions. We know the act does not necessarily follow on the thought. In fact, thought and action, word and deed, are two separate lives we lead. We need, very sin-cerely, to keep connection. But while we think, we do not act, and while we act we do not think. The great necessity is that we should act accord-ing to our thoughts, and think according to our acts. But while we are in thought we cannot really act, and while we are in action we can-not really think. The two conditions, of thought and action, are mutually exclusive. Yet they should be related in harmony.

"And this is the real point of this book. I want men and women to be able to think sex, fully, completely, honestly and cleanly."

This is more strikingly stated by the "lover", Mellors in "Lady Chatterley's Lover":

"The first girl I had, I began with when I was sixteen. She was a school-master's daughter over at Ollerton, pretty, beautiful really. I was supposed to be a clever sort of young fellow from Sheffield Grammar School, with a bit of

French and German, very much aloft. She was
the romantic sort that hated commonness. She
egged me on to poetry and reading: in a way,
she made a man of me. I read and I thought
like a house on fire, for her. And I was a clerk
in Butterley Offices, thin, white-faced fellow
fuming with all the things I read. And about
everything I talked to her: but everything. We
talked ourselves into Persepolis and Timbuctoo.
We were the most literary-cultured couple in ten
counties. I held forth with rapture to her, posi-
tively with rapture. I simply went up in smoke.
And she adored me. The serpent in the grass
was sex. She somehow didn't have any; at least,
not where it's supposed to be. I got thinner and
crazier. Then I said we'd got to be lovers. I
talked her into it, as usual. So she let me. I was
excited, and she never wanted it. She just didn't
want it. She adored me, she loved me to talk to
her and kiss her: in that way she had a passion
for me. But the other, she just didn't want. And
there are lots of women like her. And it was just
the other that I *did* want. So there we split. I
was cruel, and left her. Then I took on with
another girl, a teacher, who had made a scandal
by carrying on with a married man and driving
him nearly out of his mind. She was a soft,
white-skinned, soft sort of a woman, older than
me, and played the fiddle. And she was a demon.
She loved everything about love, except sex.
Clinging, caressing, creeping into you in every
way: but if you forced her to the sex itself, she
just ground her teeth and sent out hate. I forced
her to it, and she could simply numb me with
hate because of it. So I was balked again. I

loathed all that. I wanted a woman who wanted me, and wanted *it*."

Lawrence elsewhere marks the keynote of his sexual philosophy: "Sex is really only touch, the closest of all touch. And it's touch we're afraid of."

The story of "Lady Chatterley's Lover" is starkly simple. The effect of the work lies in its vibrant characterization and pointed indictments. Lady Chatterley's husband, Sir Clifford, is a hopeless paralytic "from the hips down". Sir Clifford is symbolic of the emotional paralysis of the men of his type and class. Lady Constance chooses as her lover her husband's game-keeper, Oliver Mellors, a robust vital "rush of a man". The affair is naturally clandestine until "Connie" is so wracked with emotion that she decides to dare the conventions and live with Mellors even if Sir Clifford refuses to divorce her.

The story is, of course, completely subsidiary to Lawrence's purpose: "To-day the full conscious realization of sex is even more important than the act itself." This is strikingly shown in Lady work contains a description of the sexual ex-Chatterley's self-introspection during the act:

"It was a night of sensual passion, in which she was a little startled and almost unwilling: yet pierced again with piercing thrills of sensuality, different, sharper, more terrible than the thrills of tenderness, but, at the moment, more desirable. Though a little frightened, she let him have his way, and the reckless, shameless sensuality shook her to her foundations, stripped her to the very last, and made a different woman of her. It was not really love. It was not voluptuousness. It was sensuality sharp and searing as fire, burning the soul to tinder.

"Burning out the shames, the deepest, oldest shames, in the most secret places. It cost her an effort to let him have his way and his will of her. She had to be passive, consenting thing, like a slave, a physical slave. Yet the passion licked round her, consuming, and when the sensual flame of it pressed through her bowels and breast, she really thought she was dying: yet a poignant, marvellous death.

"She had often wondered what Abélard meant, when he said that in their year of love he and Héloise had passed through all the stages and refinements of passion. The same thing, a thousand years ago: ten thousand years ago! The same on the Greek vases, everywhere! The refinements of passion, the extravagances of sensuality! And necessary, forever necessary, to burn out false shames and smelt out the heaviest ore of the body into purity. With the fire of sheer sensuality.

"In the short summer night she learnt so much. She would have thought a woman would have died of shame. Instead of which, the shame died. Shame, which is fear: the deep organic shame, the old, old physical fear which crouches in the bodily roots of us, and can only be chased away by the sensual fire, at last it was roused up and routed by the phallic hunt of the man, and she came to the very heart of the jungle of herself. She felt, now, she had come to the real bed-rock of her nature, and was essentially shame-less. She was her sensual self, naked and una-shamed. She felt a triumph, almost vainglory.

So! That was how it was! That was life! That was how oneself really was! There was nothing left to disguise or be ashamed of. She shared her ultimate nakedness with a man, another being."

Lawrence's closeness to nature is symbolized throughout his work. He states in the introduction:

"Sex is the balance of male and female in the universe, the attraction, the repulsion, the transit of neutrality, the new attraction, the new repulsion, always different, always new. The long neuter spell of Lent, when the bood is low, and the delight of the Easter kiss, the sexual revel of spring, the passion of midsummer, the slow recoil, revolt, and grief of autumn, greyness again, then the sharp stimulus of winter of the long nights. Sex goes through the rhythm of the year, in man and woman, ceaselessly changing: the rhythm of the sun in his relation to the earth. Oh, what a catastrophe for man when he cut himself off from the rhythm of the year, from his unison with the sun and the earth. Oh, what a catastrophe, what a maiming of love when it was made a personal, merely personal feeling, taken away from the rising and the setting of the sun, and cut off the magic connection of the solstice and the equinox!"

This is exemplified in "Lady Chatterley's Lover" by a stirring incident in which Constance and Oliver pay homage to Mother Earth:

"She opened the door and looked at the straight heavy rain, like a steel curtain, and had a sudden desire to rush out into it, to rush away. She got up, and began swiftly pulling off her stockings, then her dress and underclothing, and he held his breath. Her pointed keen animal breasts tipped and stirred as she moved. She was ivory-coloured in the greenish light. She slipped on her rubber shoes again and ran out with a wild little laugh, holding up her breasts to the heavy rain and spreading her arms, and running blurred in the rain with the eurythmic dance-movements she had learned so long ago in Dresden. It was a strange pallid figure lifting and falling, bending so the rain beat and glistened on the full haunches swaying up again and coming belly-forward through the rain then stooping again so that only the full loins and buttocks were offered in a kind of homage towards him, repeating a wild obeisance.

"He laughed wryly, and threw off his clothes. It was too much. He jumped out, naked and white, with a little shiver, into the hard slanting rain. Flossie sprang before him with a frantic little bark. Connie, her hair all wet and sticking to her head, turned her hot face and saw him. Her blue eyes blazed with excitment as she turned and ran fast, with a strange charging movement, out of the clearing and down the path, the wet boughs whipping her. She ran, and he saw nothing but the round wet head, the wet back leaning forward in flight, the rounded buttocks twinkling: a wonderful cowering female nakedness in flight."

37.

Famous Works on Flagellation

The Racial English Vice in the Art of Love

NGLAND is the classic land of flagellation. In no other country at any time has the mania for flagellation been so highly developed.

Delightful sport! whose never failing charm
Makes young blood tingle and keeps old
blood warm.

The rod may well be the national symbol of England; all classes and all ages bow beneath its sway. A few extreme examples will show the truth of the above statement. Ward, in his "The London Spy" (1704) describes the whipping of prostitutes which in his day was a public spectacle for the edification of the Londoners:

"From thence my Friend conducted me to Bridewell, being Court-Day, to give me the diversion of seeing the Letchery of some Town Ladies cool'd by a Cat of Nine-tails. We follow'd our Noses and walk'd up to take a view of their Ladies, who we found were shut up as close as Nuns; but like so many Slaves, were under the Care and Direction of an Over-seer, who walk'd about with a very flexible Weapon of Office, to Correct such Hempen Journeywomen, who were unhappily troubled with the Spirit of Idleness. These smelt as frowzily as so many Goats in a Welsh Gentleman's Stable, or rather a Litter of Piss-tail Children under the Care of a Parish Nurse; and look'd with as much Modesty as so many Newgate Saints Canoniz'd at the Old Baily. Some seem'd so very Young, that I thought it strange they should know Sin enough at those Years to bring them so early into a State of Misery. My Friend reconducted me back into the first Quadrangle, and led me up a pair of Stairs into a Spacious Chamber, where the Court was sitting in great Grandeur and Order. A Grave Gentleman, whose Awful Looks Bespoke him some Honourable Citizen, was mounted in the Judgment-Seat, Arm'd with a Hammer, like a Change-Broker at Loyds-Coffee-House, when selling Goods by Inch of Candle; and a Woman under the Lash in the next Room; where Folding Doors were open'd, that the whole Court might see The Punishment Inflicted; at last down went the Hammer, and the Scourging ceas'd; that I protest, till I was undeceiv'd, I thought the Offenders had been Popish Penetents, who by the

Delusion of their Priests, were drawn thither to buy Lashes by Auction. The Honourable Court, I observed, were chiefly Attended by Fellows in Blew-Coats, and Women in Blew-Aprons. Another Accusation being then deliver'd by a Flat-Cap against a poor Wench, who having no Friend to speak in her Behalf, Proclamation was made, viz. All you who are willing E....th T....ll, should have present Punishment, Pray hold up your Hands: Which was done accordingly: And then she was order'd the Civility of the House, and was forc'd to shew her tender Back, and tempting Bubbies, to the Grave Sages of the August Assembly, who were mov'd by her Modest Mien, together with the Whiteness of her Skin, to give her but a Gentle Correction."

"Whipping Toms" and "Flogging Cullies" were also common occurrences in eighteenth century England. We read of the former in "Whipping Tom Brought to Light and Exposed to View":

"Whipping Tom for some weeks past, has lurked about in Alleys, and Courts in Fleet-street, Chancery-lane, Shoe-lane, Fetter-lane, the Strand, Holburn, and other places, and at unwares seizes upon such as he can conveniently light on, and turning them up as nimble as an Eel, makes their Butt ends cry Spanko; and then (according to the Report of those who have felt the weight of his Paws) vanished; for you must know, that having left the Country, he has not the advantage of getting Rods, and therefore is obliged to use his Hands instead thereof: His first Adventure, as near as we can learn, was on a Servant Maid in New Street, who being sent

out to look her Master (sic), as she was turning
a Corner, perceived a tall black Man standing
up against the wall, as if he had been making
water, but she had not passed far, but with
great speed and violence seized her and in a
trice, laying her across his knee, took up her
Linnen, and lay'd so hard upon her Backside,
as made her cry out most piteously for help, the
which he no sooner perceiving to approach but
he vanished; and although diligent search was
made, no person could be found."

The art of handling the rod is no less important. We learn in the "Exhibition of Female
Flagellants": "Know then, you silly girl, there
is a manner in handling this sceptre of felicity,
that few ladies are happy in; it is not the im-
passioned and awkward brandish of a vulgar female that can charm, but the deliberate and elegant manner of a woman of rank and fashion,
who displays all that dignity in every action,
even to the flitting of her fan, that leaves an in-
delible wound."

It is impossible in the confines of the present
volume to give even a faint idea of the many
thousands of books, brochures and pamphlets
that have been printed in England on the subject of flagellation. Every conceivable position,
class and art must have been depicted in these
works. Yet almost all such books are written in
a uniform manner and have much the same content. There are few that are distinguished by
style and intellect. Perhaps the best writer on
the subject was St. George H. Stock, a lieutenant
in the Queen's Royal Regiment. He used the
pseudonyms "Expert", "Major Edward Mark-

ham", and "Dr. Aliquis" in his writings, all of which discussed some phase of flagellation. The more important of his many works are: "Plums without Dough; or 144 Quaint Conceits, within the bounds of becoming mirth" (1870), "The Charm, The Night School, The Beautiful Jewess and The Butcher's Daughter" (1874), "The Sealed Letter" (1870), "The Nameless Crime, A Dialogue on Stays, Undue Curiosity, The Doll's Wedding, The Way to Peel, The Jail and the Stiff Dream" (1875), "The Romance of Chastisement; or, the Revelations of Miss Darcy" (1866), and "The Romance of Chastisement; or, Revelations of the School and Bedroom" (1870).

Henry Thomas Buckle, the famous author of "History of Civilization in England", is often said to be the editor of a series of works on flagellation. This is untrue. In 1872 J. C. Hotten, a publisher of erotica, collected seven pamphlets on flagellation and gave them the title: "Library Illustrative of Social Progress. From the Original Editions collected by the late Henry Thomas Buckle". In an accompanying circular Hotten asserted that Buckle had been a collector of curiosa and had a special collection of works on flagellation. The following seven works were supposed to have been taken from Buckle's private library:

1. *Exhibition of Female Flagellants.*
2. *Part Second of the Exhibition of Female Flagellants.*
3. *Lady Bumtickler's Revels.*

4. *A Treatise of the Use of Flogging in Venereal Affairs.*

5. *Madam Birchini's Dance.*

6. *Sublime of Flagellation.*

7. *Fashionable Lectures.*

The truth of the matter is that the above works were obtained from the library of a well-known London collector who bound them together in one volume. Hotten borrowed the work, had it reprinted and used Buckle's name for prestige and sales-possibility without the knowledge of the collector.

Perhaps the best written and most famous work on flagellation in English is the "Exhibition of Female Flagellants, in the Modest and Incontinent World, Proving from Indubitable Facts that a number of Ladies take a secret Pleasure in whipping their own, and Children committed to their care, and that their Passion for exercising and feeling the Pleasure of a Birch-rod, from Objects of their Choice of both Sexes, is to the full as Predominant as that of Mankind" (1777?).

We hope, at some later date, to present a complete account of the history and development of this strange mania for flagellation in England.

38.

Erotic Folk Lore and Song

NGLAND is celebrated in the annals of anthropology and ethnology for its valuable contributions to the study of folk lore, the connection between sexuality and religion, and the curious sexual customs of England as well as foreign lands.

R. P. Knight (1750-1824) was the first student of modern times who conducted original research into the problem of the sexual origin of religion. Knight, a poet and archaeologist of high repute, resided for some time in Naples, made extensive explorations in the ruins of Pompeii and Herculaneum and collected an extraordinary number of valuable relics on the sex life of the classical period. This collection is now guarded in the British Museum and is available only to recognized students.

Knight's main work is: "A Discourse on the Worship of Priapus. And its Connexion on the mystic Theology of the Ancients" (1786). The work treats of priapic cults in great detail and is to be found in most large libraries. Knight's work was supplemented by John Davenport in two books that also dealt with sexual curiosa. The first is: "Aphrodisiacs and Anti-aphrodisiacs: Three Essays on the Powers of Reproduction; with some account of the Judicial 'Congress' as practised in France during the Seventeenth Century" (1869). The first essay is on "Ancient Phallic Worship"; the second, on "Anaphrodisia, or Absence of the Productive Power"; the last on "Aphrodisiacs and Anti-aphrodisiacs".

The second volume by Davenport is titled: "Curiositates Eroticae Physiologiae; or, Tabooed Subjects Freely Treated" (1875). This work contains six essays: 1. Generation. 2. Chastity and Modesty. 3. Marriage. 4. Circumcision. 5. Eunuchism. 6. Hermaphrodism, followed by a closing essay on death.

The serious nature of Davenport's research is evidenced not only by the high tenor of his work but also by his expressed purpose: "Let it not be supposed from these remarks that the author's intention has been that of writing an obscene book, or even to employ obscene words. He holds that the grand subject — the Reproduction of the Human Race — which runs more or less through all the Essays in this volume, is in itself most pure, and that the words which are necessary, adequately and correctly to describe it in its various phases and ramifications, have acquired the stigma of obscene only in modern times, and, through an ultra-fastidiousness, which would hesitate to apply the word breech to a man's small clothes, but would rather designate them as unmentionables, indescribables, or femoral habiliments."

England is richer than any other country in the number and variety of its ballads, folk and street songs. The majority of these poems naturally treat of love, and many are of marked erotic and obscene content. A complete list of works on this subject would run to many pages and we can here mention only the three most famous collections with a representative selection from each one.

A famous collection of songs set to music is that by Thomas Durfey. It was originally published under the title: "Songs Compleat, Pleasant and Divertive" (Six Volumes, 1719) but is better known as "Wit and Mirth: or Pills to Purge Melancholy; being a collection of the best Merry Ballads and Songs, Old and New". One of the better known songs by Durfey is "Phillis Awakes":

> Phillis at first seem'd much afraid,
> Much afraid, much afraid,
> Yet when I kiss'd, she won repay'd;
> Could you but see, could you but see,
> What I did more, you'd envy me,
> What I did more, you'd envy me,
> You'd envy me.
>
> We then so sweetly were employ'd
> The height of Pleasure we enjoy'd;
> Could you but see, could you but see,
> You'd say so too, if you saw me, etc.

Ladies, if how to Love you'd know
She can inform what we did do,
But cou'd you see, but cou'd you see,
You'd cry aloud, the next is me,
You'd cry aloud, the next is me,
The next is me.

Thomas Percy, Bishop of Dromore, was the author of "Reliques of Ancient English Poetry, consisting of old heroic ballads, songs, and other pieces of our earlier poets, together with some few of later date" (Three Volumes, 1765). A characteristic Old-English ballad is that of the London Goldsmith Shore and his unfaithful wife, Janet, mistress to King Edward IV:

To Matthew Shore I was a wife
Till lust brought ruine to my life;
And then my life I lewdly spent,
Which makes my soul for to lament.

In Lombard-street I once did dwelle,
As London yet can witness welle;
Where many gallants did beholde
My beautye in a shop of golde.

I spread my plumes, as wantons doe,
Some sweet and secret friende to woe,
Because chaste love I did not finde
Agreeing to my wanton minde.

At last my name in court did ring
Into the ears of Englandes king,
Who came and like'd, and love requir'd,
But I made coye what he desir'd.

Yet Mistress Balgue, a neighbour neare
Whose friendship I esteemed deare,
Did saye, It was a gallant thing
To be beloved of a king.

Jane Shore is then beguiled into becoming mistress to the king. For a short period she reigns in splendor, but, at the death of her royal lover,

Richard III ascends the throne and sentences her to public disgrace:

> I then was punisht for my sin,
> That I so long had lived in;
> Yea every one that was his friend,
> This tyrant brought to shamefull end.
>
> Then for my lewd and wanton life
> That made a strumpet of a wife,
> I penance did in Lombard-street,
> In shamefull manner in a sheet.
>
> Where many thousands did me viewe,
> Who late in court my credit knewe;
> Which made the teares run down my face
> To thinke upon my foul disgrace.

Bereft of friends and fortune, she walks through the streets of London, a wretched beggar, until she dies on a street-corner which is named "Shoreditch" after her. This miserable end affords the following moral to the ballad:

> You wanton wives, that fall to lust,
> Be you assured that god ist just,
> Whoredome shall not escape his hand,
> Nor pride unpunish'd in this land.

Robert Burns, the illustrious Scotch poet, collected in his time the many erotic and obscene folk songs of the old Scots. He purified these in his famous versions, but the originals were preserved and published after his death under the title of "The Merry Muses of Caledonia; a collection of Favourite Scot Songs" (1800). This collection had much influence on English poetry in point of rythmic technique. Byron, in particular, was much impressed by the lightness and quickness of the verse. One of the merrier songs follows:

HOW CAN I KEEP MY
MAIDENHEAD

How can I keep my maidenhead,
My maidenhead, my maidenhead,
How can I keep my maidenhead,
  Among sae mony men, O.

The captain bad a guinea for't,
A guinea for't, a guinea for't;
The captain bad a guinea for't,
  The colonel he bad ten, O.

But I'll do as my minnie did,
My minnie did, my minnie did,
But I'll do as my minnie did,
  For siller I'll hae nane, O.

I'll gie it to a bonie lad,
A bonie lad, a bonie lad;
I'll gie it to a bonie lad,
  For just as gude again, O.

An auld moulie maidenhead,
A maidenhead, a maidenhead,
An auld moulie maidenhead,
  The weary wark I ken, O.

The stretchin' o't, the strivin' o't,
The borin' o't, the rivin' o't,
And ay the double drivin' o't,
  The farther ye gang ben, O.

39.

Erotic and Obscene English Magazines

Contents of Hundreds of Periodicals

NGLAND is best known among collectors of curiosa for its wealth of erotic and obscene magazines. No other country approaches England in its number and variety of such productions. The first of these erotic magazines appeared in 1774 and similar works have appeared up to the present date. A list of the more important publications follows:

1.   *The Covent Garden Magazine, or Amorous Repository, calculated solely for the entertainment of the polite world* (1774). This original production contains accounts of court-trials, lists of prostitutes, and erotic poetry.

2.   *The Rambler's Magazine; or the Annals of Gallantry, Glee, Pleasure, and the Bon Ton; calculated for the entertainment of the Polite*

World; and to furnish The Man of Pleasure with a most delicious banquet of Amorous, Bacchanalian, Whimsical, Humorous, Theatrical and Polite Entertainment (1783). The more interesting articles are: "Lecture on Procreation", "Essay on Woman" (in prose), "Art of the Lover", "Notes on Dr. Graham", descriptions of marriage ceremonies in various countries, letters on flagellation, a "Dialogue on Divorce", and a "Cytherean Discussion". There are also memoirs on the sex life of Cecil, Lord Burleigh, Peter Abelard, Miss Bellamy, the Duchess of Kingston, Miss Ann Catley; also reports of divorce and separation cases, and finally a great number of erotic tales such as the "Adventures of a Dancing Master", "Adventures of an Eunuch", "Memoirs of an English Seraglio", "Adventures of a Man About Town", etc., etc. There is even a complete drama, "The Coffee-House Medley, a comedy".

3. *The Bon Ton Magazine; or Microscope of Fashion and Folly* (Five Volumes, March 1791-March 1796). The "Bon Ton Magazine" is the most important gallant magazine England has ever produced and plays a role in the "High Life" of the period quite similar to that of the "Gentleman's Magazine" in the more serious subjects. The editorship is falsely ascribed to a John or Jack Mitford. The more important subjects are: three treatises, "The Adventurer", "The Rake", and "The Essayist"; a "Vocabulary for High Tone" or the "Savoire vivre Vocabulary", a "Fashionable Dictionary of Love", "The Love Affairs of the Kings of France", "Love Anecdotes", biographies of actresses, robbers, a

"History of the Theatre", a series of historical essays on eunuchism, reports of scandals, erotic novels such as "Elmina; or the flower that never fades", "Life of a Modern Man of Fashion", "Adventures and Amours of a Bar-Maid", "The Black Joke", "The Modern Lovers, or the Adventures of Cupid", and the usual run of descriptions of marriage rites, scenes of flagellation, queer clubs, personal accounts of prostitutes, erotic poems and letters.

4. *The Ranger's Magazine; or the Man of Fashion's Companion; being the Whim of the Month, and General Assemblage of Love, Gallantry, Wit, Pleasure, Harmony, Mirth, Glee, and Fancy. Containing a Monthly list of the Covent-Garden Cyprians; or, the Man of Pleasure's Vade Mecum — The Annals of Gallantry — Essence of Trials for Adultery — Crim. Con. — Seduction — Double Entendres — Choice Anecdotes—Warm Narratives — Curious Fragments — Animating Histories of Tête-à-Têtes — and Wanton Frollicks. — To which is added the Fashionable Chit Chat, and Scandal of the Month, from the Pharaoh Table to the Fan Warehause* (January-June 1795). The title sufficiently illuminates the nature of the contents.

5. *The Rambler's Magazine; or, Fashionable Emporium of Polite Literature, The Fine Arts — Politics — Theatrical Excellencies — Wit — Humour — Genius — Taste — Gallantry — and all The Gay Variety of Supreme Bon Ton* (January-December 1822).

From grave to gay, from lively to severe,
Wit, truth and humour shall by turns appear.

The editor adds in the introduction: "Our theme is love for, as Moore says, the whole world turns round on't." Especial mention should be given to "London Hells Exposed", "The Cuckold's Chronicle", "Fashionable Gallantry", selections from the "Golden Ass", and an incomplete erotic novel "The Rambler; or the Life, Adventures, Amours, Intrigues and Excentricities of Gregory Griffin".

6. *The Rambler; or, Fashionable Companion for April; being a complete Register of Gallantry. Embellished with a beautiful engraved Frontispiece of the Venus de Medicis* (April 1824-January 1825).

> *Art, Nature, Wit, and Love display*
> *In every page a Rambler's gay.*

This magazine had a successful run but its career was broken short by suppression because of indecent reference to contemporary personages. Its general contents: notes on the theatre, scandalous stories, reports of trials, Canto XVII of Byron's "Don Juan", and an erotic tale, "Maria, or, the Victim of Passion".

7. *The Original Rambler's Magazine; or, Annals of Gallantry; an amusing miscellany of Fun, Frolic, Fashion and Flash. Amatory Tales, Adventures, Memoirs of the most Celebrated Women of Pleasure, Trials for Crim. Con. and Seduction, Bon Ton, Facetious Epigrams, Jeu d' Esprit, etc.* (1827). This work contains mostly biographical articles, among them, "Loves of Col. Berkeley", "Life, Amours, Intrigues, and professional career of Miss Chester", "Amours of the Duke of Wellington", "Amours of Mrs.

Thompson", "Amour of Napoleon Buonaparte and Mrs. Billington", "Memoirs of Miss Singleton with a Portrait of this Beauty of Arlington Street in the State of Nudity", Amourous Memoirs of Lady Grigsley", and a "Description of London Bordels".

8. *The Rambler's Magazine; or, Annals of Gallantry, Glee, Pleasure, and Bon Ton*: *A Delicious Banquet of Amorous, Bacchanalian, Whimsical, Humorous, Theatrical, and Literary Entertainment* (Two Volumes, 1827-1829). The editor was John (Jack) Mitford, a man of respectable rank and classical education; he served with distinction under Hood and Nelson in the English Navy, rose to a Captaincy, then fell into debauchery, want, prison, and died in 1831 in St. Gile's Work House in London. The chief articles in this new "Rambler's Magazine" are: "Salon Sirens", and the "Bazaar Beauties", two series of biographies of easy ladies and courtesans of the period, an essay on Madame Vestris, the "Loves of Lord Byron", the gossip columns "Cuckold's Chronicle" and "Amatory and Bon Ton Intelligence" and the following erotic novels, "Helen of Glenshiels; or, the Miseries of Seduction", "Amours of London, and Spirit of Bon Ton", "The Confessions of a Methodist; or pictures of sensuality", and "The Cambridge Larks".

9. *The Crim. Con. Gazette; or, Diurnal Register of the Freaks and Follies of the Present Day* (November 1830-April 1831). Reports of "Crim. Cons." (criminal conversations, i.e., the technical, legal term for cases of divorce which charge adultery) have always been the favorite

reading of London society, especially since they
may be printed in full, as a matter of court-rec-
ord, including the scabrous and indecent details.
There are, in addition, memoirs of Sally Mac-
lean, Madame Vestris, Clara Foote, Mrs. Jor-
dan and an article on the secret amours of the
Duke of Wellington.

10.   *The Quizzical Gazette and Merry Companion* (August 1831-January 1832). This a
worthless collection of contemporary facetiae.

11.   *The Exquisite: a collection of Tales, Histories, and Essays, Funny, fanciful and facetious,
Interspersed with Anecdotes, Original and Select. Amorous Adventures, Piquant Jests, and
Spicey Sayings, Illustrated with numerous Engravings, published weekly* (Three Volumes, 145
numbers, 1842-1844). The contents are mainly
comprised of erotic novels and tales but there is
also a sufficient number of erotic miscellanea of
all sorts. Each number contains a poem, among
them John Wilkes' "Essay on Woman". Under
the headings "Stars of the Salon", "Sketches of
Courtesans", and "Unveiled Seductions" there
are mentioned names, addresses, appearances,
tastes and perversities of the favorite prostitutes
of the day, after the notorious "List of Ladies"
by Harris. "The Exquisite" also furnishes memoirs of Madame Vestris, Mrs. Davenport, Mlle.
de Brion, Madame Gourdan, Marie Antoinette,
and the "Original Anecdotes and Sketches of
Charles II and the Duchess of Portsmouth".
The "art of love" is treated in the following essays: "The Bride's Vade Mecum", "A Trustworthy Guide through Venus' Domain", "Venus
Physique", "The New Way of Loving", and a

"Physical Consideration of Man and Woman in the State of Marriage". There are also selections from Parent-Duchâtelet on prostitution in Paris, a Malthusian treatise, "Seven Years' Experiences on the Practice of Limitation of Children according to the Best Known Method", letters on flagellation, articles on eunuchs and phallic cults, and innumerable erotic tales from the French and the Italian, mostly translated by James Campbell, among them the three notorious romances of Andréa de Nerciat, "Les Aphrodites", "Félicia", and "Monrose". Of the original English stories in "The Exquisite" we mention: "Nights at Lunet; or a budget of amorous tales", "Where shall I go tonight?", "The Loves of Sappho", "Wife and no Wife, A Tale from Stamboul", "The Child of Nature, Improved by Chance", "The History of a Young Lady's Researches into the nature of the Summum Bonum", "The Practical Part of Love exemplified in the personal history of Lucy and Helen, eminent priestesses of the Temple of Venus", "The Illustrious Lovers; or, secret history of Malcolm and Matilda", "Julia; or, Miss in her Teens", and "The London Bawd".

12. *The Pearl, a Monthly Journal of Facetiae and Voluptuous Reading* (Three Volumes, July 1879-December 1882). "The Pearl" is the most obscene and best known English magazine of its kind. It contains for the major part poetry, facetiae and obscene stories. In the last group are to be named: "Lady Pokingham, or they all do it", "Miss Coote's Confession, or the voluptuous experiences of an old maid" (a series of flagellation scenes whose "heroine" is the aunt

of the famous general Sir Eyre Coote in service in East India), "Sub-Umbra, or sport among the she-noodles" (also on flagellation), "La Rose d'Amour, or the adventures of a gentleman in search of pleasure", "My Grandmother's Tale, or May's account of her introduction to the art of love", "Flunkeyana, or Belgravian Morals".

These obscene novels are shocking to the extreme; all contain a series of horrible scenes in the manner of the Marquis de Sade. An analysis of the first named story, "Lady Pokingham, or they all do it", should suffice in indicating the trend of the magazine.

The heroine Beatrice begins her story with an account of the usual onanistic and tribadic practices in school. She then tells the details of the rape of her young friend Alice Marchmont. She leaves with Alice for the city and they take up quarters in a Catholic home. A parody of an episode from Lord Beaconsfield's "Lothair" now follows, including an imitation of the convent whipping-scene from "Gamiani". We next meet a pornologic society which delights in portraying every imaginable vice, somewhat in the style of "120 Days of Sodom". The famous "Berkeley Horse", the whipping machine, is also brought into the picture. When the respectable gentlemen at these orgies refuse to undergo such mechanical punishments the good ladies have recourse to the servants. Lady Beatrice Pokingham is now introduced to the Earl of Crim-Con, an "old man of thirty who looks as if he were at least fifty years old". She courts and marries him although his impotence can be momentarily conquered only by the strangest and severest stimulants. This unnatural marriage cannot help but end in discord. His Lordship forsakes his lady for his two young pages. Beatrice surprises him with the two young men but takes advantage of the opportunity to join the orgy, at the height of which the Earl of Crim-Con is seized with heart failure. Beatrice then seduces his brother and heir, all her waiting-men, a steward, two pages and her servant girls. Her health is undermined by reason of these grandiose exploits and she is sent to Madeira, but not before she seduces the physician who gave her this advice. On the ship she flagellates and seduces the cadets until none is left sound and whole. After a short stay in Madeira she returns to England and dies of "galloping consumption".

Supplementing "The Pearl", and without which this magazine cannot be considered complete, are the following four publications:

1. *Swivia; or, The Briefless Barrister. The Extra Special Number of "The Pearl", Containing a Variety of Complete Tales, with Five Illustrations, Poetry, Facetiae, etc.* Christmas, 1879. In the main this is a description of a frenzied orgy of four young men and two servant girls. Strange erotic dreams are told and obscene songs are sung in this party.

2. *The Haunted House or the Revelations of Theresa Terence. 'An o'er true tale.' 'There are more things in heaven and earth than are dreamt of in our philosophy.' Being the Christmas Number of "The Pearl"* (1880). This work contains a description of the sexual ex-

ploits of Sir Anthony Harvey, who is surprised by three young men, and who then take part in his private orgies. Defloration and flagellation form the plot. The "Revelations of Theresa Terence" announced in the title do not appear in the book.

3. *The Pearl, Christmas Annual* 1881. *Containing New Year's Day, The Sequel to Swivia, Vanessa, and other Tales, Facetiae, Songs, etc.* The chief feature of this number is the erotic tale of "Vanessa", whose heroine is a modern Fanny Hill with "modern ideas".

4. *The Erotic Casket Gift Book for* 1882. *Containing Various Facetiae omitted in "The Pearl" Christmas Annual for Want of Space.* This small brochure contains eight extremely obscene anecdotes and a few short stories of no particular distinction.

"The Pearl" seems to mark the swan-song in English obscene magazines for only two other similar publications have followed in its bold path. These are:

13. No. 1., Jan. 1851. *The Cremorne; A Magazine of Wit, Facetiae, Parody, Graphic Tales of Love, etc.* (Real date of issue: August 1882). The stories in this number are: "The Secret Life of Linda Brent", "A Curious History of Slave Life and Slave Wrongs", and "Lady Hamilton: or Nelson's Inamorata. The Real Story of her life".

14. *The Boudoir; A Magazine of Scandal, Facetiae, etc.* (June 1883). This is composed mainly of short anecdotes and "eccentricities" in prose and verse.

40.

Ideal Sex Life
in English Utopias

Bernard de Mandeville's
Revolutionary Sex Systems

THE British nation is noted for its profound interest in political economy. It is even called the country par excellence for Utopian theory and we can therefore expect the intimate relations of the sexes, the core of social life, to receive a full and reasoned treatment in the realm of sociologic theories.

Sir Thomas More (1478-1535) in his "Utopia" (1516) analyzed very keenly the relations of the sexes in this first of modern ideal republics. More especially distinguished himself by recognizing the extreme significance of sexual love in producing a healthy posterity, a purpose which he held to be so fundamental in a state that he proposed an audacious plan:

"For a sad and an honest matron showeth the

woman, be she maid or widow, naked to the wooer. And likewise a sage and discrete man exhibiteth the wooer naked to the woman. At this custom we laughed and disallowed it as foolish. But they on the other part do greatly wonder at the folly of all other nations, which in buying a colt, whereas a little money is in hazard, be so chary and circumspect, that though he be almost all bare, yet they will not buy him unless the saddle and all the harness be taken off, lest under those coverings be hid some gall or sore; and yet in choosing a wife, which shall be either pleasure or displeasure to them all their life after, they be so reckless that, all the residue of the woman's body being covered with clothes, they esteem her secretly by one handbreadth (for they can see no more but her face); and so do join her to them not without great jeopardy of evil agreeing together, if anything in her body afterward do offend and mislike them."

This drastic method would indeed lead to a more natural and "ideal" sexual relation between a couple, and is highly to be recommended from the standpoint of the public weal. In modern times, More's ideal system has been approximated by a medical examination of the individuals to ensure the health and potency of the couple. To be sure, the four-century old idea of More of a mutual examination is too "modern" for our times. Prudery will have to be vanquished in a far greater degree before More's dream can come true.

In no other country, both in early and modern times, has polygamy (mainly in the form of bigamy) appeared so frequently as in England. Even Chaucer has the Wife of Bath humorously interpolate:

> "Thou hast yhad fyve housbondes," quod he,
> "And thilke man, the which that hath now thee,
> Is nought thyn housbond;" thus seyde he certeyn;
> What that he mente thereby, I can nat seyn;
> But that I axe, why that the fifthe man
> Was noon housbond to the Samaritan?
> How manye mighte she have in mariage?
> Yet herde I never tellen in myn age
> Upon this nombre diffinicioun;
> Men may devyne and glosen up and doun.
> But well I woot express, withoute lye,
> God bad us for to wexe and multiplye;
> That gentil text can I wel understonde.
> Eek wel I woot he seyde, myn housbonde
> Sholde lete fader and moder, and take me;
> But if no nombre mencioun made he,
> Of bigamye or octogamye;
> Why sholde men speke of it vileinye?
> Lo, here the wise king, dan Salomon;
> I trowe he hadde wyves mo than oon;
> As wolde god, it leveful were to me
> To be refreshed half so ofte as he.

This subject was actually discussed in the affirmative in a monograph by Th. Alethaeus (John Lyser), "Polygamia Triumphatrix" (1692). Lyser praised in glowing terms the institution of polygamy and travelled through many countries of Europe in an effort to spread propaganda for his "ideal system of marriage". He found little support. Christian V of Denmark had Lyser's work publicly burnt at the stake and threatened to hang the author if he ever dared cross the boundaries of Denmark. According to Bayle, the polygamous phantasy of Lyser was the more bizarre, since Lyser, himself, was impotent and could not satisfy a single woman, let alone a harem!

Two later English authors came out in favor

of Lyser's theory. The first was Martin Madan, doctor of theology, who showed in his "Thelyphthora" (1780) that the polygamy authorized by Mosaic Law could not logically be forbidden to the Christians. Madan's three-volumed work was also confiscated and burnt and is today an extremely rare work. Another advocate of polygamy was the famous Sir Arthur Stephen Brookes in his "Sketches of Spain and Morocco". An interesting discussion on polygamy is also be to found in Mrs. Manley's "Atalantis", where it is warmly defended by Hernando.

In the eighteenth and nineteenth centuries the cases of bigamy were so frequent that all commentators have made especial mention of this "English proclivity". Schuetz reports the following interesting case on the transgression of the law by a polygamist. "Since all laws in England must be explained literally, it is not a very difficult matter to find some loophole in the exercise of justice, for law has no force in England beyond that of its literal sense. Thus, for example, a man was once condemned to death for having married a second wife. The culprit, however, was clever enough to marry a third time! Since the law said nothing about trigamy, the cunning Englishman escaped the gallows! But at the next meeting of Parliament this error was rectified by the substitution of the word polygamy for bigamy."

A famous case of bigamy in modern times was that instituted against Earl Russell in 1901 in the House of Lords. He was declared guilty and condemned to a term in prison.

An unique phenomenon in the field of sociological theories of sex is presented by the London physician, Bernard de Mandeville (1670-1733). This amazing Englishman had an apostle of egoism canonize the "seven deadly sins" in his notorious "Fable of the Bees". This work first appeared in 1706 under the title "The grumbling hive or Knaves turned honest". The nature of its startling contents can be judged from the author's thesis.

If all men were virtuous, declared de Mandeville, the state would crumble: if all men were honest, frugal, and entirely self-controlled, the nation would soon be bankrupt. The moral of this "syllogism" is that vice is essential to civilization. This is expressed in poetical form by the author:

> Then leave Complaints: Fools only strive
> To make a Great an Honest Hive
> T'enjoy the World's Conveniences,
> Be jam'd in War, yet live in Ease,
> Without great Vices, is a vain
> Eutopia seated in the Brain.
> Fraud, Luxury and Pride must live,
> While we the Benefits receive:
> Hunger's a dreadful Plague, no doubt,
> Yet who digests or thrives without?
> Do we not owe the Growth of Wine
> To the dry shabby crooked Vine?
> Which, while it Shoots neglected stood,
> Chok'd other Plants, and ran to Wood;
> But blest us with its noble Fruit,
> As soon as it was ty'd and cut:
> So Vice is beneficial found,
> When it's by Justice lopt and bound;
> Nay where the People would be great,
> As necessary to the State,
> As Hunger is to make 'em eat.
> Bare Virtue can't make Nations live
> In Splendor; they, that would revive
> A Golden Age, must be as free,
> For Acorns, as for Honesty.

In the second edition which appeared under the title of "The fable of the bees or private vices public benefits" (1714), de Mandeville even accentuates the more this radical view of the necessity of vice for the advance of mankind, a theory which found especial favor in France with Voltaire and the Encyclopaedists and reached its fruition in the "120 Days of Sodom" of the Marquis de Sade, a complete defence of debauchery and libertinism. Other writers in England have expressed thoughts similar to that of de Mandeville and Adam Smith in the "Theory of moral sentiments" sharply criticizes the letters of Lord Chesterfield and the concluding moral in Swift's "Gulliver's Travels" as belonging to the "licentious systems" of de Mandeville.

An equally unique application of the theories of de Mandeville is contained in "A Modest Defense of public stews", which also appeared under the title "A Conference upon Whoring" (1727). This work is excessively rare and is more familiar to collectors in its French translation, titled "Vénus la Populaire ou Apologie des Maisons de Joie" (1727).

The foreword of this bizarre creation, which is dedicated to the "Members of the Society Established for the Reformation of Morals", is signed "Phil-Pornix" and attacks the activities of the "Society for the Suppression of Prostitution and Whore-Houses". The author refers to the ancient philosophers whose erotic inclinations are then recounted in detail. Prostitution is an absolute necessity and prevents the appearance of greater evils.

The text of "A Conference upon Whoring"

is a development of this notion. Bernard de
Mandeville has declared that "whoring" is far
less harmful than alcoholism, since in the former man guards his cold-bloodedness which is
lost in intoxication. The advantages of bordels
consist in the fact that they are places where
man can satisfy a sudden attack of passion without danger, or at least less danger than with an
ordinary street-walker. Bordels also prevent
any mésalliance, lessen masturbation, and limit
the intemperate frequency of sexual intercourse
with clandestine prostitutes or with private
parties, and also keep the dangers of venereal
infection within reasonable limit.

The entire work shows a marked distaste
for the institution of marriage. The author
explains that all, even the best men, are deceived
by marriage and are soon surfeited with their
wives, at least from physical connection. Thus
an effective protection against boredom in marriage is sexual intercourse with prostitutes! A
proof of this is seen in the "fact" that licentious
women make the best wives. Bordels are therefore the greatest aids to marriage. It prepares
the couple for marriage, keeps them happy and
contented during marriage, protects the wife
from the dangers of adultery as well as the innocent maiden from seduction and rape. For the
modesty of woman, says de Mandeville, is
purely artificial and conventional. In actuality,
according to him, women have as violent a
desire for sexual intercourse as the man. For
this reason the feminine resistance against the
male's storming of the fort is but slight and
negligible, with the proviso that there shall be

no danger incurred in the loss of their "good name". There then follows a cynical description of the various practical arts of seducing a woman in the quickest time possible.

Since legal punishment does not prevent men from laying snares for honorable wives and maidens, another means of satisfaction must be created for their benefit. The bordels afford such a "legal evacuation". De Mandeville wishes to limit prostitution to this form and therefore recommends either the forcing of street-walkers to enter such public places or their imprisonment in Bridewell or their transportation to the Carolinas in America! The advantages of bordels are seen in the quiet, orderly life of the inmates; the strict, sanitary precautions with which they are regulated; and in the possibility of drastically treating the sources of venereal infections; he also proposes free treatment in hospitals for the cure of venereal diseases. He believes that one hundred houses in a fixed quarter of London, stocked with two thousand girls, will be sufficient for the sexual needs of the men in London. Each bordel is to be presided over by a matron of experience and energy who shall take care of twenty girls and be responsible for their physical welfare. The bordels shall also contain restaurants where food and drink can be served at moderate prices. Two physicians, three surgeons and three commissariats complete the establishment. Bernard de Mandeville proposes a classification of bordels into four classes, according to the beauty of the girls and the price. In the first and lowest, an engagement will cost one shilling, three pence; in the second, three shillings; in the third, one-half guinea; in the fourth and highest, one guinea. The girls must pay a small tax to the state from their earnings. For the stocking of bordels with fresh beauty the author proposes the importation of foreign prostitutes from time to time as needed.

In the conclusion de Mandeville defends his proposals from religious attacks. To the moral proposition: one shall not use evil means for a good purpose, he counterposes: of two evils one must choose the lesser. He places the universal weal above the individual good. Sexual freedom is better than eternal prohibition, which indeed inevitably leads to sexual excesses. The author concludes that only if his proposals are followed will England be saved from the "country-sweeping corruption menacing the very vitals of our most sacred institutions".

41.

The Greatest
Erotobibliomaniacs
in England

Their Fabulous Erotic Treasuries
Described

N NO other country, with the possible exception of France, has bibliophilism flowered so early and been cultivated so extensively as in England, the "El Dorado of bibliophilists and bibliomaniacs". Indeed, the oldest monograph on bibliolatry is the product of an Englishman, Richard de Bury, Bishop of Durham, who wrote in the year 1344 "Philobiblon, A Treatise on the Love of Books". Chaucer also points out in the prologue to the "Canterbury Tales" that the true Englishman is a booklover. Shakespeare indicates his own temper in "The Tempest".

> *Me, poor man, my library*
> *Was dukedom large enough.*

An old English poem of the same period
reads:

> O for a Booke and a shadie nooke,
>   eyther in-a-doore or out;
> With the grene leaves whisp'ring overhede,
>   or the Streete cryes all about.
> Where I maie Reade all at my ease,
>   both of the Newe and Olde;
> For a jollie goode Booke whereon to looke,
>   is better to me than Gold.

Incomparably the greatest English bibliophile in the field of erotic literature is acknowledged by critics to be the eminent figure of
Frederick Hankey. He was the son of Sir Frederick Hankey, the English Governor of the Ionian
Islands, who married a Greek noblewoman. He
became Captain of the Guard and at his retire-
ment from active service in 1850 removed to
Paris where he died on June 8, 1882.

Hankey's collection was small, but extremely
select. In addition to obscene works it also consisted of erotic works of art and other curiosa,
such as a classic group of tribades in marble, a
bronze of a cunnilinguent satyr, a genuine chastity belt, an ivory dildo, and many other rarities.
The erotica consisted of illuminated manuscripts,
the best editions and the most costly examples of
the foremost erotic works, which were extra-
illustrated by famous artists and bound by the
finest French bookbinders.

Hankey was also an "original" in his mode of
life. He never rose before noon. He received vis-
itors only after ten o'clock at night, and then he
would be found buried among his books. He
had blond hair, blue eyes, an almost feminine

appearance, and in many other ways corresponded to the Marquis de Sade's description. De Sade was also his favorite author.

The "clou" of Hankey's collection was formed by three unique works: a single example on vellum of the "Liaisons dangereuses" by Choderlos de Laclos, with original illustrations by Monnet and Gérard; secondly, the famous "Tableaux des moeurs du temps" by La Popelinière in the original manuscript of the author, together with twenty exquisite miniatures by Monnet (this one item cost Hankey twenty thousand gold francs!); the third "opus rarissimum" was a manuscript of La Fontaine's "Contes" which was considered to be an "example of illuminated calligraphy without equal in modern times".

James Campbell (a pseudonym for J. C. Reddie) almost equalled Hankey as an erotobibliomaniac. He died on July 4, 1872 in Crieff, Scotland, at an advanced age, after he had been forced to leave London and give up his literary studies because of shattered health and failing eyesight. Campbell, without having enjoyed an academic education, read with complete ease Latin, French, Italian and German. His knowledge in this field was so prodigious that as soon as an obscene work appeared in any language he was immediately aware of it. Every new book, every new edition was immediately procured by him, collated and bibliographically compared, page by page, word by word, with the other editions of the same book! If he could not purchase an example of the rarest items, he would make a perfect copy of it by his own hand. He often stated that he considered his collection of erotic literature from a philosophic viewpoint as the "clearest illustration of human nature and its weaknesses".

William S. Potter, another noted collector of erotica, is also famous for his connection with Boucher's immortal erotic paintings. Potter was born on January 21, 1805 and died on January 16, 1879. His collection was almost as vast as that of Campbell's and also contained erotic pictures, etchings, photographs and innumerable curios which he had collected on his many journeys abroad. The highmark of his collection was the notorious erotic paintings which Boucher had executed by order of the Marquise de Pompadour. Louis XVI later had them removed from the Palais de l'Arsenal with the command: "Il faut faire disparaître ces indécences." This desire of the monarch was first literally carried out a full century later. Potter's collection was sold in Edinburgh to an American multi-millionaire. In the New York Custom House these works were declared to be "foul and loathsome" and were accordingly returned to the English port where they were burnt by the authorities! A sad fate for such glorious examples of a master genius of classic art!

The greatest bibliographer and bibliophile in the erotic field, not only in England but in the entire world, is universally acknowledged to be Pisanus Fraxi (pseudonym for H. Spencer Ashbee), the renowned author of the "Index", the "Centuria", and the "Catena", those three unique bibliographies of erotica.

Fraxi was born on April 21, 1834 and died on July 29, 1900. He was a London wholesaler and became quite wealthy through a marked talent for business. In the travels to all parts of the globe he attained a practical knowledge of social customs and human failings. His favorite country was Spain which he knew as well as his own native London. In the last decade of his life he collected every printed edition of Cervantes and published a complete bibliography of his works, for which he was signally honored by Spain.

Fraxi was one of the most successful and luckiest book-collectors of the nineteenth century. In his house in London, Bedford Square No. 53, he collected an imposing library and a very select number of paintings. His library was especially notable for its specimens of English erotica of the eighteenth and nineteenth century, the finest ever amassed by one man. He also had all the foremost foreign erotic works, including every book mentioned in his three splendid volumes of erotic bibliography, upon which we have drawn so heavily in the present work and to which we refer every student of bibliography and literature for exact and authoritative references. Fraxi's three classics are:

1. *Index Librorum Prohibitorum*: *being Notes Bio-Biblio-Iconographical and Critical, on Curious and Uncommon Books. By Pisanus Fraxi. London: Privately Printed: MDCCC-LXVII.* Quarto, LXXVI, 542 pages and 4 unnumbered pages *Additional Errata* and *Contents.* Frontispiece by Chauvet, a picture of the "Berkeley Horse" between pp. XLIV and XLV.

The main bibliographical specimens are:
works of Sellon, John Davenport, bibliography
of the "Essay on Woman", and innumerable
writings on flagellation.

2. *Centuria Librorum Absconditorum*: *Being Notes Bio-Biblio-Iconographical and Critical, on Curious and Uncommon Books. By Pisanus Fraxi. London*: *Privately Printed*:
MDCCCLXXIX. Quarto, LX, 593 and 2 un-
numbered pages *Sodom* and *Contents*. Frontispiece by John Lewis Brown, two reproductions
of flagellation pictures, "Molly's first Correction", and "Lady Termagant Flaybum", 1 facsimile of the "Gynaecologia" of Martin Schurig, 5 facsimilies of title-pages of editions of
the "Historie van B. Cornelis Adriaensen", and
1 facsimile of "The Toast" of W. King.

The main contents of "Centuria" are: complete bibliographies of Schurig, Catholic works
of sexual casuistry, King's "The Toast", Rochester's "Sodom", Rowlandson's obscene pictures
and a bibliography of flagellation.

3. *Catena Librorum Tacendorum*: *Being Notes Bio-Biblio-Iconographical and Critical, on Curious and Uncommon Books. By Pisanus Fraxi. London*: *Privately Printed*: *MDCCC-*
LXXXV. Quarto, LVII, 593 and 2 pages
Errata and *Contents* and *Arrangement*. Frontispiece by Oudart, also a portrait of Octave Delepierre and of James Campbell, including a facsimile of the title-page of Antonio de Soto-
maior's "Polygamia".

The main contents are: bibliography of various works of the seventeeth and eighteenth centuries dealing with sexual relations, followed by an exhaustive bibliography of English erotica of the eighteenth and nineteenth centuries, especially the works of John Cleland, a list of Spanish erotica, and "Varia".

No person who professes any serious interest in books should fail to read these three splendid works of a masterhand, especially the classical "Introduction" to each volume, a reprint of which is badly needed since the works of Fraxi were limited to an edition of only two-hundred-and-fifty copies! A student of bibliography cannot help but be inspired by them. As Fraxi says in the introduction to the "Index":

"It was Southey, I believe, who said that next to writing an epic poem was the talent to appreciate one; and this remark may not inappropriately be applied to bibliography. It is not in the competency of every one however fond of books, adequately to catalogue, describe and classify them. But to extract from them their pith and marrow, and to put the same in a useful, convenient, and readable form, so as to be a lasting and trustworthy record (and this I take to be bibliography in its highest sense), is a noble and elevating pursuit, which requires tact, delicacy, discrimination, perspicuity, not to mention patience and untiring assiduity."

His standards of bibliography were of the highest and he cleverly composed his principles in poetic form in the "Catena":

ON QUOTING AUTHORITIES

Unless you've read it with your eyes
Set nothing down, nor ought surmise.
Imagination leads to lies
In Bibliography. The wise
Know well this golden rule to prize.
But if a beaten path you tread,
(You surely must if much you've read)
And needs must say what has been said
Give your Authority—be terse—
Quote Author, Title, Chapter, Verse,
That each one to the fountain head
At once and surely may be led,
And read himself what you have read.

Fraxi has time and time again in his classics pointed out the importance of individual erotic and obscene books for almost every branch of knowledge, from the Academician to the Zenoist, but at the same time cautioned against the use of his works by immature youth. This was exceedingly well expressed in the "Catena":

TO THE READER

Dear brother of the gentle craft
Collector, student, "bouquiniste",
Or book-worm, virtuoso daft
As oft unletter'd dolts insist,
For thee I've writ this bulky tome
(And others twain). On topmost shelf
For it I beg a secret home,
Secure from idle, meddling elf,
Who, wanting purpose, vainly pries,
Or maiden green, or artless youth,
Or him who would, Procrustes-wise,
A limit set to search of truth,
And make all letters his own size.
No book exists, however bad,
From which some good may not be had
By him who understands to read.
May this, oh brother, be my meed:
That in thy calm, impartial sight
I may be judged to read aright.

Fraxi was ever ready to place his astounding collection of English erotica at the disposal of authentic students. We would never have been able to write this work had not Fraxi given us moral aid and encouragement as well as free rein among his rarest volumes. We deeply regret that the many years of further research on our part prevented this work from appearing during his lifetime.

Book Two

ETHNOLOGICAL
AND
CULTURAL STUDIES
OF THE
Sex Life in England
AS REVEALED IN ITS
Erotic and Obscene Art

1.

Nature of Erotic
and Obscene Art

THE principal function of art is the pictorial delineation of mankind in its activities, sensations and emotions; an essential element in this design is the natural addiction of art to the field of human love, in its ideal and physical counterparts. The question as to the advisability of the representation of the purely sexual component in art must be answered emphatically in the affirmative with the proviso: eroticism must be subsidiary to the higher artistic conception. This, in turn, is possible only by completely denuding the represented object of its "actuality" that is, the purposive dismissal of time and place by the artist for the far more important universal element of humanity.

Let us consider for a moment a practical application of sex in the "humorous" ideology of the artist. How small is the gap between sublimity and bathos! In "Die Welt als Wille und Vorstellung" Schopenhauer declares that the sexual relations of mankind could not be treated in a jocund manner unless it had a foundation of the most profound seriousness. "Hence the poet and the artist can sing of passion as well as mysticism, be Anacreon or Angelus Silesius, write tragedies or comedies, represent the most sublime or commonest notions, all according to his mood and calling. The artist is the mirror of humanity and resolves into consciousness its innermost feelings and emotion." We shall in a later chapter examine closely the greatest artist of all time in the field of "humorous" portraiture of sex, the Englishman Thomas Rowlandson. It is a Belgian, Félicien Rops, who is unparalleled for his masterful mystico-satanic conception of eroticism, especially as it is made increasingly apparent to us in the many perverse phenomena of the "normal sex life of to-day". But it is again an Englishman, the immortal genius William Hogarth, who stands supreme in the use of erotic art to promote morality.

In all artistic representation of sex, which falls into one of these categories (with the exception of such works as the obscene pictures of Carracci, artistic classics from all conceivable viewpoints), the intelligent spectator and student sees only the higher concept and importance of the work of art that has made use of sex as a background.

2.

Anthropologic Survey
of World
Erotic and Obscene Art

S AN orientation to the erotic art of England we shall here present a concise survey of the classic work in this field in other lands.

The desire to represent pictorially the sex life in all its relations is to be found among the majority of primitive races. The origin of erotic art among savages is perhaps to be found in their sexual cults and religions which first reproduced the generative organs and then the generative act. In ancient India, the lingam and the yoni were represented in a combined form as well as in the individual states. Another possible cause is to be seen in the desire to reproduce the frenzied sexual orgies and erotic festivals of primitive peoples, the principal element being the public consummation of sexual intercourse. Erotic pictures are also well known in West Africa, Japan, the Philippines, Tibet, China, Egypt, Peru, Bali, and many other fetishistic countries.

Mantegazza reports a remarkable use of erotic pictures in New Guinea and we append it at this point because of the excellent example an "uncivilized" people sets to the Western world with its vaunted Aryan superiorities:

"Such pictures as illustrations of the life-principle are usually found in religious or semi-sacred buildings, just as among the Hindus in the well-known Indian temples. The subject of such erotic scenes is ordinarily the mingling of men with gods or with the equally worshipped demons, sometimes in the form of animals, as is the case in Australia. In these painted or carved representations of the sex act the genitals are usually purposely enlarged many times the normal size, a procedure reminiscent of Chinese and Japanese erotic picture-books.

"Perhaps the best description of such sexual panoramas is that of von Rosenberg who made a detailed study of a remarkable house which, although only six feet high, was eighty-five feet in length, and was situated near the coast of south-western New Guinea in the town of Dorej. It stood in the open sea, a short distance from the shore; there was no connecting bridge.

"In the center of the interior of the building there stood a beam on which two figures, male and female, had been roughly cut in an attitude that plainly indicated the consummation of sexual intercourse. On the woodwork of the

roof were carved figures of snakes, fishes, croc-
odiles, etc.; on the two main joists were chiseled
two great figures, the ancestral parents of the
Doresi. On the open side of the building, facing
the west, were two recumbent wooden figures
four feet long, representing man and woman in
the act of coition: the male with his knees in the
air, both with painted faces and covered with
gumutu (threads from the sheaths of the sago
palm) on those parts of the body which are
usually hairy. The head of the man can be
moved in the following fashion: at the back of
the head a heavy cord is fastened, which, when
pulled upward and downward, causes it to rise
and fall on the face of the woman, simulating
the upward and downward movements in sexual
intercourse.

"The importance of such structures with plastic delineations of the sexual processes cannot
be gainsaid in the sexual education of the young,
who are permitted free access at all times. In a
world where there are no corrupting gutters,
alleys, street-urchins, etc., to contend with, the
need of sexual information is excellently filled
by this institution.

"It is only in recent years that civilized man
has begun to teach his young by such pictorial
methods. But as yet he has confined this instruction through false modesty to the animal world.
The reader must determine which of these two
methods is calculated really to instruct the child
and youth."

Erotic art customarily restricts itself to myth-
ologic or historic data or to the illustration of
novels. The obscene photography of modern

times is usually concerned with scenes from brothel life. The latter is thus infinitely more dangerous to the state, but the evil company in which erotic classic art finds itself through no fault of its own is sufficient to damn it in the eyes of the law. In antiquity, the people were as free from such hypocritical failings as the New Guineans. Every vice the ancients could imagine was portrayed and modelled on their walls, ceilings, vases, and other objets d'art. We need but remind the reader of the famous "Musée Secret" at Naples, in which were collected a representative number of classic statues of the most "indecent" nature.

The age of the Renaissance marks the first appearance of "modern" erotic art. The most famous artists were Giulio Romano, who painted the obscene illustrations to the "Sonetti Lussuriosi" of Pietro Aretino, and Augusto and Annibale Carracci who made a series of the so-called "figures", that is, the various positions of lovers in sexual intercourse. The castles and palaces of the kings, the villas and mansions of the princes and princesses were adorned with obscene frescoes and paintings, the gardens and furnishings were also embellished with lascivious sculptures. A more complete treatment of the subject will be found in our "Strange Sexual Practises", to which we refer the student specializing in this field.

3.

History of Aretino's "Figurae Veneris" in England

THE history of erotic art in France and England during the sixteenth, seventeenth, and eighteenth centuries is almost exclusively concerned with the prolific expansions of the "figures" of Aretino from the obscene illustrations of Giulio Romano and the erotic plates of Antonio Raimondi, which consisted of sixteen pictures of the different "Figurae Veneris", or coital positions, corresponding to the sixteen sonnets of Aretino. ' At the destruction of the edition by Pope Clement VII, the original plates were sent to France where innumerable editions were printed from them in the sixteenth century. Brantôme writes: "I knew a good Venetian bookseller in Paris who called himself Bernardo and who was a relative

of Aldus Manutius of Venice. He had a shop
in the rue St. Jacques and once told me that in
less than a year he had sold more than five
hundred copies of Aretino to married and unmarried couples and to high-born ladies, 'of
whom he named three very prominent ones."

Aretino later added four new "sonetti lussuriosi" which naturally correspondingly increased the number of illustrations. Within a
decade, thirty-six of such "Schemata Veneris"
were collected in one book. Brantôme declares
that at the end of the sixteenth century a nobleman presented his mistress with an obscene album in which thirty-two ladies represented the
more than twenty-seven figures of Aretino, and
the majority of these ladies only had one man
at their disposal.

In the seventeeth century all obscene paintings, sculptures, etc., were confiscated and destroyed. Thus almost all the illustrations of
Antonio disappeared. The Abbé de Marolles
boasted of his sole remaining copy, but even
that is no longer extant. A few copies were
found in the storming of the Bastille in 1789.

Aretino's illustrated sonnets also appeared in
England early in the sixteenth century. It was
only a matter of time before the traffic in this
work attained monstrous proportions, even corrupting a famous Oxford College! In a letter
by Humphrey Prideaux to John Ellis, dated
Oxford, January 24, 1674, we discover that the
masters of All Souls College were using the
printing-press of Oxford University for an edition of Aretino's "Figurae Veneris"! The horrified dean of Christ Church, John Fell, discov-

ered them one day "pulling proof of these bawdy pictures", and confiscated the edition. The masters were naturally expelled from the college, but when it was learnt that sixty copies had been printed and distributed before the discovery, the masters were allowed to resume their positions, the sole condition being the recovery of the missing copies. This was done and the honor of Oxford University was preserved!

How firm a grasp Aretino had on the English imagination may be judged from the fact that it is not until 1755 that we encounter any originality in English erotic art. An anonymous London artist made sixteen illustrations to "The Pleasures of Love: Containing a Variety of entertaining particulars and curiosities in the Cabinet of Venus". The same artist later illustrated an edition of Cleland's "Fanny Hill". Although his work is of an inferior quality it is noteworthy for the first break from tradition and the attempt to depict natural and lifelike scenes.

4.

William Hogarth: Greatest Erotic Artist in the Eighteenth Century

THE greatest artist of the eighteenth century is, in our opinion, William Hogarth (1697-1764), who drew on his full genius for moralizing in his illustration of erotic subjects.

Hogarth usually confined himself to a representation of the bestiality of mankind and the painting of the evil effects of sensuality and debauchery in the blackest of colors. He must therefore be considered essentially a moralist. "This illustrious painter," says Jouy, "was to the English what Aristophanes was to the Athenians, a corrector of the morals of his age."

He has with inimitable art represented both love and sexual love in their personal and social relations, in a coarse, naturalistic and even indecent manner that shied away from no filth in presenting a true picture of the time. In fact, his erotic series throw more light on the manners and morals of his countrymen than do a dozen contemporary histories.

Hogarth was apprenticed at a very early age to an engraver of arms on silver plate. In 1718, at the age of twenty-one, he set up for himself, his first employment being the engraving of coats-of-arms, ciphers and shop-bills. In 1724 he undertook to execute plates for booksellers, among them, prints to "Hudibras" and illustrations to "Mortraye's Travels". His first performance as a painter was a repesentation of Wanstead Assembly, the portraits being taken from life. In 1730 he clandestinely married a daughter of Sir James Thornhill, in whose academy he had studied drawing from the living figure. After gaining some pecuniary profit and fame by the publication of a series of small etchings representing London life and folly, he afterwards began to paint portraits, but soon abandoned this line of pictorial art as being too full of drudgery for a man of invention and original genius. In 1733 appeared his "The Harlot's Progress", prints which stamped his reputation at once as the greatest master of caricature the world has ever seen. The sale of engravings of his pictures, executed by himself, was so great that, notwithstanding they were largely pirated, he was assured of enough means for a comfortable life.

The inscription written by David Garrick on Hogarth's tomb reads:

> Farewell, great painter of mankind,
> > Who reach'd the noblest point of art;
> Whose pictur'd morals charm the mind,
> > And through the age correct the heart.
> If Genius fire thee, Reader, stay,
> > If Nature touch thee, drop a tear,
> If neither move thee, turn away,
> > For Hogarth's honor'd dust lies here.

We shall here emphasize only the most important erotic works of William Hogarth and begin with his most famous series, "The Harlot's Progress".

Traill justifiably declares that a characteristic feature of the grossness of the period is the election by Hogarth of the life of a whore as a subject for artistic representation. Such a theme would be completely impossible in modern English art which shrinks from "nudities and any work that smacks of sex".

But Hogarth was extraordinarily applauded by society for his work. Lichtenberg notes: "He received the unheard of number of twelve thousand subscriptions! The six plates have even been copied on umbrellas, so that they may be seen in the greatest heat of mid-day and in wind and rain."

In the first plate of "The Harlot's Progress", Hogarth depicts the arrival of the heroine of the series, Mary Hackabout, who has been brought to London by her father, a poor country parson. Hogarth, significantly enough, has the girl arrive from Yorkshire, a province notorious for sending its prettiest girls to London for whoring. He illustrates the alighting from the post in front of the inn. Father and daughter are awaited by the notorious "Colonel

Charters" one of the worst usurers, pimps and bordel owners in the first third of the eighteenth century. Charters has been castigated by Swift, Pope, and Arbuthnot as a comrade-in-arms to the devil. He always attends this particular inn to watch for these Yorkshire beauties so that he may refresh his bordel stock. Next to him stands his accomplice, John Gourlay, a "kind of bloodhound", and a respectably dressed procuress, drawn from life by Hogarth after the notorious "Mother Needham", owner of a bordel in Park Place. With the aid of this woman, Charters succeeds in enticing the poor Mary Hackabout to his "house".

In the second plate, Mary is already the mistress of a rich Jewish banker, who has furnished a private apartment for her so that he can visit her at any hour of the day. The picture depicts one of these morning visits. A lover, whom she has had in the night, is creeping to the door, sheltered by a chambermaid, while Mary is setting the breakfast table to turn the attention of the banker away from the door. All the wiles and arts of the experienced harlot are deftly drawn in Mary's portrait. With a few strokes the artist has perfectly expressed the artfulness, faithlessness and covetousness of the prostitute in the play of Mary's facial muscles.

The third plate presents the heroine in the garret of a wretched bordel in Drury Lane. We are immediately made aware of the depths to which Mary has fallen, and are convinced of her miserable state by the entrance of Judge Gonson, who has her imprisoned for stealing his watch. Among the objects strewn about the room are the ominous rod, the periwig of a notorious thief, whom Mary must harbor as her "bully", and also phials of medicine and salves, which speak clearly enough of her physical condition.

Mary in prison is the theme of the fourth plate of "The Harlot's Progress". She has been condemned by the court, not merely to be "privately whipped" but also to "hard labour" and to "beat hemp". Near her stands a domineering overseer with a rattan, and behind him a woman who mocks Mary at her work. Besides Mary, seven other persons are beating hemp, among them a ten year old prostitute, a pregnant negress, etc.

In the fifth plate, Hogarth has perfectly indicated the ailment of all prostitutes, dread syphilis in its devastating effects. Mary Hackabout has just died of its plagues and the nature of her death is recognized not only from the presence of the quack-doctors but also from the entire apparatus of a mercurial cure.

The sixth and last plate shows Mary in her coffin, surrounded by many prostitutes and a few dubious lads who have come to pay their last respects.

Hogarth also finds in his second famous work, the eight plates of "The Rake's Progress" (1735), fertile field for satirizing the worldly vices and corruptions of London society in the figures of a coarse parvenu and conscienceless seducer, the repulsive ecstasy of castrates, the horrible orgies in the bordel, alcoholism and gambling vices, wealthy marriages, the debtors' prison, and the interior of the Bedlam Insane Asylum.

Hogarth's "Marriage à la Mode" (1745) introduces us to the "respectable society" whose moral decay is no less great than that of "the lower classes". A deeply indebted lord marries off his son, who is already exhausted by his revelries, to the pretty and healthy daughter of an alderman of the city. They are coupled like two passing dogs. Such a state cannot exist. After the birth of a girl, they separate. The wife takes a young robust advocate as her lover, the lord contenting himself with immature girls. This solution is also not maintainable. The wife is surprised by her husband. An encounter between the advocate and the young lord follows in which the latter is stabbed. While the murderer flees through the window the unfaithful wife kneels and begs her dying husband for pardon. The advocate is caught, and condemned to death. The wife returns to the philistine boredom of her father's home. As her gallant is led to the gallows she commits suicide by taking poison. The only person who remains master of the situation is her father. In the tragic hour of her death, he withdraws the marriage-ring from her finger lest "the body snatchers rob the corpse".

That Hogarth did not disdain the use of obscenities in his satiric caricatures is shown by the ninth plate of "Industry and Idleness", where the grenadier draws with coal a picture of the male organ on the wall, also the drawing of the faeces in "A Midnight Modern Conversation", and the indecent pictures, "The Complicated R——n" and "The Frontis-Piss".

5.

Greatest Erotic Artist
on Flagellation:
James Gillray

"ENGLAND," says Eduard Fuchs in his "Die Karikatur der europaeischen Voelker," "is the home of caricature." It is little wonder that the three greatest English caricaturists, James Gillray, Thomas Rowlandson and George Cruikshank, also extended their talent into the realm of erotic art. For caricature offered such marvelous possibilities in eroticism that the masters of the field made full use of the opportunity of expressing themselves, disdaining possible shocks to English prudery.

Thus James Gillray (1757-1815) is noted not only for his excellent caricatures of the French Revolution and Napoleon I, but also for his many caricatures with a distinctly erotic tinge. Of these the most famous are: "The Latest Lady's

Costume", a chaffing at Madame Tallien's "Garment of Nudity", the "Wedding Night", a caricature of the marriage of Princess Mathilda of
England, the mockery of the sexual debaucheries of the Prince of Wales and the Duke of
Clarence, "Dido in Doubt" (Lady Hamilton),
"The Fashionable Mama or the Conveniences
of Modern Dress", and "The Former Profession" in which Madame Tallien and Josephine
Beauharnais dance in the nude before their lover
Barras.

But James Gillray is best known for his two
masterful illustrations of scenes of flagellation.
The first and more famous appeared in 1786 under the title of "Lady Termagant Flaybum going to give her stepson a taste of her dessert after
dinner". It pictures a respectable Englishwoman
of imposing appearance at the point of applying
the rod to her little son, who is being brought in
by the parlormaid.

The second is bolder in treatment: a lady with
an exceedingly high hairdress and with a bared
bosom is forcibly applying the rod on the nude
posteriors of a young lad who is lying on her
capacious lap. A pretty girl is behind the sofa
on which the above couple are seated and is holding the left leg of the boy with her left hand.
On the right side of the foreground another little
girl is satisfying herself in a very indecent manner. The entire scene is executed in an exceptionally vivid manner.

We here take the opportunity of mentioning
a third famous caricature of English flagello-
mania. It was the work of H. F. Gravelot (1699-
1773), a French artist residing in London, and

satirized the passion of Englishwomen for the use of the rod. We see a gathering of four women, one of whom, with a richly developed bosom, reaches for her rod, as in the background a fifth woman is finishing her chastisement of a little girl on her bared backside. We can also see beyond the door a number of children who are plainly awaiting the same punishment. This engraving was reproduced under the title of "Molly's First Whipping, after the very rare original by Hogarth". The work however is not Hogarth's but Gravelot's.

6.

Thomas Rowlandson:

Greatest of All Artists
in the Depiction of Eroticism
in England

THOMAS ROWLANDSON is universally acknowledged to be the greatest artist in the representation of eroticism that the history of art can offer before the appearance of Félicien Rops. None before him and none after, not even Rops, has shown such a masterful hand as Rowlandson in the purely humorous delineation of sex and obscenity. This humor is expressed by the addition of the artist's personal touches to the representation of sexual intercourse, the droll treatment transforming it into an excellent specimen of the artist's handwork. The diverting peculiarities may be expressed in the act itself, the couple, their clothing, the odd situation or position, or the surrounding scene.

Although Rowlandson at times exaggerates the obscenities, which undoubtedly add to the impressiveness of the work, he never exceeds the boundaries of naturalness and humanness. He is never bestial or perverse and limits himself to the variegated patterns of the natural sex act. This is an important distinction between Rowlandson and the majority of the modern erotic artists who have sought to express themselves in the most involved and ingenious complications of the "Figurae Veneris" by multiplying the most unnatural and improbable positions.

To be sure, one does not find in Rowlandson's work the finesse of execution and detail, so usual among his contemporary French colleagues. He threw the entire force of his fertile phantasy into the planning of the central idea, and placed less weight on the fineness of execution and the precision of line.

Thomas Rowlandson was born a year before James Gillray, in July 1756 in the Old Jewry in London and died in his house in the Adelphi on April 22, 1827. In early childhood he was sent to the London Academy, and then to Dr. Barvis' private school in Soho Square where he numbered among his school-fellows such figures as Richard Burke, the son of the eminent Edmund Burke, the dramatist and actor J. G. Holman, the actor John Bannister and his later very intimate friend Henry Angelo. At the age of sixteen, Rowlandson was sent to Paris where he was supported for two years by a rich French aunt who also left him at her death seven thousand pounds sterling and other properties.

In Paris, Rowlandson had zealously studied French art and when he returned to London he just as zealously "sowed his wild oats", reversing the usual procedure. He gambled day and night, drank continually, spent his "leisure hours" in the famous "pleasure palaces" of London, especially the Vauxhall, and in general cavorted with a reckless company of men-about-town.

This life of dissipation left its artistic mark on Rowlandson. His intimacies with all walks of life attracted him to the field of caricatures where the actual drawing followed fast on the heels of the conception. Rowlandson now revelled in his artwork, gave up all his time to perfecting his bold but clear style, and like Dr. Syntax searched out the picturesque that he might turn the full force of his devastating humor on its pecularities.

It is indeed difficult to find another artist as expressive as "Master Rowley" (his nickname) with as few graphic methods. Such experts as Sir Joshua Reynolds and Sir Benjamin West declare that many of his illustrations are worthy of a Rubens or any of the great masters of the old schools. Bates, in modern times, has expressed himself in somewhat similar terms. "In originality of humour, vigour, colour, drawing, and composition, he exhibits talents which might, but for the recklessness and dissipation of his character, his want of moral purpose, and his unrestrained tendency to exaggerate and caricature, have enabled him to rank with the highest names in the annals of art. In his tinted drawing with the reed pen, as in the productions of his inimitable and too facile needle, his subjects seems to extend over the whole domain of art, and remind one in turn of the free and luxuriant outlines of Rubens, the daring anatomy of Mortimer, the rustic truth and simplicity of Morland, the satiric humour of Hogarth, and perhaps, even, the purity and tender grace of Stothard. I have seen artists stand astounded before the talent of his works, and marvel at their own utter ignorance of one whose genius and powers were so consummately great."

The greatest erotic work of Rowlandson is contained in a small brochure with the title: "Pretty Little Games for Young Ladies and Gentlemen. With Pictures of Good Old English Sports and Pastimes. By T. Rowlandson. 1845. A few copies only printed for the Artist's Friends." This work was actually published by Hotten in 1872 from the ten erotic engravings issued singly by Rowlandson in 1810. Hotten also added erotic explanatory verses to the plates. A description of this rare classic, as far as is consistent with propriety, follows:

No. 1. *The Willing Fair, or Any Way to Please.* An interior with view of a garden from an open window. A young man, sitting on a stool is sexually engaged with a very plump and almost naked girl. On the floor, to the right, stands a wash-basin and an ewer, and in the background, left, a dog is stealing some object from the table. Underneath the picture is the verse:

The happy captain full of wine
Forms with the fair a new design:

Ah! happy captain, charming sport!
Who would not storm so kind a fort?

No. 2. *The Country Squire New Mounted.* Interior, two tables and two chairs, an erotic picture on the back wall. A man and woman are engaged. The woman, almost completely nude, has a feather in her hair. The Squire wears only a frock-coat. The verse:

The Country Squire to London came,
And left behind his dogs and game,
Yet finer sport he has in view,
And hunts the hare and cony too.

No. 3. *The Hairy Prospect or the Devil in a Fright.* Interior, a bed at the left, an open door at the right. A young girl raises her dress and petticoat up high. Satan stares astounded and frightened. The devil is equipped with horns and wings. The verse:

Once on a time the Sire of evil
In plainer English call'd the devil,
Some new experiment to try
At Chloe cast a roguish eye;
But she who all his arts defied,
Pull'd up and shew'd her sexes pride:

So much it made old Satan stare,
Who frightened at the grim display
Takes to his heels and runs away.

No. 4. *The Larking Cull.* Bedroom, left, a toilette table; right, a wall-mirror; in the background a flower-vase on a small table; all very prettily designed. A youth with an elephantine member is engaged "inter mammas".

No. 5. *The Toss Off.* A representation of an engagement between an old Jew and a young, coarse maiden. The man gazes very seriously at their reflection in a mirror at the left. On the back wall, a painting of the city of Jerusalem and the Temple of Solomon. The verse:

> As Maramount her music grinds
> Levi a pleasing passion finds
> He calls the little wanton in
> And tells his wishes with a grin.

No. 6. *New Feats of Horsemanship.* Representation of an engagement between man and woman upon a trotting horse; a barking hound follows them.

No. 7. *Rural Felicity, or Love in a Chaise.* An engagement in a post-chaise.

> The winds were hush'd, the evening clear,
> The Prospect fair, no creature near,
> When the fond couple in the chaise
> Resolved each mutual wish to please.
>
> What couple would not take the air
> To taste such joys beyond compare.

No. 8. *The Sanctified Sinner.* Through the back window of a prettily decorated room an old, ugly man is watching another old man being whipped by a pretty young girl. On the left, foreground, a broken candle in a holder and an opened book with the title "The Hypocrite Display'd", and "Crazy Tales". An excellent engraving.

> For all this canting fellow's teaching
> He loves a girl as well as preaching.
>
> When flesh and spirit both combine
> His raptures sure must be divine.

No. 9. *The Wanton Frolic.* A well furnished room. A young girl's charms are inspected by an onanistic young man. The verse:

> Upon the carpet Chloe laid,
> Her heels toss'd higher than her head.
> No more her cloaths her beauties hide
> But all is seen in native pride.

No. 10. *The Curious Wanton.* A bedroom.
A girl bends over the bed, while a friend holds
a mirror before her so that she can gaze at her
own charms. A dog leaps at her from the back.
The verse:

> Miss Chloe in a wanton way
> Her durling (sic) would needs survey.
> Before the glass displays her thighs,
> And at the sight with wonder cries:
> Is this the thing that day and night
> Make (sic) men fall out and madly fight,
> The source of sorrow and of Joy
> Which king and beggar both employ,
> How grim it looks! Yet enter in
> You'll find a fund of sweets begin.

This verse is a wretched paraphrase of Hilde-
brand Jacobs' original poem "The Curious
Maid":

> And is this all, is this (She cry'd)
> Man's great Desire and Woman's Pride;
> The Spring whence flows the Lover's Pain,
> The Ocean where 'tis lost again,
> By Fate for ever doom'd to prove
> The Nursery and grave of Love?
> O Thou of dire and horrid Mien,
> And always better felt than seen!
> Fit Rapture of the gloomy Night,
> O, never more approach the Light!
> Like other Myst'ries Men adore,
> Be hid. to be rever'd the more.

7.

107 Erotic and Obscene Engravings by Rowlandson

THE world of art is eternally in Pisanus Fraxi's debt for having gathered together in one collection the one hundred and seven erotic and obscene engravings by Thomas Rowlandson and thus preserving them for posterity. Many specimens of Rowlandson's erotic work are also to be found in the Library of the British Museum and in the South Kensington Museum. We shall here shortly describe the most interesting and characteristic of Rowlandson's work:

No. 3. *The Star Gazer.* Motto: "I have known many a man who was cuckolded by the brilliance of a star." Interior. An arched room. On the floor, books and two globes. A dog is in the foreground. An old man, in night-gown and slippers, gazes open-mouthed through a spyglass, while in an adjoining room a couple are engaged in bed. The moonlight streaming through the open window is a splendid touch by the artist.

No. 4. *Carnival at Venice.* A street-scene. Many persons stand in a circle about a young girl who is completely naked and is kneeling "on all fours". Another nude girl collects money from the spectators, while a man plays a hand-organ. Libidinous scenes are portrayed in three windows facing the street. On the corner of the street a quack is giving an enema to a woman who is kneeling on the platform. The compo-sition is harmonious, very witty and satiric, and an excellent specimen of Rowlandson's talent.

No. 6. *Lady Hamilton's Attitudes.* Interior of an artist's studio. An old man draws back the curtain and displays a pretty young girl who is posing nude before a youth, sitting at an easel, brush in hand. In the background two figures are in close embrace, and on the left front, on the floor, two heads are pressed to each other in an eternal kiss. The composition is very spirited and represents the original of the famous "attitudes" of Lady Hamilton, which later degenerated into frivolous "poses plas-tiques" and "tableaux vivants".

No. 9. *French Dancers at a Morning Re-hearsal.* Interior of a barn. Seven persons; a girl clothed with feathers in her hair dances with a similarly dressed man who is playing a violin; another violinist is busily engaged with a girl who kneels before him; at the right, another nude girl is standing before a wash-tub; in the center, background, a man sits on a chamber-pot, while the girl next to him beats a tambourine. The dancing girl is very prettily drawn, the other persons are only roughly sketched.

No. 13. *Inquest of Matrons or Trial for a Rape.* Interior. At the right section a nude woman is being searched by an old matron. On the left section is the court trial of the rapist. An old man of frightful ugliness peeps through the door at the woman's investigation for marks of rape. The work is mediocre but the composition is highly original.

No. 17. *Meditation among the Tombs.* A very fat person is reading the last rites over a fresh grave, surrounded by mourners, as, from the left through a church window, a peasant and a buxom maiden are fondling one another. The grave-stone bears a phallic ornament with the following inscription, taken from the actual one of John Gay in Westminster Abbey:

> Life is a jest and all things shew it
> I thought so once but now I know it.

A splendid work.

No. 18. *Les Lunettes, from les Contes de La Fontaine.* Interior of a convent. An old nun in an armchair, surrounded by ten young nuns in varying stages of disarray. Before them stands a young man, in a nun's garb, who "threatens the eye" of the old nun in a very obscene fashion. The composition is highly original.

No. 19. *Such Things Are or a Peep into*

Kensington Gardens. A highly curious and bizarre composition. Various figures of grotesque appearance, some of them representing gigantic phalli, disport themselves in very lascivious positions. A young woman, all aghast, is running away. On a bench, left, are seated two phalli. The background is formed of phallic trees. The entirety is of the most original humor.

No. 20. *Lord Barrymore's Great Bottle Club.* This has the following couplet:

> With Women and Wine I defy every care
> For Life without these is a volume of care.

Interior. Six couples seated about a table. A nude girl holding a punchbowl dances on the table. Drunkenness and debauchery are the keynotes of the scene, which is quite vivacious.

No. 21. *In Front of a Hut.* An old woman is separating two coupled dogs with a broom, as another woman from a window is endeavoring to scare away two coupled cats. The animals are badly drawn.

No. 23. *Harlequin and Colombine* as they are surprised in a confidential tête-à-tête by Pierrot.

No. 24 *The Juggler.* In a public square a well developed man is balancing a vase on a part of the body usually used for other purposes. A girl in décolleté is catching the money thrown her in her raised skirt. A little devil is beating the tambourine and dances with a trumpet which is very indecently fastened to his posteriors. A very extravagant and difficult composition well carried out.

No. 25. *The Turkish Choice.* A Turk sits

on a rug, a pipe in his left hand, inspecting a great number of women who stand in two parallel rows before him.

No. 28. *Convent Life.* A monk is busily engaged with two nuns. In the background are altar and crucifix. A very bold composition, excellently engraved.

No. 29. *Rural Sports or Coney Hunting.* A clearing surrounded by trees. Three pretty girls allow their charms to be inspected by an old man with a periwig and tri-cornered hat. Behind the old man, who is sitting on a fence, hides a youth who is also drinking in the beauties of the girls. At the left is a large tree, the branches of which delicately obscure three-quarters of the picture. A very carefully executed work.

No. 30. *The Love Knight.* A couple engaged on a couch are rudely surprised by a ghost clad in armor who threateningly swings an axe over their heads. Immense fright is painted on the faces of the guilty couple for disturbing the quiet of the old castle. At the left is a statue of an armed knight. The expression of the couple is excellent.

No. 31. *The Connoisseur.* A pretty woman is being examined by an old man with a large periwig and hat. He is holding a pair of spectacles before his eyes.

No. 33. *Foolish Toys.* A woman is holding in her right hand the arm of a little boy who is standing behind her. At the left a girl and a statue of Priapus, at the right a statue of Silenus.

No. 34. *The Classic Period.* A pretty,

though coarse, girl is seated on a couch of classic style. In the foreground a figure is seated on a pedestal near the bust of a woman and a dildo. In the background, right, are numerous priapic statues. An excellent imitation of the classics.

No. 35. *Fantocinni.* Interior. A man is leaning against a barrel-organ, before him stands a woman watching a puppet-play. He is holding a trumpet to her posteriors. Another girl in the back is beating a tambourine. At the right is a monstrous ape. A curious work.

No. 36. *The Trial.* A girl is being inspected by ten men with very large periwigs.

No. 37. *The Tease.* A laughing girl is being ogled by two old men.

No. 38. *The Musical Swing.* A girl is swinging herself in gay abandon. Four curiously costumed musicians watch from below and play various instruments. A highly original composition.

No. 39. *Love Aloft.* An old man and a girl are swinging in two different swings. The girl wears two feathers in her hair. The old man is very ugly, wears glasses and boots with spurs. A distant stream with two sailboats can also be seen.

No. 40. *Nun at Home.* A convent interior. A nun using a dildo. An old man peeps through the cell-window.

No. 41. *The Choice.* A young girl is inspected by six leering men. On the floor, right, a vase filled with dildoes. An open book lies near a bed.

No. 42. *A Midnight Treat.* An ugly old man smoking a long pipe, holds a bottle in his left hand, a glass in his right. Before him stands a young and very pretty girl with a broad-brimmed hat. In the foreground are a coffee pot and a bowl of fruit.

No. 43. *Love in a Stall.* An intimate scene between a hunter and a pretty woman. Next to them are a horse and two cocker spaniels.

No. 44. *Rich Young Blood.* An aristocratic parlor with many statues and a large antique vase. A love scene between a youth and a girl. A spirited illustration in the style of the Italian masters.

No. 45. *Empress of Russia reviewing her Body Guards.* Her soldiers are all tall, well-built men with closely fitting uniforms that reveal their bulging privates.

No. 46. *A Painful Exit.* An old man with periwig and spectacles applies a clyster to a woman. At the left, three women sit around a table. Right, a night table. Behind the doctor a box with the inscription "medicine-chest".

No. 47. *On the Sea Shore.* Two couples in a boat which is partly on the strand, partly on the water. At the left, a very corpulent woman is shrieking for aid. A very original work.

No. 48. *Down the Wine Cellar.* An old man engages a young girl. A pitcher, overflowing with wine, is underneath the first keg. The stairs are at the left.

No. 49. *Essay on Quakerism.* Interior of a well decorated bedroom. A Quaker engages a girl who wears a long feather in her hair. Quite humorous in scope.

No. 50. *The Music School.* A gouty old man with spectacles hanging on his nose plays the violin from his music-book which lies on the back of a young girl kneeling before him. Another girl plays the violin-cello, a third beats a tambourine. All four are singing. At the right, a violin chest, at the left on the floor, a fruit-bowl, a wine glass and a bottle with the label "Rumbo". Original and accurate in treatment.

No. 51. *The Merry Traveller and the Kind Chambermaid.* A bedroom. A young officer and a pretty chambermaid who is placing a "comforter" in the bed. On the floor a lighted candle. The libidinous expression of the girl is masterfully portrayed.

No. 52. *Connoisseurs.* Interior of a hut. A girl and three old men. The faces of two express delight, the third disgust. A fourth old man peeps through the half-opened door. The girl's face is jovial and entrancing.

No. 54. *Lost Labour.* Interior. A youth and a girl are sleeping on a sofa. An old man, whose face expresses extreme ire, is at the point of stabbing the youth. A woman is entering the half-closed door.

No. 55. *Garden Fruits.* A man on a ladder is trimming a tree, which is in the form of a phallus. Two women watch him closely. One holds a parasol over her shoulder. The other sits on the ground. Another couple are seated on a nearby bench. Near them are two pots, in each of which a phallus is growing. A notable work of clever design.

No. 56. *Pitched in the Haystack.* A soldier and a prostitute in a field behind a haystack, surprised by a farmer with a pitchfork in hand. Perfect perspective and amusing expressions.

No. 58. *How It's Done.* Man and woman sitting on a stool, playing the same harp together. She has two feathers in her hair. At the left an old woman slumbers before a fire. Near her are a bottle and glass. A notebook has fallen to the floor. Simply and prettily executed.

No. 59. *Flight of Love.* A young man and a girl in a boat on a stream. The girl is at the rudder as they row away from an old man who stands with a cane in his hand on the left bank and makes threatening gestures after them. At the right bank stands an Italian temple, surrounded by trees. Two swans are floating along. A very delicate drawing.

No. 60. *After the Prize.* Interior. A man and three girls, one of whom is in a swing. A little dog barks at her. In the foreground is an antique jug.

No. 61. *The Sacrifice.* Two girls present a third woman to a man, behind whom is a fourth woman. In the foreground on the floor are a sword, shield and an antique dish. A very characteristic illustration.

No. 62. *The Dairy Maid's Delight.* A country girl and a negro in a love-bout. At the right a cat is stealing milk from a table.

No. 64. *Turkish Delight.* A Turk is sitting on an ottoman and is being regaled by five girls.

No. 66. *The Navy's Delight.* Four sailors are engaged with three mermaids in a cave on the seashore. Another sailor draws up the boat to shore, while a second stands with oar in hand ready to beat off a sea-monster who shakes his fists at them in token of his wrath.

No. 68. *A Lucky Peep.* A girl admires the

reflection of her body in the mirror, as an old man peeps from behind the dresser.

No. 69. *A Lucky Pair*. A youth is engaged with two girls.

No. 70. *The Sermon*. A preacher is engaged with a girl under a tree. In the background a church. Very spirited.

No. 72. *Cause for Disgust*. Two busy loving couples. In front of them a woman is vomiting. A very daring work.

No. 73. *With Grapes and Vine*. Bacchus and a girl are engaged under a tree. Both are completely nude and crowned with grapes and vine-leafs. In the background can be seen five satyrs and nymphs dancing and frolicking. A classical treatment.

No. 74. *A Burnt Offering*. A bedroom. A very corpulent man engaged with the chambermaid who is singeing his hair with a candle held in her right hand. A "foot-warmer", in the form of a phallus, is at the foot of the bed and is steaming heavily. At the left a cat is on a stool. A burlesque composition.

No. 75. *After the Hunt*. Two women, plainly tired by the hunt, rest at the foot of a tree. A quiver and spear are at their side. They are surprised by two satyrs. Behind a tree, left, the head and shoulders of a third woman are visible.

No. 76. *Amour Refused*. A young and pretty woman repulses the advances of a naked cupid who is grasping her right hand. Three obscene satyrs surround her, ready to help the cupid.

No. 77. *Leda and the Swan.* Leda sits in a cave and presses the swan to her body. In the background are two nude children.

No. 85. *The Sad Discovery or the Graceless Apprentice.* Interior. A woman implores three men and a woman for mercy as they try to push the apprentice from under the bed. In the confusion the chamber-pot is tossed about. Very realistic.

No. 86. *Lust and Avarice.* A pretty girl begs an old, wrinkled man for money. He sticks his tongue out and rolls his eyes about.

No. 87. *Liberality and Desire.* Pendant to the above. An old one-eyed pensioner with a wooden leg gives the girl his purse as he firmly presses his other hand on her breasts.

No. 92. *A Dutch Academy.* Interior. A very fat and ugly woman sits upon a high bench, surrounded by twelve men, some are painting and some are smoking. Angelo praises this work very highly and describes it as "a Dutch Life Academy, which represents the interior of a school of artists, studying from a living model, all with their portfolios and crayons, drawing a Dutch Venus of the make, though not of the colour, of that choice specimen of female proportion, the Hottentot Venus, so celebrated as a public sight in London a few years since. This very whimsical composition, however, cannot fairly be classed with caricature, for we may refer to the scarce print, scraped, or scratched, on copper, by Mynheer Rembrandt, now in the custody of Mr. John Thomas Smith, at the British Museum, as a grave refutation of such an aspersion of the verity of an English artist. In this favourite print of the peering old connoisseurs, Madame Potiphar is represented according to the gusto of Dutch epic design, twice as voluminous of flesh as even the beauties of Rubens. Rowlandson, then, is rather within, than without the prescribed line of Dutch and Flanderkin beauty."

No. 93. *Intrusion on Study or the Painter Disturbed.* Interior of an atelier. Two men suddenly enter as the artist is painting a girl sitting on a sofa. The artist raises his hands as if to implore them to leave. The girl is crying.

No. 94. *Connoisseurs.* Interior of an art-gallery. Four old men gape at a picture of Venus and Cupid. The composition is not indecent but the old men register the height of lasciviousness.

No. 95. *Symptoms of Sanctity.* Interior of a convent. An ugly monk gazes lustfully at a pretty girl who stands next to him with folded hands in prayer. The holy man's hands rest on her breasts as he listens to her confession.

No. 96. *Touch for Touch, or a Female Physician in full practice.* Interior. A pretty girl takes money from an old man as he registers lust in every facial muscle.

No. 97. *The Ghost of my Departed Husband, or Whither my love, ah! whither art thou gone.* A churchyard. An ugly old woman frightened by the watchman has fallen on her back. Under her body lies a naked ghost flat on the ground. A weird effect.

No. 98. *The Discovery.* An old man has caught a couple in an engagement. He carries a heavy poker in his hand.

No. 99. *Washing Trotters*. Interior of a poorly decorated room. An ugly man and a pretty young girl are washing their feet in the same bucket. An erotic song, "The Black Joke", hangs on the wall.

No. 100. *Work for Doctors-Commons*. Two men, one of them plainly the husband, helplessly watch a couple making love on the sofa. The picture represents General Upton and Mrs. Walsh whose affair caused great scandal at the time.

No. 102. *Rural Sports. Or a Pleasant Way of Making Hay*. In a hayfield two youths and three girls are tumbling about, as a fourth girl is about to throw hay on them.

No. 105. *Neighbourly Refreshment*. A young man and a young girl lean from two partly opened doors and kiss each other. The youth's left hand grasps the girl's right breast for support. Behind the boy is an old woman, behind the girl an old man. A dog leaps upon a hen engaged with a rooster. A frightened cat runs past the doors.

No. 106. *A Spanish Cloak*. The captain of the guard is engaged with a young woman. An old officer turns the corner and surprises them.

No. 107. *Puss in Boots. Or General Junot Taken by Surprise*. A tent. A young, powerful maiden swings a sword about as the general in bed appears to be calling on his adjutant for aid.

Besides these plates, which mostly appeared in colors, Thomas Rowlandson left behind a great number of erotic and obscene drawings and sketches, almost all of them displaying the same delicate and gracious talent. These works are to be found in the British Museum, South Kensington Museum and in the hands of wealthy English collectors. We shall here briefly describe the seven most characteristic and interesting examples of Rowlandson's work.

No. 1. *Antique Dream.* A pretty, naked girl lies on a rug underneath a tree; her head rests on a tambourine. Two nude children: one kneels and plays the flute; the other, winged, also plays a flute and beats a tambourine. Classic manner.

No. 2. *English Custom.* Interior. Fourteen persons in couples around a table. At the right, the president with a glass and a bottle. At the left a man is vomiting, near him a very drunken woman. The other couples are engaged in various positions.

No. 3. *The Road to Ruin.* Interior. A young squire sits at a table. Next to him is his mistress with bared breasts. Both are drinking. Opposite the squire, a captain is dealing cards. Between them is a fat, old chaplain with a very sensuous expression, busily engaged in drinking from a gigantic punch-bowl.

No. 4. *The Inspection.* An old procuress demonstrates the charms of a young, innocent girl to an old rake who inspects the beauty through an eye-glass.

No. 5. *Ardent Flames.* Five firemen are trying to extinguish the flames in a burning house from which a fat old woman is escaping. She carries a few household utensils in her raised petticoat. The sweating firemen gaze lustfully at her. The entire composition is spirited and robust.

No. 6.   *Leda and the Swan*. In the background another swan follows a nude woman as Leda is engaged with her own private swan. Very delicate workmanship.

No. 7.   *Cricket Matches at the 3 Hats, Islington*. This scene, replete with humor and life, is quite in style of the great artist. The game is being played by women of all figures and sizes. Their expressions and actions are exceptionally droll.

But besides the erotic and obscene caricatures, Rowlandson is to his age what Hogarth was to the first half of the eighteenth century, the greatest illustrator of the morals and customs of the English people. In his extensive work Rowlandson has critically examined all the social and sexual relations of all the classes of English society. We can here mention only the most important of Rowlandson's general work in its sexual significance.

"Charity covereth a multitude of sins" (1781) shows a bordel in Cleveland Row, London. From a window two prostitutes are interestedly gazing at a young officer who is about to enter.

"The Devonshire, or most approved manner of securing votes" (1784) represents the activities of the Duchess of Devonshire in procuring votes for her favorite, Charles Fox. She is kissing a fat butcher in a public mart in return for his vote for Fox. Another famous work on the same subject is "Wit's Last Stake, or the cobb-

ling voter and abject canvassers" in which the
Duchess sits in Fox's lap as the crowd cheers.

We see the hidden gallantries of society in the
many sketches of the "Opera Boxes" (1785); the
luxurious voluptuousness of the Orient in "The
Polish Dwarf or Count Boruwloski Performing
before the Grand Seigneur" (1786) and "Love
in the East" (1787); the filth of English taverns
and inns in "Damp Sheets" (1781); the common custom of tight stays in "A Little Tighter"
(1791); the modish stupidities in the English
bath-houses is presented in the illustrations to
Christopher Austey's poetic description "The
New Bath Guide" (1798), the abduction and
sale of English girls in foreign lands is satirized
in "A Sale of English Beauties in the East In-
dies" (1810) and the notorious adultery trials
of England in "The Secret History of Crim.
Con." (1812).

8.

Erotic Art of
the Cruikshank Family

LMOST all the contemporaries of Rowlandson in the field of caricature have sought
to imitate his success in erotic and obscene
art. Among such followers, the first that
deserves mention is the famous Cruikshank
family.

The illustrious father, Isaac Cruikshank, contributed a title-picture to the erotic work "The
Cherub: or Guardian of Female Innocence"
(1792). It represents a young maiden standing
before a haggard old soothsayer who traces a
magic symbol on her body with a gnarled stick.
Another erotic title-picture, among many others
by Isaac Cruikshank, called "The Invitation"
decorates the collection of anecdotes titled:
"Useful Hints to Single Gentlemen respecting

Marriage, Concubinage and Adultery" (1792). It represents a prostitute sitting on a sofa as she speaks to a young man peering through the open window. She is inviting him to enter the house so that he may the better inspect her charms. The man appears to be declining the invitation.

Isaac's son, the great George Cruikshank (1792-1878), made a series of engravings for John Cleland's notorious novel "Fanny Hill, or the Memoirs of a Woman of Pleasure". Inasmuch as this work is exceptionally rare we have been unable to determine the exact number and content of the illustrations beyond their obscene nature.

It was George Cruikshank's illustrations of the manners and customs of the people in Pierce Egan's well-known "Life in London" (1821) which firmly established the fame of the artist as one of the greatest caricaturists.

9.

Erotic Art of George Morland

N artistic conception of eroticism similar to that of Rowlandson is found in the work of his friend and colleague George Morland (1763-1804). The representation of the feminine body is especially similar in both artists. Morland, however, like Gainsborough, is a "rococo master", who conjures up a "small, separate, esthetic world", formed of "pale blue bands and gigantic yellow straw hats, white caps and aprons, rosy silk dresses and bared shoulders".

George Morland, mostly with the aid of his cousin William Ward and the engraver John Raphael Smith, made a great number of highly obscene illustrations to the famous novels of the eighteenth century. One of his most interesting series of mezzotints accompanied Fielding's "Tom Jones":

No. 1. *Tom Jones and Molly Seagrim in the Grove* as they are watched by Thwackum and Square.

No. 2. *Tom Jones and Molly Seagrim in an Engagement* as they are surprised by Square.

No. 3. *Tom Jones and Mrs. Waters in the Inn at Upton after the Battle.*

No. 4. *Lady Bellaston and Tom Jones after their return from the Masquerade.*

No. 5. *La Fleur taking leave of his sweethearts,* an obscene caricature from Sterne's "Sentimental Journey".

No. 6. *Rousseau and Madame de Warens* in a love scene. From Rousseau's *Confessions.* Highly obscene.

No. 7. *St. Preux and Eloisa.* "I feel you are a thousand times more dear to me than ever — O my charming Mistress! my Wife! my Sister! my Friend! By what name shall I express what I feel?" From Rousseau's *Nouvelle Héloïse.* Highly obscene.

Morland also illustrated the real erotic works. His best known are the five superb mezzotints to John Cleland's *Memoirs of a Woman of Pleasure*:

No. 1. *Fanny Hill and Phoebe.* Phoebe is initiating Fanny into tribadic practices.
and Fanny Hill. Fanny secretly observes the fat Mrs. Brown being engaged by a lusty soldier.

No. 3. *Fanny Hill, Louisa, and the Nosegay*

Boy. The youth is engaged with the two prostitutes. In the foreground a basket with flowers. At the right, a rod on a stool.

No. 4. *Harriet ravish'd in the Summer House.* A powerful drawing of a forcible rape.

No. 5. *Harriet and the Barronet* (sic). A couple engaged on the ottoman, while two other couples stand behind and watch them.

Another obscene mezzotint by Morland illustrates a scene from Courtney Melmoth's (Samuel Johnson Pratt) erotic work, *The Pupil of Pleasure.* It bears the title *Mrs. Homespun and Sedley. Pupil of Pleasure* and represents Harriet stroking Sedley's cheek with her right hand as she is drawing him closer to her in a very indecent manner with her left hand.

Three other famous works of Morland are:

No. 1. *Mock Husband.* A Lesbian scene between two girls. A third girl whips one of the "lovers" with a rod on her bare posterior.

No. 2. *The Nobleman's Wife and the Taylor's Crazy Tale.* A very fat man seeks in vain to engage a woman. This "Figura Veneris" is impossible because of the corpulence of the male.

No. 3. *The Female Contest; or my* . . . . . *larger than thine!* Five young girls are privately examined by a sixth who endeavors to decide which girl has been most favoured by nature.

John Raphael Smith, in his own right, produced the following ten obscene mezzotints:

No. 1. Interior. Love bout between a youth and a pretty girl upon a sofa.

No. 2.   Interior. A robust youth engages a coarse girl. The upper part of her body is covered. Her left foot dangles on the floor. In the right corner a chamber-pot.

No. 3.   Interior. A girl with a phallus. A cupid inserts his staff from the back and titillates the woman.

No. 4.   A woman dejectedly rests her head in her left hand. She sits on a tousled bed which has apparently been forsaken by her lover.

No. 5.   Interior. A monk engages a pretty young girl.

No. 6.   Dutch interior. A man in a high hat, pipe in hand, caresses a woman who is apparently sleeping on a chair.

No. 7.   Interior. A woman sits on a stool. She presses her left breast firmly with her right hand and gesticulates to a man with her left hand.

No. 8.   Interior. A young violinist titillates with his bow a pretty girl sitting next to him.

No. 9.   A young lady with a high hairdress is sleeping in a park under a tree. Her position is that of gay abandon and invitation to the passerby.

No. 10.   Interior. A man sits on a stool and undresses himself. At the left, an occupied bed. A cat scurries about.

10.

Erotic Art of
Richard Newton

OHN GRAND-CARTERET, in his "Le Décolleté et le Retroussé", draws an interesting
parallel between English and French eroticism in art at the end of the nineteenth
century and places Richard Newton on an equal
footing with Rowlandson as a master of naturalism in this field.

In support of this judgment he cites three
very characteristic caricatures by Newton. The
first, "Which way shall I turn me"? (1791), depicts the difficult choice of a "bon vivant". He
must choose between the joys of the table and
the joys of love (in the form of a handsome
woman reclining on a divan). The second, "Old
Goats at Sale of a French Kid" (1796), parodies
the business methods of the London pimps. Amor

is auctioning off a Parisian beauty who is displaying her charms in a very coquettish fashion to the gaping oldsters. Amor cries: "Twenty pounds a year, a cabriolet and a pony was the last bid. Come, come, gentlemen, you'll have to do better with your bids for this Parisian beauty. Just look at her! What grace! what elegance! I see you are all suitably astounded. Ah! five hundred pounds a year! Thanks your grace. Sold for five hundred!" The third work, "After the Battle", is a very realistic illustration of the physical weariness after the pleasures of sexual love in the form of an attractive woman who reclines listlessly in an armchair.

Richard Newton is also supposed to be the author of the following ten obscene mezzotints:

No. 1.   Interior. A love scene between a man and a woman. A boy kneels on one leg and watches them in amazement. His left hand clenches his cap while his right hand makes a gesture signifying astonishment.

No. 2.   An engagement under a tree in a park between a young man and a girl. Her head rests on a very large book.

No. 3.   An engagement from the rear.

No. 4.   Interior. An old man sitting on an ottoman fondles a girl who has her back turned to him. He supports her with his left hand while his right caresses her breasts.

No. 5.   Interior. A man and a woman represented in a state of violent sexual excitation.

No. 6.   Love scene between a youth and a maiden in a forest.

No. 7.   Interior. A perverse love scene between a man and a woman on an ottoman.

No. 8.   Interior. A man indicates with his left hand the markedly developed callipygean charms of a young girl, while his right hand is indecently engaged.

No. 9.   Representation of an engagement "a posteriori". The young man is supposed to represent George IV as the Prince of Wales. A painting "Leda and the Swan" hangs on the wall.

No. 10.   Bedroom. A love scene between a very pretty young man and a girl. They are also clasped in a divine "seraph-kiss".

11.

Erotic Art
in the Nineteenth Century

FTER the first two decades of the nineteenth century there were few erotic illustrations of any actual artistic value. The fashion seemed to turn to badly colored lithographs which literally flooded the market. There are only a few exceptions to this wretched taste.

An unknown artist made a series of fourteen obscene mezzotints to Sterne's "Life and Opinions of Tristam Shandy". The frontispiece represents a parson whose nose and upper lip form a phallus. The plates bear the following individual titles: *Such a silly question, Par le moyen d'une petite Canulle, Right end of a Woman, A Limb is soon broke in such Encounters, I will touch it, The Intricacies of Diego and Julia,*

Whiskers, Take hold of my Whiskers, Widow Wadman, Yes, Yes, the duce (sic) *take that slit, I seiz'd her hand,* and *Tom's had more gristle in it.*

The only significant colored lithographs of this period are contained in an erotic album which is ascribed to H. K. Browne, an artist of significance. The title of this old erotic album reads: "The Pretty Girls of London; Their Little Love Affairs, Playful Doings, etc." (n.d.). The craftsmanship is excellent and the subjects are very freely, though not obscenely, treated. The portraits are of a ballet-girl on the stage, between acts, as oyster-girl, the lady in her loge, the waitress, the orange-girl, the cigarette-girl, the chambermaid, the servant-girl, the confectioner's "mamsell", the bar-girl and the nursery-maid. A short verse accompanies each plate.

An edition of "Fanny Hill" issued in 1877 is also notable for the rare excellence of its illustrations. But, in general, publishers contented themselves with reproducing the old illustrations until the very engravings and plates disintegrated. It seemed as if no artist worthy of his name was willing to adorn such works, even under a pseudonym. The reason is not far to seek.

12.

Nudity in Art

HE renaissance of puritanism in the Victorian era swept all fields as a reaction from the coarse naturalism of the former century which carried over its influence until about the 1830's. English art was particularly affected.

All "nudities" in art were strictly interdicted. The slightest physical contact between a man and a woman was considered indecent. "In the representation of nudity," says Muther, "English art shows how close were the restrictions on freedom of expression. Contrast this condition with France and its yearly publication, 'Le nu au Salon'; think of Degas, Carrière, Besnard, who found so fertile a field in the play of light on the nude body of woman. Compare an England of a former age, when Hogarth was allowed the grossness of a 'Marriage à la Mode'. Even in 1860 Etty, Eastlake and Hilton lived in the world of Titian and Rubens. The Victorian fig-leaf morality sent this entire colony to Coventry. The spirit of puritanism held sway over the entire country. Even Watts was called on to explain in public why he could not have clothed his Psyche and the young girl of the famous Mammon work! And the last of the classicists, Poynter, Tadema and Crane, were able to proceed with their work only by robbing their women of all reality, transforming them into cold, lifeless, marble statues, lest Victorian morals be even slightly offended. In no other way might nudity be displayed: babies, toddling to their baths; children playing about the surf in their shirts — in God's name, what stupidities Victorians inflicted on English art! Of course an exception had to be made for the church! Such a religious motivation was found by Philipp Calderon in the 'Saint's Tragedy' of Kingsley, where the young girl, kneeling before the crucifix, renounces the vanities of the world so that she might 'naked follow her naked Lord'. The public could not very well expect the artist to clothe his subject. This is the single nudity, with the exception of Watts and Leighton, to be found in the entire Tate Gallery! That a priest in the picture holds his hand before his eyes lest he see the graceful body of the maiden is also an excellent English nuance. Artists were obliged to forsake a realm of infinite beauty."

The movement against nudity in art was indeed the most powerful imaginable. The many

Mrs. Grundys of the period denounced the un-
clothed body as shameless, indecent, immoral,
foul, loathsome, etc., and thus indirectly accused
the Creator, as Hector France wittily puts it,
of "bad taste and immorality!" A super-pietist
even wanted to pierce with his umbrella some
paintings in the Exhibition of the Royal Academy for fear other people might be shocked at
the sight of such innocent nudities.

13.

Eroticism Among the Pre=Raphaelites:

Dante Gabriel Rossetti
Edward Burne=Jones

ECAUSE of this condemnation of the representation of the nude human body in English art in the second half of the nineteenth century, eroticism turned to a new field for the expression of the universal sexual element in mankind. Since love could no longer be depicted with the naive naturalism of a Hogarth, Rowlandson, Morland, etc., there arose that artificial eroticism which, apart from the purely physical element, sought to express the purely psychic features, but was here necessarily betrayed into a highly developed sensuality that found itself more and more verging on the representation of actual sex acts.

This movement proceeded from the school of the so-called "Pre-Raphaelites", whose most famous representatives were Holman Hunt, Dante Gabriel Rossetti and Edward Burne-Jones. Psychic states, sensations, emotions, psychologic experiences, these were the chief materials of the Pre-Raphaelites in their art movement, which in this respect rested completely on the early Italian and Gothic school.

Dante Gabriel Rossetti (1828-1882), the "soul" of the Pre-Raphaelite brotherhood, is also the founder of an entirely new conception of eroticism in English art. In his love scenes from the Bible, "Le Morte d'Arthur", the "Decameron", the "Divine Comedy", the "Roman de la Rose", there is plainly evident a new style of "ecstatic sensuality", completely foreign to the early English artists.

"Rossetti," says Muther, "does not treat sensuality in the classical sense, but as the sultry, sinful passion which Christianity first introduced into the world. Languishing and yearning, incestuous love, over which sways a fateful doom — that is the theme of the work. There is no end to the kissing. But these kisses are not the dilly-dallying ones of a Fragonard. In a painful soul-piercing kiss the lips meet. 'I drink thy soul, death is insatiable.' All the concupiscence of his imagination is poured by Rossetti into his artistic moulds. He paints 'la bella mano' — the Venus Astarte of England in all its variegated forms, but always with that lustful carnality . . . Never before in England have there been paintings of so profound a sensuality."

Rossetti is, indeed, a modern psychologist of love who sees in it the fervent ardor of the soul from out the grayness of ordinary life, longing for new beauty, and incorporates this conception in the figure of woman as priestess of this "soul's desire".

The natural development of this movement necessarily leads to mysticism and asceticism, as we find in the work of Edward Burne-Jones (1833-1898). His ethereal feminine figures turn from mundane joys to heavenly raptures. They are transported to elysium in mystic voluptuousness. The physical sensuality still apparent in Rossetti is replaced by a purely psychical image, the luxurious forms of the feminine bodies must yield to ethereal slenderness. Thus Burne-Jones became the idol of the esthetes who found a "piquant charm in enthusing over slenderness after they had been satiated by corpulency. Life itself seemed to follow the style of Burne-Jones. Nature, as Oscar Wilde said, produced like a clever publisher thousands of copies of what a painter had devised."

14.

The Erotic Genius of
Aubrey Beardsley

HE artistic conception of eroticism by Rossetti and Burne-Jones were fused in the
individual genius of Aubrey Beardsley,
the English Félicien Rops, and in his own
right one of the foremost of modern erotic artists. At Beardsley's early death (1872-1898) he
had not yet attained the full power of his imagination, although he had already perfected his
style. Beardsley displays all the modern refinements of sexual love and has clearly followed
the path of Rops in expressing the satanic element, in "singing the song of sex as a demonic,
cosmic, creative and destroying power". From
the immature "priest of sin" he developed into
the "philosopher of sex".

"At the end of the old century when the time-

worn doctrines were already moribund, there
appeared the bold, attractive and wondrous
death-blow, the adventurer of the line, who dared
all, and united in his phantasy a delicate corruption with a precious boldness." These words of
Edmond de Goncourt on Fragonard apply in an
even higher degree to the work of Beardsley. In
his early work he shows the decided influence of
his teacher, Burne-Jones, in his chaste delicacy
and tenderness. Then Félicien Rops burst into
the young master's ken, Rops the satanist, Rops
to whom woman signified the incarnation of passion, the daughter of darkness, the accomplice
of the devil. And thus in Beardsley's work there
gradually appeared the "note macabre", the line
of perversity. Heaven and hell, asceticism and
passion, old English bigotry and the most modern corruption united in forming a demonic potpourri. What was formerly divine, became common. The unworldly women of Burne-Jones
change to prostitutes. It is as if an angel were
suddenly to utter obscenities! "This is what gives
Beardsley's work that sinister and infernal quality. While all other artists have celebrated the
delicacy and grace of the English soul, Beardsley dares to expose the slime that lies on the bottom of the sea which, from above, appears so
pure."

In the first period, under the influence of
Burne-Jones, Beardsley drew woman essentially
as the priestess of asceticism, in "Adoramus te",
"A Christmas Carol", "A Head", and others,
completely in the style of the early Florentine
renaissance.

In the second period, influenced by Rops, he

developed his peculiar style of line-drawing to
the height of his amazing genius. But Beardsley
studied Rops only to orient his theories of art.
Sexual love in all its viciousness appears more
clearly, more painfully and more suggestively
than in the plastically constructed idiosyncrasies
of Rops.

Never in the history of art has the beast in
woman, the savage obscenity of "pure sex" been
more powerfully expressed than in the "Incipit
vita nova", "Messalina", and "The Wagnerites",
those three supreme classics by Aubrey Beardsley.

"It is night; to the fevered woman there appears the horror of the embryo conceived in the
abomination of her womb: Incipit vita nova.

"It is night; like a devilled glittering gigantic
fury, swollen with a thousand sucking lusts, the
priestess of Baal bares the rape: Messalina.

"It is night; an army of horrendous, denuded
Vampyre-women drink in the Tristan music
with their blood-sucking lips in a state of maddened satyriasis: Wagnerites."

In the last period of his short life of creation,
Beardsley advanced from the description of
"vice in love" to a more restrained conception of
eroticism. Woman becomes luxurious, but without sin. The lusts of the body are means, and not
the final purpose. The breasts are full, no longer
an object of sterile passion. Woman becomes a
symbol of blessed fecundity, a healthy Cybele,
replete with Hindu solemnity. Its apogee is
reached in a Volpone initial. At the left and
right are an Indian Hermes. Under the head six
turgescent breasts. In the ornamented letter, it-

self, is a woman, half Michelangelo, half Hindu. No trace of sin, of vice. The body in the last stages of pregnancy, and a child longingly stretches its hands to the mother.

The work of Beardsley is collected in "The Early Work of Aubrey Beardsley", "The Later Work", "A Book of Fifty Drawings", and "A Second Book of Fifty Drawings".

15.

Spread of Erotic and Pornographic Art

THE sexual instinct is not satisfied with the sole representation of eroticism by the usual channels of art, but demands its excitative force in the common and everyday objects. All countries exhibit this desired erotic stimulation in the form of obscenely decorated objets d'art, furniture, phallic ornaments and decorations, etc. England naturally has had and still has a wealth of such artistic works with a sexual motivation.

We shall here, however, briefly describe those erotic forms indigenous to England, or those which she has developed to inordinate lengths: in early times, this was true of the gigantic traffic in obscene playing cards and snuff boxes, in the last two centuries the limitless number of obscene lithographs, and in modern times the gigantic industry of obscene photographs.

Playing cards, which were introduced to England at the end of the fifteenth century were frequently decorated with erotic subjects. Thomas Heywood of Pendleton, Manchester, possessed an example of such cards. The back of the ace of hearts represented a cupid, plucking a rose with the subtitle "In love there is no pleasure without pain" and the following verse:

> As when we reach to crop ye blooming rose
> From off its by'r ye thorns will interpose;
> So when we strive the beauteous nymph to gain,
> Ye pleasures we pursue are mixed with pain.

In later times, Ryan reports an exceptionally wide use of obscene playing cards. These are mostly in the form of transparent cards, which must be held to the light for the obscene pictures to be seen.

Since the beginning of the nineteenth century a favorite place for obscene pictures was the snuff-boxes. Both the exterior and interior covers were decorated with lascivious scenes. The traffic was so great that all the tobacco-stores kept them as a matter of course for the convenience of their patrons.

In modern times, England has distinguished itself as being the leader in the manufacture and sale of obscene photographs. Just as in the former centuries obscene lithographs were common currency among the bookstores, the advance of invention has transformed this industry into a most highly developed business, dealing in thousands of thousands of copies of a single print! The dangers to society of such wretched and miserable products can easily be imagined, yet the authorities prefer to busy themselves in suppressing works of artistic and literary merit because of the greater publicity attached to them. Eroticism is a healthy force in life, and when it is curbed in its most beneficent forms, it shows its Gorgon and Cerberean head in its more virulent forms. If modern scientific research has proven anything, it has at least conclusively demonstrated that the sexual impulse must find expression in creative as well as physical forms, and so long as a society forces it into underground channels, the more rotten and corrupt will be the core of that society.

Bibliography

Of Reference Works Only

I.

Bibliographical, Historical and Scientific Works

1. PISANUS FRAXI, *Index Librorum Prohibitorum*. London, 1867.
2. PISANUS FRAXI, *Centuria Librorum Absconditorum*. London, 1879.
3. PISANUS FRAXI, *Catena Librorum Tacendorum*. London, 1885.
4. J. GAY, *Bibliographie des ouvrages relatifs à l'Amour, aux Femmes, au Mariage et des Livres Facétieux, Pantagruéliques, Scatologiques, Satyriques, etc.* Six Volumes. Turin, 1871.
5. HUGO HAYN, *Bibliotheca Germanorum Erotica. Verzeichniss der gesammten deutschen erotischen Literatur mit Einschluss der Uebersetzungen, nebst Angabe der fremden Originale.* Leipzig, 1885.

6. HUGO HAYN, *Bibliotheca Germanorum Gynaecologia et Cosmetica.* Leipzig, 1886.

7. EDUARD GRISEBACH, *Weltlitteraturkatalog eines Bibliophilen mit litterarischen und bibliographischen Anmerkungen.* Berlin, 1898.

8. BERNHARD STERN-SZANA, *Bibliotheca Curiosa et Erotica.* Vienna, 1920.

9. THOMAS BABINGTON MACAULAY, *History of England.* London, 1849-1858.

10. THOMAS WRIGHT, *A History of Domestic Manners and Sentiments in England During the Middle Ages.* London, 1862.

11. THOMAS WRIGHT, *A History of English Culture. From the earliest known period to modern times.* London, 1874.

12. JOHANNES SCHERR, *Geschichte der englischen Literatur.* Leipzig, 1874.

13. H. A. TAINE, *History of English Literature.* Two Volumes. London, 1878.

14. EDW. FORBES ROBINSON, *The Early History of Coffee Houses in England.* London, 1893.

15. I. D'ISRAEL, *Curiosities of Literature.* Three Volumes. London, 1895.

16. GEORGIANA HILL, *Women in English Life. From Mediaeval to Modern Times.* Two Volumes. London, 1896.

17. IWAN BLOCH, *Strange Sexual Practises.* New York, 1933.

18. IWAN BLOCH, 120 *Days of Sodom.* New York, 1934.

II.

𝕷𝖔𝖓𝖉𝖎𝖓𝖊𝖓𝖘𝖎𝖆

(CHRONOLOGICALLY)

19. JOHN STOW, *A Survey of London, written in the year* 1598. London, 1842.

20. (Misson de Valbourg), *Mémoires et Observations faites par un Voyageur en Angleterre.* Hague, 1698.

21. *The Foreigner's Guide, or a necessary and instructive Companion Both for the Foreigner and Native in their Tour through the Cities of London and Westminster, etc.* London, 1730.

22. *The Midnight Spy, or, a View of the Transactions of London and Westminster.* London, 1766.

23. *L'Observateur français à Londres.* Four Volumes. Paris, 1769.

24. RICHARD KING, *The Frauds of London detected, or a new Warning-Piece against the iniquitous practices of that Metropolis.* London, 1770.

25. J. W. V. ARCHENHOLTZ, *England und Italien.* Five Volumes. Leipzig, 1787.

26. *Offenherzige Schilderung der Muessiggaenger und Taugenichtse in London zur Warnung fuer deutsche Muessiggaenger und Taugenichtse.* London, 1787.

27. THOMAS PENNANT, *Beschreibung von London.* Nuernberg, 1791.

28. *Les Sérails de Londres, ou les Amusements nocturnes.* Paris, 1801.

29. *Sittengemaelde von London.* Gotha, 1801.

30. JOHANN CHRISTIAN HUETTNER, *Englische Miscellen.* Two Volumes. Tuebbingen, 1802.

31. CHRISTIAN AUGUST GOTTLIEB GOEDE, *England, Wales, Irland und Schottland.* Five Volumes. Dresden, 1806.

32. JAMES PELLER MALCOLM, *Anecdotes of the Manners and Customs of London.* Two Volumes. London, 1810.

33. WILHELM BORNEMANN, *Einblicke in England und London.* Berlin, 1819.

34. *L'Hermite de Londres.* Three Volumes. Paris, 1820.

35. *London wie es ist, oder Gemaelde der Sitten, Gebraeuche und Charakterzuege der Englaender.* Leipzig, 1826.

36. *Skizzen aus England.* Four Volumes. Frankfurt am Main, 1830.

37. A. V. TRESKOW, *Leiden zweier Chinesen in London.* Two Volumes. Quedlinburg, 1838.

38. MICHAEL RYAN, *Prostitution in London, with a Comparative View of that of Paris and New York.* London, 1839.

39. MAX SCHLESINGER, *Wanderungen durch London.* Two Volumes. Berlin, 1852.

40. J. VENEDEY, *England.* Three Volumes. Leipzig, 1845.

41. JULIUS RODENBERG, *Kleine Wanderchronik.* Two Volumes. Hannover, 1858.

42. JULIUS RODENBERG, *Tag und Nacht in Lon-* Berlin, 1862.

43. JOHN TIMBS, *Curiosities of London. A New Edition.* London, 1867.

44. JULIUS RODENBERG, *Studienreisen in England.* Leipzig, 1872.

45. GUSTAV RASCH, *London bei Nacht.* Berlin, 1873.

46. JULIUS RODENBERG, *Ferien in England.* Berlin, 1876.

47. WALTER THORNBURY, *Haunted London,* London, 1880.

48. JACOB LARWOOD, *The Story of the London Parks.* London, 1881.

49. *La Société de Londres.* Paris, 1883.

50. MAX O'RELL, *Les Filles de John Bull.* Paris, 1884.

51. HECTOR FRANCE, *Les Va-Nu-Pieds de Londres.* Paris, 1884.

52. HECTOR FRANCE, *En "Police-Court".* Paris, 1891.

53. H. D. TRAILL, *Social England.* Six Volumes. London, 1893.

54. GUSTAF F. STEFFEN, *Aus dem modernen England.* Stuttgart, 1896.

55. WARWICK WORTH, *The London Pleasure Gardens of the Eighteenth Century.* New York, 1896.

56. WALTER BESANT, *London.* London, 1898.

57. H. BARTON BAKER, *Stories of the Streets of London*. London, 1899.

58. PIERCE EGAN, *Life in London. A New Edition*. London, 1900.

59. HECTOR FRANCE, *La Pudique Albion. Les Nuits de Londres*. Paris, 1900.

60. ARTHUR H. BEAVAN, *Imperial London*, London, 1901.

61. WALTER BESANT, *East London*. London, 1901.

62. EDWARDS, ROBERT. *The English Manner*. London, 1909.

63. KERVANI, JEAN. *La Société de Londres*. Paris, 1912.

64. D'AUVERGNE, EDMUND B. *The Light Side of London*. London, 1916.

65. HELIP, MARC. *La Vie Anglaise*. Paris, 1918.

66. HOLITSCHER. ARTHUR. *Der Narrenbaedeker*. Berlin, 1925.

67. MORTON, HENRY. *The Nights of London*. London, 1926.

68. BENJAMIN, LEWIS S. *The London Scene*. London, 1926.

www.ingramcontent.com/pod-product-compliance
Lightning Source LLC
Chambersburg PA
CBHW022112080426
42734CB00006B/103